Sara Wheeler read Ancient
Greek, at Oxford. She lived in Athens for eighteen months, and since then has worked in publishing and journalism in London. Her next book will be about her travels in Chile. She lives in Mornington Crescent, London.

AN ISLAND APART

Travels in Evia

Sara Wheeler

An *Abacus* Book

First published in Great Britain by Little, Brown and Company 1992
This edition published by Abacus 1993

A CIP catalogue record for this book
is available from the British Library.

ISBN 0 349 10346 1

Printed in England by Clays Ltd, St Ives plc

Abacus
A Division of
Little, Brown and Company (UK) Limited
165 Great Dover Street
London SE1 4YA

For Louis Mackenzie-Smith

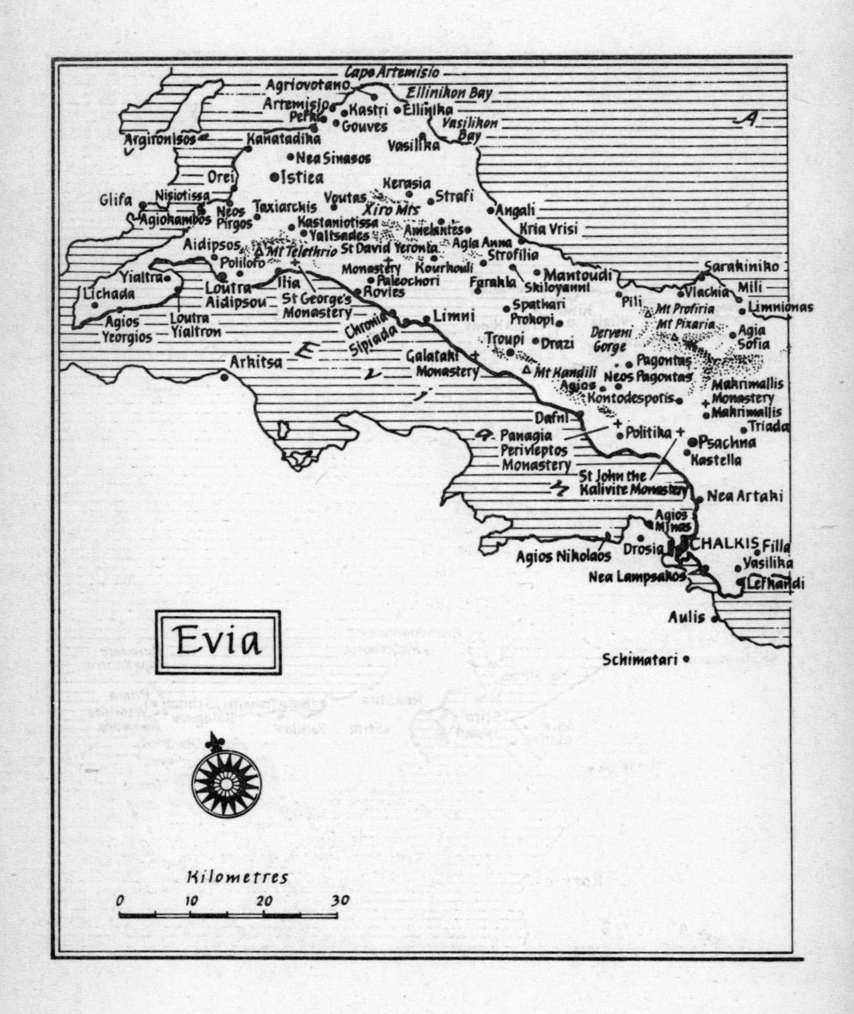

Cape Artemisio
Agriovotano
Ellinikon Bay
Artemisio
Kastri
Ellinika
Pefki
Gouves
Vasilikon Bay
Argironisos
Kanatadika
Vasilika
Nea Sinasos
Orei
Istiea
Kerasia
Glifa
Nisiotissa
Voutas
Strafi
Neos Pirgos
Taxiarchis
Xiro Mts
Angali
Agiokambos
Kastaniotissa
Yaltsades
Amelantes
Kria Vrisi
Aidipsos
Mt Telethrio
St David Yeronta Monastery
Agia Anna
Polilofo
Kourkouli
Strofilia
Sarakiniko
Yialtra
Paleochori
Farakla
Mantoudi
Mili
Loutra Aidipsou
Ilia
Rovies
Skiloyanni
Lichada
St George's Monastery
Pili
Vlachia
Limnionas
Loutra Yialtron
Limni
Spathari
Mt Profiria
Agios Yeorgios
Chronia
Sipiada
Prokopi
Mt Pixaria
Agia Sofia
Troupi
Drazi
Dervení Gorge
Arkitsa
Galataki Monastery
Pagontas
Mt Kandili
Neos Pagontas
Makrimallis Monastery
Agios
Kontodespotis
Makrimallis
Dafni
Triada
Panagia Perivleptos Monastery
Politika
Psachna
Kastella
St John the Kalivite Monastery
Nea Artaki
Agios Minas
CHALKIS
Filla
Drosia
Agios Nikolaos
Vasilika
Nea Lampsakos
Lefkandi
Aulis
Evia
Schimatari
Kilometres
0
10
20
30

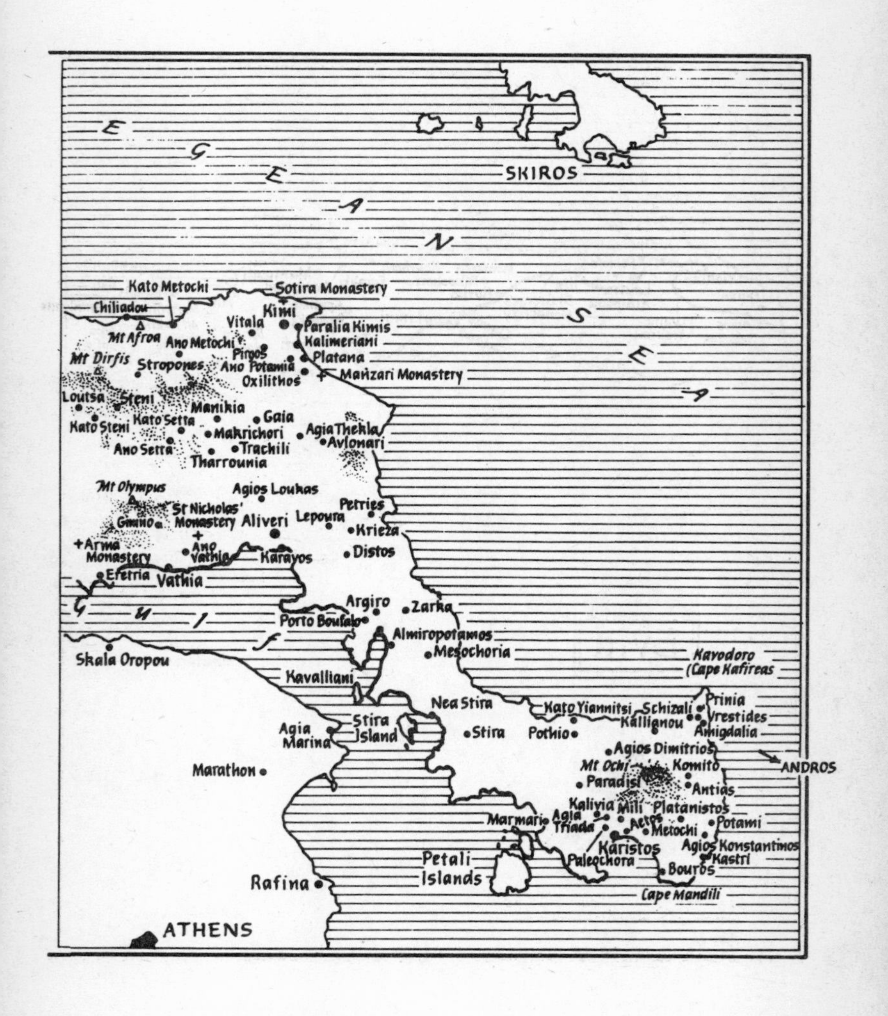

E G E A N S E A
SKIROS
Kato Metochi
Sotira Monastery
Chiliadou
Kimi
Vitala
Paralia Kimis
Mt Afroa
Ano Metochi
Kalimeriani
Mt Dirfis
Piroos
Platana
Stropones
Ano Potamia
Manzari Monastery
Oxilithos
Loutsa
Steni
Manikia
Gaia
Kato Steni
Kato Setta
Makrichori
Agia Thekla
Avlonari
Ano Setta
Trachili
Tharrounia
Mt Olympus
Agios Loukas
St Nicholas' Monastery
Petries
Gimno
Aliveri
Lepoura
Krieza
Arma Monastery
Ano Vathia
Karavos
Distos
Eretria
Vathia
G U L F
Argiro
Zarka
Porto Boufalo
Almiropotamos
Skala Oropou
Mesochoria
Kavodoro
(Cape Kafireas
Kavalliani
Nea Stira
Prinia
Kato Yiannitsi
Schizali
Vrestides
Kallianou
Amigdalia
Agia Marina
Stira Island
Stira
Pothio
Agios Dimitrios
ANDROS
Marathon
Mt Ochi
Komito
Paradisi
Antias
Kalivia
Mili
Platanistos
Marmari
Agia Triada
Aetos
Metochi
Potami
Karistos
Agios Konstantinos
Petali Islands
Paleochora
Kastri
Bouros
Rafina
Cape Mandili
ATHENS

Acknowledgements

I owe a great deal to travellers who have written about Evia in centuries past. Not only did they provide information, but they entertained me and kept me company too. We agreed on a number of things, but there were rather radical cultural differences between us. I always thought fondly of Jacques Peeters, a Dutchman toiling round Evia in the late seventeenth century. He talks of Evian wine admiringly in his book, though suggests it is 'not for our delicate ladies'. How times change.

I would like to thank Patrick Leigh Fermor and John Murray Ltd for permission to quote from *Roumeli* on page 96.

There are many people to whom I owe a debt of gratitude. I must mention in particular Alan Samson, my editor, who told me I should write this book; my parents, Diane and John; Chris Coles, who gave me a home when I had to rent my own out; and Nann du Sautoy at Little, Brown for her support. Father Meliton (Richard Oakes) answered masses of questions both verbally and by post, always with enthusiasm and scrupulous attention to detail. Dr Peter Mackridge, who runs the Modern Greek department at Oxford University, taught me as a recalcitrant student in the early eighties and still had the generosity of spirit to read my typescript and offer a great deal of valuable advice and correction. Clare Shine, Phil Kolvin, Jane Walker and Garry

Emmerson also read portions of the typescript and helped me grapple with it. Diamantios Sampson, Evian expert *par excellence*, had a clearer conception of the island's identity than anyone else I met, and on many occasions gave up a good deal of his time to discuss it with me; it was tremendously helpful, and always a pleasure. Finally there are four people in Greece whose friendship and support throughout the course of both journey and book were of superlative importance. Aris and Monica Berlis simply embraced me as the fourth member of their family, and Aris helped me realize what kind of book I wanted to write. Denise Harvey and Philip Sherrard first showed me this island, many years ago, and their unstinting hospitality and hundreds of hours of late-night discussion ever since extend beyond anything thanks on a page can convey.

Transliteration

I have used the standard transliterations of Ancient Greek words. These are based on the Roman method of converting Greek into Latin, or simply on traditional usage. Some Anglicisms are also too entrenched in the modern language to be dug out, for instance Corfu, Crete and Rhodes.

As far as Modern Greek generally is concerned I have tried to facilitate pronunciation by non-Greek-speakers, thus the transliterations are more or less aural. They are also based as far as sensibly possible on Modern Greek orthography, thus k not c, f not ph and so on. As pronunciation and simplicity were my first rules, however, I have used the English i to render the vowel sound ee, which in Greek is represented by several different vowels and diphthongs. Purists will regret that this entails the loss of the y representing the Greek upsilon (Karystos, Kymi): I am sorry for that, but I think it is the most user-friendly way of dealing with a knotty old problem.

This two-tier system of Ancient and Modern leads to confusion over the name of the island itself, which is written Euboia in Greek and which appears in a multitude of versions in contemporary English. Following my Modern Greek rule I use Evia, which is how it is pronounced (with the stress on the first syllable). I cannot, however, use this in any ancient context: the standard name of the island in translated ancient texts is Euboea, and the weight of scholarship that lies behind it has defeated me. Thus in *An Island Apart* the land mass in question metamorphoses in about AD 330 from Euboea to Evia. This date is arbitrary (besides being the year Constantinople was dedicated as the new capital of the Roman Empire), but anything more precise would involve a delving into an issue far too complex for the confines of a non-academic book.

Having said my piece about facilitating pronunciation, I then spoilt the whole thing by not using accents. I'm afraid I think that they look too peculiar in what is meant as a reading book and not a reference book, and simply get in the way.

Introduction

Although Evia is the second largest Greek island (after Crete), it is often optimistically referred to in Greek books as the third. This is because they count Cyprus. When I travelled around it and then sat down to write a book, my first intention was simply to draw a picture of an island and its inhabitants. The lines might not join up, but that didn't matter: it was going to be my picture. With this objective in mind I set out to discover an island culture, and the first thing I found was that there isn't one – there are many. Internal geography has fostered the development of a series of isolated regions rather than one coherent whole. At first I was depressed about this, but I gradually realized that it was the lack of homogeneity which made the island so rich and complicated and unique, quite unlike the hundreds of other islands, and I hope I have managed to convey at least some of the scintillating diversity which captivated me.

Secondly, I was aware that I was travelling in a period of drastic social change. I saw a world that is fading, and that is being replaced, ultimately, by nothing, because that which is replacing it has no meaning. I have tried to explore that in *An Island Apart*. I don't simply mean that a traditional and rural society is giving way to a fragmented and mechanized one. That is the superficial transformation, if you like, but below it the new world order is fundamentally altering the way people perceive themselves. This means that the journey and the book are as much about time as place.

Thirdly, I was trying in my very small and hesitant way to see through that world to my own. In this way travelling is a condition of mind, and as Plato says in *Epistle VII*, 'For in learning these objects it is necessary at the same time to learn both what is false and what is true of the whole of existence.' In modern parlance he might have said, 'Life is not a rehearsal', and this was always in my mind.

Chapter One

νησός τις ἐστι
(There is an island . . .)

AESCHYLUS. The Persians

I once heard an American on the Acropolis say. 'Look. you can see the Hilton from here.' He was a hopeless case. actually. but it nonetheless exemplified the tendency of travellers to see everything in relation to themselves. The thought arrived unbidden in my head as I stood on a quay on the Greek mainland south of Athens on a shimmering day at the beginning of June 1990. screwing up my eyes at the horizon: I badly wanted to see the island that had. in the complicated months leading up to the start of this journey. become a vital part of my life. I had always assumed that I was going to be objective. With the delicious imminence of departure. however. I realized that I was on some subliminal level that Acropolis American. It all gets refracted through a personal lens before you can do anything with it. Anyway. I couldn't see a thing.

The boat from Rafina to Karistos was cancelled. I sat at a café with a middle-aged Greek woman who was clutching a hessian sack bulging with chickpeas. and we decided to take the 3.30 to Marmari. up the coast from Karistos. and then make our way south. After three minutes she asked me if I was married. and looked depressed when I said I wasn't. She then asked how old I was: learning I was 29 seemed to make the situation much worse. and she ordered me a slab of synthetic gateau and some gritty coffee by way of consolation. While I was tackling them a man appeared beating a tambourine and trailing a chimpanzee dressed in a loincloth. A pungent smell of fresh fish hung on the air and boxes of bright-eyed and barely-dead corpses glistened on the waterfront. The boat eventually lumbered into dock and we boarded. It was huge, made in Spain, and had a special contraption in the toilet for being sick into. I went out on deck and saw some of the Petali islands: Laperousa, Avgo, Makronisi and Chersonisi, and on Evia the Ochi mountains faded into gradations of obscurity. I felt lighthearted with relief that the journey had begun at last.

It was a journey I had been turning over in my mind for years, but it had still been difficult to decide where to begin. I had discovered Evia through friends when I was living and working in Athens eight years previously: we used to sneak off to their house in the north for weekends. But I had only ever been to their village, and my plan was to make a journey through the whole of the island. The little I had seen made me want more. To begin with it was extraordinarily beautiful. There were few tourists, and no airport. It was a long, slender and graceful shape, exactly like a seahorse with a flicked-back tail. I began to read up about it, and I discovered that this shape had formed its history and much of its character: it was almost part of the mainland, but not quite. It was an island, but an island apart from the rest.

I had decided to start at the tail and make my way up to the snout, as that way I would have my friends to look forward to at the end, and everything else would be new. There was something natural about a steady progression northwards, and I could make detours as and when I liked. I planned to take about five months, and I thought I could probably find rooms to rent in most villages. As I was hoping to do much of the journey on foot I had little luggage – just a capacious and much-loved carpetbag (the mental baggage I was carrying around was more cumbersome).

There are no cities on Evia. The capital, Chalkis, is an urban centre (with all the attendant horrors conjured up by those words) but not large enough to qualify as a city. Near it there are two satellite towns, and besides that the island has a spa town and a small commercial town. Three places hover on the boundary between town and village; Istiea, on the top of the seahorse's head, Kimi on its back and Karistos at the end of its tail, and with Chalkis they constitute the focal points of the four wildly divergent areas that make up the island.

So it was that I made hopefully for Karistos.

When we docked, Marmari seemed too small for such a big boat. We disembarked, and five of us piled into a taxi. The others were all elderly Greek women, and they discussed my accommodation prospects with keen interest. (My friend from Rafina quickly imparted the bad news regarding my marital status.) The journey took about 20 minutes and was punctuated by the tobacco-stained voice of the beaming taxi driver, who irritatingly insisted on repeating 'Thatcher, Thatcher'. *You're supposed to be telling me quaint local stories.* I thought, *not reminding me of that.*

We climbed up, then down, and quickly reached the fertile Karistos plain, its horizons still liquid in the heat.

Karistos (population approximately 4000) was a delight, although it had no right to be as the newer additions to its streets were an architectural disaster. I found a room overlooking the bay, all high ceilings, peeling pink paint and vast mahogany furniture, and made friends with the proprietor, a dark-skinned, statuesque young woman called Litsa. I was the only guest in the house. The french windows next to my bed overlooked the long stone jetty and a yard in which a dozen fishing boats were propped up by tree trunks. The front consisted of an enormously wide road, lined with mulberry trees on one side and brightly painted fishing boats on the other, and behind the trees a row of tavernas and cafés sprawled their tables over the road, shaded by awnings draped with drying octopus.

After unpacking I discovered that there was no hot water at any time; I supposed I might as well rehabilitate myself to cold showers, as I had a lot of them ahead of me. I went out, choosing a small taverna in a backstreet where appetizing piles of the food I had forgotten circled above my head in waiters' swift hands: blood-red, meaty tomatoes glistening with oil and studded with purple onions, creamy mounds of *tsatsiki* mottled a delicate pale green, plump, tar-shiny olives, puckered and slippery charcoal-grilled peppers, moist and pitted slices of feta dusted with oregano, squidgy, comfort-smelling bread, tender rings of baby squid and succulent, pink-gilled fish. I ate some squid, drank some good retsina and spoke to no one. The people at the next table were celebrating the Greek victory in the World Subbuteo Cup in Rome.

During the night the room lost some of its attraction when the entire population of Karistos seemed to be in animated conversation right under my window, and fishermen started up their motors until dawn and beyond. I lay awake for a long time listening to the rats in the roof and staring at the ceiling.

The more I uncovered of Evian history the more the island seemed, in ancient times at least, like Greece in microcosm, a bundle of separate settlements struggling to resist all comers and to acquire territory. Again and again I found too that the story of Evia shed light on the development of Greece itself, whether it was the part about the first settlers, or the pioneering colonists it sent to what has become Italy, or the triumphs and catastrophes of Classical and Roman times, or the long course of Byzantium, or the occupation of the Venetians and Lombards (in feudal residence for 265 years), or the four centuries of Turkish rule, or 1821 and after, when the Greeks won their independence. Few countries, and fewer islands, have such an extraordinary history. There too was the paradox of ancient Greece, so revered by the west and such a thorn in the flesh of the still-young new Greece which chafes against its own inadequacy like a son who can't live up to his father.

On another level the island's history revealed its individuality, and this was nowhere clearer than in the case of Karistos, whose extraordinary relationship with ancient Athens was of the intensity and volatility of a centuries-long love affair. The settlement was, the tradition goes, named after the son of the centaur Chiron (although for every mythological explanation there is a pedestrian equivalent, and it may derive from a word meaning chestnuts after the abundance of chestnut trees in the vicinity). The land was inhabited by 3500 BC at the latest. Among its first residents were Dryopes who migrated from the mainland; southern Euboea is closely associated with Dryopes by most ancient historians. Who exactly they were is unclear, but later Greeks did not consider them to be Ionians or Dorians. By the time of the Trojan War (approximately 1200 BC) the city-state of Karistos was well established, and in the Catalogue of Ships in the *Iliad* Homer lists Karistians among the participants on the Greek side.

The ancient community prospered, not least because of its strategic position at the tip of the Cycladic chain. This may have been its downfall at the beginning of the fifth century BC, however, as it was the obvious place for the Persians to stop on their way to subjugate Eretria and Athens. The Karistians were quickly forced to capitulate, and in the subsequent campaign other Greeks were suspicious of their relationship with the Persians; when the latter lost the war, therefore, retribution was swift in the shape of Themistocles and a squadron of Athenian sailors who set fire to Karistos. In 479, however, another Athenian force landed in Karistos and was beaten. Soon the Karistians were forced to submit again, and during the Peloponnesian Wars between Athens and Sparta later in the tumultuous fifth century BC they went off to fight for the

Athenians. There were serious rifts in the relationship whenever the Karistians dared to raise their collective voice in opposition, but they couldn't make the break definitive and Athens retained a foothold among the Karistians long after they had achieved nominal independence.

It was after a Euboean rebellion against Athens in 411 BC that the notion of a federal arrangement on the island appears to have manifested itself in the formation of the Euboean League. On the one hand, given the precarious nature of life in those days of frequent wars, invasions and broken alliances, it is surprising that the various groups of islanders hadn't already capitalized on their geographic unity to gain the safety of numbers. On the other hand it was a geographic unity that existed only on a map, as the mountains meant that communication by road was virtually impossible and that it was easier for almost everyone to hop over to the mainland than to visit potential allies on their own soil. The geographic factor was particularly significant in the case of Karistos, which even now is relatively isolated from the rest of the island.

The Euboean League is something of a faded leaf of Greek history, barely discernible in most places. It was probably around for half a millennium, but the only primary sources extant are inscriptions and a dodgy passage in Aeschines. Its establishment constitutes just about the only evidence of the islanders' conception of unity and identity. Despite the fact that Athens never really ceased dealing with the Euboean city-states individually, if it hadn't been for the Romans, and this nascent tendency had been permitted to mature, the island's history might have been very different.

It is most likely that the League was formed by Chalkis and Eretria alone. It was a logical move, as the break from Athens must have made the islanders chronically insecure. The League was closely associated with the Spartans in its early stages. This is hardly surprising either, as having alienated one of the superpowers it was natural that the other should be involved in the affairs of the island to some extent, for safety's sake. Karistos does not appear to have joined for over a hundred years, and the first reason must have been its geographic isolation from its fellow island communities. Secondly, although its position was commercially beneficial, it made it much more vulnerable to Athenian attack. The Karistians may have hesitated before joining an alliance guaranteed to annoy Athens when their home was far more exposed to Athenian aggression than the northern city-states. Thirdly, everyone seems to have been aware that the Karistians were of Dryopian stock, whereas the three other important city-states of ancient Euboea (Chalkis, Eretria and Histiaea) were populated largely with Ionians; it probably created a natural barrier. Karistos remained an Athenian ally until about the end of the fourth century.

By the beginning of the third century BC, however, Demetrius Poliorcetes (the Besieger), soon to be King of Macedonia, was almost certainly in control of most of the island, and he patronized the League. Karistos finally joined around that time. Whatever the role of the League was during the ensuing years of Macedonian rule, there is no reason to suppose that it was ever formally dissolved. Then the spectre of Rome became a reality – though the transformation was long and painful. The Karistians and their Macedonian reinforcements did manage to repulse the Romans once, but they couldn't hold out, and after Eretria was taken in 198 BC the Karistians surrendered. They were granted an illusory independence by the Roman Senate, like the rest of the island. At this point it emerges that the League entailed dual citizenship (of the home city-state and of the island), the four main settlements were members, and both a kind of local government and a centralized League government were in operation. In the later years of the Roman period it had little power, and disappears from the records.

The Roman Empire brought prosperity to Karistos. The smart

set back home grew exceedingly keen on the green and white marble found in various spots in southern Euboea, and it was quarried extensively. Karistos was also known then for its asbestos, used for sailcloth and winding sheets. Asbestos is not what a town wants to be associated with now, however, and people boasted to me instead of its fine meat and excellent mineral water, which they fondly claimed was good for the nerves.

During the first century AD some Christian converts who had heard St Paul speak in Athens arrived on the island and started talking to the Euboeans about Jesus, but the news probably didn't percolate through to Karistos for some time. The centre of the Roman Empire shifted east, and in AD 330 Constantinople was dedicated as its capital. Little is known of Karistos during the murky centuries of early Byzantium. When the Emperor Heraclius came to the throne in 610 he began subdividing his territory, using the military term *thema* (theme) for the regions he created. In the administrative reorganization of the following century Evia became part of the Theme of Hellas along with mainland Greece – it was never allowed to be a proper island. When the Crusaders took possession of Byzantium in 1204, the port of Karistos was assigned, in the Partition Treaty which swiftly followed, to Venice, which had secured itself three-eighths of the Empire as a reward for shipping the Crusaders east. But in 1205 the ambitious Bonifacio, Marquis of Montferrat and latterly King of Thessaloniki, unilaterally sliced Evia into three fiefdoms which were later parcelled out into baronies. He bestowed the southern third, with Karistos as the capital, upon the Veronese Ravano dalle Carceri, who went on to become ruler of the whole island. The territory was united, at that time, with the island of Aegina in the Saronic Gulf, also on paper a Venetian possession. (Aegina was already historically linked with Evia; it had been the only other island in the Theme of Hellas.) Ravano was quite a character. He managed to get himself excommunicated after having an affair with a married woman. He seemed to enjoy annoying the Catholic Church (not an uncommon pursuit) and had put his nose into property bequeathed by other feudal lords to the Templars, some of whom had settled in Evia; he can't have been surprised when they complained to the Pope.

Ravano appealed to Venice for feudal protection in 1209 when he was lord of all three fiefdoms, and accordingly acknowledged its sovereignty over the whole island. At first Venetian involvement was minimal, but as the years rolled by the powerful Republic insinuated itself into Evian affairs and became increasingly anxious to acquire the barony of Karistos, which was home to an array of Latin lords. Alfonso Fadrique, leader of the dreaded Company of Catalans and son of the King of Sicily, acquired the territory in 1317 when he married the baron's daughter (the baron having conveniently died the same year). Venice had been warring with him, supported by the Lombard lords, and in the truce of 1318 surrendered all claim to Karistos. It eventually got its way though (as it almost always did), and in 1365 bought the barony, serfs and all, from the incumbent Catalan for 6000 ducats. It was a pyrrhic victory as the financial returns were so disastrous that in 1386 the Republic was obliged to let it as a fiefdom to three Venetians, the Giustiniani brothers, for a very low rent. It declined further, like much of the island, and during the dying years of the Latin occupation the rent was continually decreased. By that time the Turks were raiding with appalling frequency, and many Evian Greeks simply packed up and left. Albanian colonists were encouraged to come over to bolster productivity, and many did. But the attrition was already irredeemable – and then there was a severe plague in 1432. The Turks gave what little remained of the barony a final battering in 1469, the year before they took the island.

Karistos duly became the second largest Turkish settlement

on Evia, after Chalkis – the only other, in fact, of any significance. By the end of the eighteenth century there were 1600 Turkish families and 400 Greek in the area. The 'system' of government required the landowning Turk to provide each Greek family on his estate with a cottage, a yoke of oxen and seed; the tenant was then obliged to remit half the harvest. The Greeks had a wretched time. According to an eyewitness account published in London's *Penny Magazine* in 1833 the Turks would ride around at their leisure with a group of attendants and settle down for the night at whichever tenanted homestead took their fancy. The Greek would be required to furnish their every need without remuneration for as long as they chose to stay. The cottages were built with ridiculously low doors, the story goes, so as to prevent, at the very least, the entrance of the Turks' horses too. The south of the island in general was so sparsely populated that Karistos was the see of a diocese extending miles to the north. A certain J. Hawkins, among the crustiest of my predecessors writing and travelling on the island, was in southern Evia in 1797, and Robert Walpole included a piece he wrote about it in the second volume of his anthology *Memoirs of European and Asiatic Turkey*. Of the bishopric at Karistos Hawkins wrote, '... on account of the barbarous state of society here it has remained unoccupied from the period of the conquest of the island until the present Bishop bought the see; of which he heartily repents.'

The whole of Greece at that time was in a state of confusion as the Ottoman Empire, over the course of the century, had been fast losing its grip on power. Not coincidentally, the nationalist movement was gaining momentum, spurred on by the ideals and drama of the French Revolution. But Evia, though full of freedom-fighters, was one of the last regions of the first modern Greek state to see the Turks off. In 1821 – a critical year – the island was virtually under the complete control of Omer Bey of Karistos, and despite numerous outbreaks of violence throughout the 1820s he held on, even when other regions of southern Greece were falling like ninepins. It was a measure of the high regard in which the Turks held the island, and of the extent and prosperity of their many estates upon it. The question of compensation payable if they did leave was always being raised, as it was in 1830 when President Ioannis Kapodistrias sent a three-person delegation to Evia setting an agenda for Turkish departure. The Great Powers had, of course, included Evia in official Greek territory, and the revolution was all but over, but after these last talks had broken down it was still to be a full three years before the Turkish leadership capitulated. (In true Greek style, domestic strife among the factions jostling for power was responsible for at least some of the delay.) In the spring of 1833, a month after Prince Otto of Bavaria had been installed as the first King of Greece, the government sent Iakovos Rizos Neroulos over to Evia in a British ship and his men took Chalkis castle. Immediately afterwards they went down to Karistos and it too was liberated.

It was during that period that a very curious document was fermenting inside the head of the Reverend Samuel Sheridan Wilson, an Englishman of that most beloved of species, the missionary. He was stationed in Malta for 16 years for the Bible Society, and travelled the length and breadth of Greece attempting, entirely unsuccessfully, to foist Protestantism upon the Orthodox Greeks. This man selected Evia of all the regions of the country as the location for a 'colony of decidedly pious Britons'. The plan was to teach the children of these colonists Greek and dress them like the natives so that the third generation 'would be Greeks in name, costume and language, yet Protestants in faith and morals.' What exactly was involved in 'Protestant morals' he chooses not to reveal. (He loathed the Pope, of course.) He sets the document down at the end of his *magnum opus, A Narrative of the Greek Mission*, published in 1839, supporting his case with the *Penny Magazine* extract which, curiously enough, recommends exactly the same fate for Evia.

Wilson really loved Evia, and describes it in fulsome detail in his book. He chose it for his new Eden because of its outstanding beauty, its fertility and its sparse population; looking down on it now from his heaven he must be pleased that it is still as beautiful as ever, and relatively unmolested – compared at least with the islands frequented by his colleagues who exercised their zeal upon the likes of Corfu, Rhodes and Mykonos. Although a horde of western missionaries descended upon Greece in the post-liberation years, Evia seems to have escaped most of them. They were all wasting their time, because the new-born country identified its precious nationalism so closely with the Orthodox Church – which had, after all, played a vital role in keeping the flame of Greek culture and tradition alive during 400 years of slavery, and which they were not likely to abandon at this juncture in their history.

In the morning I set out intending to make a day trip to Platanistos, a remote village to the southeast, but when I got to the *souvlaki* shop which doubled up as the bus station no one could tell me when a bus might go there. A bus was about to depart, however, for Agia Triada, and I decided to make the most of the opportunity and get on it, particularly as everyone else was energetically doing so.

The bus laboured up rough gravel roads until the sea looked as big as the plain, and through the other window the extravagant Red Castle appeared on top of a mottled hill. Agia Triada (Holy Trinity) was named after a small church built next to a series of dank, plum-coloured caves. A crone informed me that it was the holy day of Agia Triada, which after a good deal of toothless explanation I finally established was the Monday after Whitsun, and this explained the crowds. There were so many people on the bus that the steeper inclines could have been walked more quickly, and when we arrived the grove was swarming with yet more. Blessed bread was being noisily dispensed and everyone was squeezing sweatily through the church to kiss first the hand of a priest in a gold robe and second an icon. Then they had a party. *Souvlakia* were piled high on charcoal braziers, kids were roasted, tomatoes sliced, feta oiled, olives eaten and by 10.30 am the empty cans of Amstel beer were already heaped under a vast canopy of plane branches. A couple of groups of musicians started up a few yards apart and began playing simultaneously. It was a wonderful party, but not for one alone, and I left before moroseness set in.

The track I walked down was perfumed by lemon trees and large oleander bushes. I made for the Red Castle, a silent two hours away through desiccated fields and ghostly villages. Halfway up the hill it was perched on I crossed a small pine wood roofed with immense nests, and after stepping over rings of ruined walls I was in front of a huge and desolate fort with a jagged edge on one side and crenellations on another, built of a pale brown stone with a reddish tinge. Inside I found a silent maze of stone topiary.

I walked down to the village of Mili, and sat contemplating the castle at a tiny table under an enormous plane tree, crushing lemon verbena leaves between my fingers and relishing the scent. It was built at the beginning of the thirteenth century by the incumbent Lombards. It has been called Red Castle in the language of whoever has occupied it (Kokkino Kastro in Greek, Castel Rosso in Italian and Kizil Hissar in Turkish), either because of the colour of the stone or because of its bloody history. It was the HQ of the barony of Karistos, and bitterly fought over, so strong that it could be defended by only 30 soldiers. The

Burgundian Othon de Cicon held it as Lord of Karistos in the mid-thirteenth century and he was able to organize the obstruction of the channel between Evia and Andros when he was at war with the Venetians and Lombards. The knight Likarios got Othon out with the help of Byzantine troops, but the Lombards retook it, and in 1317 Fadrique moved in. It was always an ideal base for piratical raids (a favourite occupation of the lords) as it offered such a clear view of the straits.

During the fifteenth century Castel Rosso declined, but it revived once the Turks were established, and a little community huddled on the slopes below it. Bernard Randolph, who came in the 1670s, wrote in his book *The Present State of the Islands in the Archipelago* that all passing boats stopped off there for news of pirates, still very much at large. (They seem to be endemic in this channel. A grisly piece appeared in *The Times* as late as 1844 reporting that pirates had captured two merchant vessels there and that the headless corpses of 20 of the victims had been washed ashore at Karistos.) Castel Rosso had already established a reputation as an important commercial centre under the Latins. It controlled the only port in the area, and the surrounding land was fertile, so it became a natural trading post, especially for cipollino marble and dye-yielding molluscs, both renowned local products. Much of the trade during that period was conducted by a small group of Jewish merchants. In 1452 they complained to the Venetian governor of persecution.

Mili was an oasis in a crackingly arid landscape. I persuaded a man on a donkey to sell me some of his apricots. A group of middle-aged women at the only other table outside the café were discussing a brand of diet pills. Their eyesight was not up to reading the price on the box, and it was brought over to me so that I could illuminate them. The expiry date was June 1983.

In the evening I strolled around Karistos and looked up at the three sky-blue domes of St Nicholas' cathedral. In a neat garden next to the town hall opposite they had put up a chalk-white bust of Neofitos, a magnificently-bearded bishop of Karistos and central figure in the Evian revolution. He was a member of the *Filiki Etairia* (Friendly Society) founded by Greeks in Odessa in 1814 with the aim of liberating the motherland from the Turks, and his tireless campaigning and leadership during the 1820s is indicative of the crucial role of the Church in the Independence movement.

It was already hot when I woke the next day. I took a walk along the coastal track to the west for a few miles. The beach stretched round the bay, but there were only three people on it: a couple sunbathing, and a man in the water catching octopus with his hands. I disturbed a number of Caspian turtles sunning themselves on cracked mud around a pool; I barely saw them beneath their camouflage, but they heard me and plopped in, met by their glinting reflections. Days began to pass.

The bus to Platanistos left at 1.50. The man sitting in front of me had a voice like a megaphone which he used constantly. He got off at Aetos, the first village we came to, and as he did so he turned and said goodbye to the whole bus, as if he was aware that we had all been silently participating in his monologue. The road soon ran out of asphalt and snaked on, slithering north of the coast and ascending inland through dramatic passes. Although Platanistos was only 16 miles away, it took us well over an hour to get there. I had intended to hitch, but Litsa and her mother became nearly hysterical at the prospect. 'I know the Karistians,' warned Litsa, 'and they are worse than anyone else anywhere.' (Wherever you hitch in the world the local women think that the local men are the worst on the face of the earth: a happy little comment on sexual politics.) I was glad that I hadn't attempted it as we didn't pass a single car after Aetos, only two donkeys. This made me nervous about my accommodation prospects, and I asked the girl sitting next to me, who looked very doubtful but suggested I try Potami down on the coast, a mile or two further on. So we waited in the bus for half an hour while the driver had a drink at Platanistos, and shortly after I was deposited at the end of a track.

A very old couple also got off the bus, and we all started down the track together. Although I only had a small bag, they had 16 items between them, including a sack of potatoes and three plastic buckets. They were barely mobile, and yet proudly pointed out their village – a mere speck in the distance. As I was grappling with the relationship between their baggage and the distance to be covered, the man veered off and produced a donkey tethered behind a bush. All our bags were either hung on the saddle or tied on with a rope. I asked what the donkey's name was, and they looked at me as if I were barking; it must have been like asking a workman what his van was called. The man, who had a sun-cured face and wore a blue cap embroidered with yellow Roman letters spelling 'captain', revealed that he had a room I could rent in his taverna, and we struck off in good humour with the sun on our backs. The track wound down to the sea where Andros, geologically an extension of Evia, soon loomed out of the strip of Aegean once ironically known as Silent Mouth to intrepid medieval westerners. We met a labourer who was working the wheat, and he said that it was a very poor year, because of the drought. This produced long speeches from my companions about the wretched state of the dried-out village, but they were interrupted by the appearance of a shiny grey snake about three feet long. The donkey was halted and the woman threw stones at the snake while the man jabbed at it with a stick; they eventually debilitated it and the woman finished it off with a rock. Five minutes later the donkey got a stone in its hoof. My Swiss Army knife had been waiting all its life for this moment, but it was not to be – the man cast a suspicious look at it in my outstretched hand and used a sharpened stick instead.

The village consisted of 25 scattered houses, a church on a hillock and a bay lined with half a mile of sandy beach. Much shrunken over the past few generations by the unwillingness of young people to live so far from the new world of video games and other forms of cultural toxic waste, there was only one child under 16. Not so long ago there was a school for 30. The disappearance of children always presages the death of a village. When we arrived we agreed a price for the room and full board, and sat on the terrace outside the taverna drinking coffee and ouzo, shaded by a trellis of vines and mulberry branches and hailed by passing villagers asking news of Karistos. Before the sun set I walked down to the beach and sat on a warm rock; the sea, with a sharply sloping, pebble-laden bed, was transparent ultramarine, and there was no sound except the distant cries of a man urging his donkey on. They had actually contemplated building a nuclear power plant there once. I wandered back up as the shadows thickened, and after a meal of fried fish three men came in and everyone sat around talking about the petrol strike, the appalling price rises and the vagaries of politicians.

I was woken at 7.00 the next morning by a knock on my window and Andonis, my host, shouting that someone was going to Agios Konstantinos (which I wanted to visit to find the remains of a pre-Classical site) and did I want a lift? Travelling in the eastern corner of south Evia is extremely difficult – few roads, fewer houses, dodgy maps and virtually no signposts – so I leapt at the opportunity.

A man called Vangelis in his thirties was waiting in the taverna, and after swallowing some coffee with Andonis we set off in his battered red pickup. We turned off the track to collect an old woman who was standing on the edge of a field waiting for us, surrounded by baggage which included a porcelain toilet bowl. She squeezed in the front while Vangelis loaded her gear.

and she told me that she had been staying at her brother's for seven years nursing her husband, who had recently died, and was now returning to her home at Mourtia. During the 15-minute journey there I made the mistake of pointing out a snake on the road, at which Vangelis swerved wildly, nearly tipping us off the edge, ran over it, and then reversed back over it three times. He claimed that if you disturb them while they are mating the male leaps for your throat, and enthusiastically demonstrated. We stopped above a vineyard and began the descent to the woman's house in relays, ferrying her things. She pointed out her *patriko* (the rural Greek equivalent of the ancestral home), where she was born, in ruins next to her present one, which overlooked the valley above two huge peach trees. People were always showing me their *patrika.* The family houses were loaded with meaning, constituting the all-important link with the past, a symbol of continuity, tradition and the solidity of the family. I noticed the islanders were all plugged into their past, and their attitude towards it was totally alien to anything floating around in the modern western sensibility. As the old woman was struggling to unlock the door – which she eventually managed by pouring olive oil into the padlock – I realized that she had not been back there for the whole seven years. It quickly became apparent that her plans to move straight back in, toilet and all, were to be foiled: firstly, a cloud of bats flew at us as we went in, and then the kitchen roof fell in.

Agios Konstantinos consisted of three or four goatherds' shacks, one smart house painted white and the small eponymous church overlooking the valley. We eventually found the ruins of the ancient site: a wall and a half of massive stones, perfectly cut and as long as 10 feet each, on a kind of terrace, earthed up at the back and barely visible, but exposed at the front where the ground sloped away. Further along Vangelis found the remains of another corner. Called Elliniko (after an inscription I failed to locate), the few people who have ever recorded a visit can't agree on its function; most date it between 750 and 500 BC. A student from the American School of Classical Studies in Athens went there in 1899 and the locals told him that they frequently heard 'mutterings and groanings' coming from a hole in the wall. Then they gave him a bowl of goats' milk 'tasting of the green shoots of arbute and heather'. The position was superb, commanding a view that can scarcely have changed since the first settlers tamed a corner of it. Obscure sites may lack the artistic and architectural appeal of their intact peers, but often the lack of paraphernalia like fences, people, roads, litter and noise means the lone visitor responds more easily and more intensely. These places meant more to me, aesthetically as well as emotionally, than Delphi or Mycenae ever had.

After we got back I swam, read on the beach for a couple of hours, had an unsuccessful shower (only three of the pinholes in the showerhead actually spouted water) and sat outside the taverna to wait for Vangelis, with whom I had arranged to set off in pursuit of another benighted ancient site. The susurration of the sea drifted up to the terrace, and a Swiss man appeared who had been sailing and said that he thought that a day without human contact was '*un jour perdu*'. How wrong you are, I thought.

We were heading for Kastri, a natural harbour a few miles south of Potami. A road had recently been cut between them, though it was so appalling I wondered why they bothered: it could hardly have been worse for the car's suspension if we had driven straight over the scrub surface of the mountain. We climbed up first, above an exotic quilt of neat and burnished squares of wheat and corn. The water was so clear that from the top of the mountains I could see the formation of the rocks under the surface. We drove down and up again, and then the Kastri bay appeared with a handful of houses dotted around it. At this point Vangelis stopped the car and unilaterally decided to lunge towards the passenger seat, apparently unclear of exactly what he planned to do first but presumably with a very precise idea of what he would do last. I wasn't surprised by this: it was one of those mildly irritating interruptions that have to be dealt with, like stepping in a small dog turd. I pushed him off and explained that he'd got the wrong idea, etc., and after a few token protests we set off again, he apparently happy now that he had fulfilled his moral responsibility to Greek manhood by having a go.

It was at Kastri, the uninspired modern name of ancient Geraestos, that the Greeks stopped on the way back from the Trojan War. In the *Odyssey* Nestor recalls the numerous bulls' thighs they sacrificed at the temple to Geraestos Poseidon which gave the settlement its name (the epithet is from a verb meaning 'venerate' or 'honour'). The harbour supported Karistos' flourishing sea trade and brought prosperity to the area even before the Classical period. We searched around for the remains of the temple and eventually found a site which may or may not have been it, overgrown and fenced off with barbed wire. A column lay on its side down the middle. A villager told us there were more stones up on the hill, but Vangelis was getting tired of traipsing around looking at next to nothing so we went for a beer with a man who had a gas fridge instead; I was secretly glad.

The sun was setting on the journey back. The mountains inland turned a purply colour, and the rocks sloping down to the water were tinged with apple green. A fox ran in front of the car. The first layer of Andros lay like a flat stone on the water, and the mass beyond evanesced into haze.

Only one bus a day went back to Karistos, and it passed the Potami turnoff between seven and eight in the morning. This meant setting off on foot at six and walking uphill for three miles. The air was so crisp and pure that it made the inside of my nose hurt. I collapsed at the top and waited for the bus, which eventually appeared, several loops of the road higher, as ridiculously small as a Dinky toy. Ten hoary passengers murmured greetings and stared at me suspiciously.

When we reached Karistos I reclaimed my room where Litsa, clucking with delight to see me safely back, had let me leave my things. Later I decided to find Paleochora, the ancient site of the town, and in particular the Byzantine church of the Archangels Gabriel and Michael. The road branched off near a fort called the Bourtzi at the eastern end of the seafront. The base of the wall was built of blocks of marble from the temple of Apollo, the emaciated ruins of which I later found fenced off and ignored in one of the main shopping streets. I struck off north through lemon groves and scorching, shadeless roads lined with dusty myrtle, and found what I assumed was Paleochora – but no sign of the Byzantine church. I asked some children playing in the road, and discovered it was actually in Kalivia, further up the mountain. Abandoning the search for ancient remains I pressed on, trailed by the children, and soon I could at least see the sandy-coloured church with its striking pale blue dome. The giggling children asked me a series of questions and after discussing my nationality among themselves for a while the leader cleared his throat.

'Is it true that Britain has a woman prime minister because all the men are homosexuals? Our teacher told us so in our history lesson.' This was a difficult question to answer, and I reflected on whether the episode revealed more about the Greek attitude to foreigners or the standard of the national education system. (It is certainly true that the lack of an effective infrastructure in Greece clobbers any hope of healthy exponential growth in vital areas, notably education.)

Turning off the road at Kalivia I staggered up mountain tracks, lost the church among the trees, and eventually asked an old woman the way. She invited me in to her little house, which was surrounded by bushy pots of basil. She turned out to be the caretaker of the church, and spun a great yarn about how the Turks used it to put their sheep in for the night, but the first time a Turk slept in there he was struck down in a swoon, and after that they were ordered not to use it as an overnight stop. Then she gave me a preserved walnut in syrup and some small peaches and showed me a photo of her son, who lived in California.

The church was in fact two interconnecting churches. St Nicholas was small and crude with a simple wooden altar and crooked flagstones. Near some very flaky old icons in the sanctuary I found a collection register: the first entry was for October 1919 and recorded a donation of 95 drachmas 40 lepta. In the Archangels' church next door a series of 24 nasty icons dated 1905 betrayed a time when the Greeks were mad keen on the sickly western style, all tears and realism; fortunately for the aesthetic sensibilities of their descendants they collectively grew out of it. The old woman appeared and began hosing down the tombs outside. She pointed out her husband's, which had just been 'opened', a practice still common among people not wealthy enough to own a family tomb, at least in the country. After a period of time (not less than three years) the grave is smashed open and if the body has decomposed the bones are dug up, washed and placed in a box which is in turn placed in a charnel house; you often see these in the corner of churchyards. (If the body has not decomposed sufficiently it gets put back for a spell.) The boxes are usually adorned with a photograph of the departed. When the smell of these charnel houses becomes intolerable they are cleared out and the bones placed in a common grave.

I thanked her and set off. It was still baking, and I resolved to hitch back. After an hour a vehicle passed, and the driver picked me up. He turned out to be Tzimi, who owned Jimmy's Café and *souvlaki* shop on the front in Karistos, and he exuded the confidence of a big fish in a small pool. He had tiny eyes and must have weighed about 20 stone. At one point he clapped me on the back and said he could see I was a good person because I was nice and big like him; he didn't trust thin people. The comparison set my morale back about five years. When we arrived he insisted on offering me a cold drink in his café, and asked me all the usual questions: was I married and why not, how much was I paying for my room, did I have any brothers and sisters and were they married and the rest of the instinctive protocol routine. I could see he was a fixer, so I told him I wanted to visit Kavodoro, the eastern tip of south Evia, by boat, and he immediately summoned a friend from the other side of the bar. 'I'll take you tomorrow,' said Kirios Bouyoukas. 'Meet me at 4.30 am by the big boat with the red stripe down the side.'

Feeling pleased with this arrangement, and avoiding any mirrors, I went off to my hair appointment. I had asked Litsa in the morning where the best place was to get my hair cut. 'It's not the best place,' she said, 'it's the only place.' The hairdresser, also called Litsa, was making the most of a difficult situation: the 'salon' was in her aunty's flat and we squeezed into the tiny dilapidated and yellow-stained bathroom to wash my hair. I arrived at 4.55 and was washed (in hot water – it was worth it just for that) cut, dried and out by 5.15. She was distressed at signs of premature ageing, and had a great line in paranoia-inducement:

'Your hair has gone white! Come and look at this, aunt, this young girl has got so many white hairs! It's amazing! Why don't you dye it?'

'Well, it doesn't really bother me, actually ...'

'We could dye it now.' (Hand reaches for dye bottle.) 'You're not married, are you? It would be better if you dyed it.'

Thinking that it had cost me a lot of hard stress to get that many white hairs I managed to dissuade her, and the haircut was fine, although I did look quite a lot like Friar Tuck.

The *Dimitrios One* was a brightly painted 60-foot boat, conspicuously larger and in better condition than its harbour companions. I sat and froze on one of the long benches on deck until Kirios Bouyoukas signalled me into the cabin. When he felt cold he put an extra pair of trousers on top of the ones he was already wearing; he took them on and off numerous times over the next couple of hours, and it made me nervous. Although it was before five in the morning there were plenty of *kaikia* (small wooden fishing boats) about, and further out at sea the shipping channel between Evia and Andros was rarely without the tiny black silhouette of a cargo vessel. We chugged out of the bay and just as we rounded Cape Mandili, the southernmost point of the island, the sun rose and poured its watery luminosity over the solid blocks of dark sea. We passed the uninhabited island of Mandilou on the right; to the left sheer pale red and green cliffs sloped down to inaccessible sandy coves. In the deserted expanses further east Kirios Bouyoukas pointed out the site of the ancient town called Archampolis. There were caves there which one local guide gravely reported to an archaeologist were inhabited 'before the flood'. Bouyoukas said the town fell into the sea after an earthquake, but he didn't know when.

Three hours after setting off we arrived at the beach below the tiny village of Amigdalia. It transpired that Kirios Bouyoukas was paid by the state to call at these remote spots three times a week, and on this occasion we had brought a load of steel rods and a long aluminium pipe. These were piled onto the clapped-out rowing boat towed along behind the *Dimitrios One* and taken ashore by Yannis, Kirios Bouyoukas's mate, who had been lurking in the bowels of the boat all morning. As soon as he was on board again we turned around and started back. On the return trip I mentioned that I wanted to visit a village on the eastern end of Karistos bay called Bouros, about eight miles from the town itself, and Kirios Bouyoukas offered to drop me off. As it turned out this must have been his idea of a practical joke, as it was hideous as well as deserted. I assumed we would stop at some kind of little harbour, but suddenly he switched off the engine at a point where the bare rock sloped less steeply, and I was motioned into the rowing boat.

'But where *is* Bouros?'

'It's around the corner, but it's more difficult to stop there. You can climb around the rock.'

So I did, and a workman on the track at the top of the rock a few hundred yards further on looked stricken as I suddenly rose up, apparently out of the sea. Bouros comprised a dozen empty houses and a hotel, with a large holiday apartment complex further on. The season hadn't yet begun. A horrible statue of a woman riding a centaur stood inexplicably at the water's edge. All along this road to Karistos construction was in ominous progress. It was as if Frankenstein was being put together and the land was enjoying its last days of freedom until the moment life was breathed into him, when nothing would be the same again.

The track, everywhere splashed with the ubiquitous pink oleander, joined the asphalt at Aetos, where a woman asked me in for some water. We sat on the porch outside her little house, and she complained about local unemployment. Her brother-in-law pulled up and asked if she wanted a lift into town; she didn't, but I did, and he took me. He was eager to tell me that in Greece they had a special name for the British prime minister, which was 'the iron lady', and he chortled at the ingenuity of this Hellenic invention all the way to Karistos.

Most evenings I sat on the front with Litsa and her parents outside the shop they kept underneath the rooms, watching the ferryboat come in from Rafina. It docked twice or three times a day right in the middle of the front, and disgorged its passengers directly onto the road. The town beat to the rhythm of that ferry schedule. The family were always hopeful that the boat would bring more takers for their rooms, but it never did. An endless provision of gossip sustained them as the populace eddied around the front, their chatter frequently punctuated by neighbours stopping for a few words. The fishmonger reported his short visit to Chalkis, which everyone agreed they didn't like, though it turned out that many of them had never been. It was quicker to get to Athens, and they obviously felt a greater affinity with the mainland than with the unknown territories away to the north of their own island.

On Saturday evenings they shut the seafront street to facilitate the *volta* (evening stroll, but so much more besides), when everyone meandered up and down in their best clothes. It started in earnest at about 9.30. Although I have often participated in the ritual in various Mediterranean towns and villages, I never really understood it until I walked up and down with Litsa after a day lolling in Karistos. It seemed to form a natural whole with all the other routines and rituals of the day. We had just had an extended conversation with Litsa's mother on the subject of marriage. Litsa was 25 and single, and she said she didn't want to get married until she met the right man. I said that I didn't know if I wanted to get married at all. Litsa's mother said quite firmly that this was wrong; it's not natural to remain single, and you should follow the natural rhythm of life which includes having children, for if you don't fit into this structure you won't be happy.

I have heard all this said before many times, and although there is a particular obsession with marital status in Greece it is visible in the couple culture of western Europe, too, in a liberalized form. In Greece the role of tradition is crucial: whereas the whole complex social and domestic structure is intimately linked to a spiritual dimension endowing it with meaning, if the spiritual withers then the family/marriage/children routine becomes an end in itself. Rural communities always set more store on the importance of marriage and procreation in any country, but in particular in Greece; the urban jungle offers other kinds of distractions.

The same evening about 25 cars, lorries, trucks and even a bus suddenly came hurtling along the front (a passenger in the first one got out to remove the road blocks) with all their drivers' hands permanently on the horn. It was a wedding, and this was the procession following the groom. Twenty-five minutes later exactly the same thing occurred, this time following the bride's car. The bride's father had really blond hair. I was constantly amazed at how many blond people there were in certain parts of Evia; you hardly ever see one on the mainland, except in Athens, where it's always out of a bottle. It could be the Albanian influence. Up in the north, where blond hair is frequently seen around an estate owned for generations by foreigners, all the locals will tell you that it dates back to the time when the *droit de seigneur* was exercised on brides.

The next morning I went to have a proper look at Marmari up the coast. The bus, due to leave at 9.15, was delayed, and I sat waiting next to an old man wearing a black leather cap drinking ouzo and eating pistachios. The road was lined with vines as we approached Marmari, high above two Petali islands squatting in the small bay directly in front of the village. I asked the woman next to me if they were inhabited, and was told no, they are owned by *plousii* (rich people) who use them for holidays. They turned out to be shipowners.

Marmari, as you might guess, was in ancient times rich in marble, but this was little in evidence in the modern village, except in the church on the front, which had a beautiful wide marble floor. At the northern end of the bay a wooded path threaded between whitewashed houses splashed with bright blue paint and guarded by geraniums in earthenware pots. On the southern side the houses straggled behind a narrow shingle beach which stretched right around the bay, partially shaded by a row of pine trees. I was about to swim when a jellyfish was washed up at my feet, four fat tentacles wobbling on a base like a translucent fried egg. The music at the café on the front was provided by the owner's car, parked with the door open and the radio on. I travelled back to Karistos on the bus in high good humour as my Australian friend Christopher Emmerson was arriving on the evening boat. I was looking forward to speaking English, to our trip out to the wilds beginning the next day, and to a break from that most morose of activities, solitary drinking.

Kavodoro is one of the last regions of Greece to be transformed by what is commonly called progress. Although western-style modernizations have made incursions into its inaccessible villages, the inhabitants of its heart are still leading a life unrecognizable from that of their urban compatriots, and not so very long ago would come into Karistos on occasion to swap a goat for a pair of trousers.

Evians used to speak reverentially to me of a region shrouded in the mystique of the unknown with an enigmatic history of mythological gold seams, shipwrecks and strange folk customs. Furthermore, the first language of Kavodoro is Albanian, not Greek. Later in the summer I took to the archives of Athenian libraries to find out more. The name derives from the Venetian Cavo d'Ouro (Gold Cape); besides the gold seams, people used to say that there were once golden houses in the valleys. The Cape is actually the headland at the tip of the flicked-back crook of the seahorse's tail – but the name Kavodoro has come to designate anything from the headland alone to the whole southern trunk of the island.

Christopher had arrived on schedule, and he sauntered down the gangplank of the *Karistos Queen* with a broad smile, looking like a surfer fresh from Bondi. We had a celebratory drink and I told him we were leaving for Kavodoro immediately; nothing ever fazed him. People warned us against the trip. 'It's far, very far. There is nothing there. It's the black place,' said the bus driver outside the Karistos 'bus station'. The only way to travel to Kavodoro is to go as far as possible by bus and then walk. In Evia the type of bus you get is generally determined by the quality of the road it serves, and sure enough we boarded a thin tin shell with a kind of open-plan engine and bent seats. The driver was reluctant to let us on ('What are you going to do there?') and vague about the final destination of the bus, which apparently spent the night at whichever village suited him and the passengers.

The journey to Amigdalia in the heart of Kavodoro is 11 miles as the crow flies. The bus dropped us somewhere nearby after four hours; it had contended with the Ochi mountain range, dramatically plunging valleys, hairpin turns and broken stone tracks which would have defeated the heaviest-duty scrambling bikes. The first leg had taken us past the turning to Potami, and not long after we went through Antias, the only village in Kavodoro where Albanian isn't spoken. I often tried to find out why, but besides a confused story about the Persians leaving a settlement there after the Greek-Persian wars 2500 years ago I didn't get very far. It is also the village where the shepherds communicate by whistling across their isolated valleys, and the system has evolved to such a degree of sophistication that a complex whistling language has emerged which even uses grammar and which has attracted the close attention of linguists and social anthropologists. At Komito a beer stop was announced. It was a tiny, relatively affluent village with modern second storeys built onto the old stone cottages, creating a curious architectural fracture. Ten years ago it was the only village in Kavadoro with a policeman.

The bus struggled on up craggy mountainsides and down into breathtakingly precipitous valleys where a bright emerald line of trees marked the course of a river like a vein through dark flesh. The most spectacular valley of all was dotted with a handful of tiny villages – about 10 houses apiece – most of which (Simikouki, Drimonara, Thimi) have never appeared on a map. Then a pass cut through the mountainside into another wild abyss where the tottering houses of Zacharia were dwarfed by their primeval surroundings. Besides the odd yellow squares of harvested barley and oat stalks, grown for fodder, the occasional hillside was elaborately terraced for crops, and large expanses of dried-out fern broke up the green, along with clumps of oaks, planes and chestnuts.

When J. Hawkins was there he found that the 'frightful succession of chasms and precipices' corresponded to the 'savage reputation of the inhabitants', who were inhospitable and rapacious, and had been known to murder shipwrecked sailors. He hadn't been very impressed with the Turks around Karistos either. He watched them as they gathered on a beach during a storm looking forward to seeing a good shipwreck.

We eventually reached a fork where the bus driver ordered us to get off, flapping his hand towards the sea. 'Amigdalia is down there. I'll be coming through on Friday at 6.30 am if you want to come back.' It was Tuesday. We stumbled out apprehensively and began walking towards the sea. Thirty or forty small flat-roofed stone huts came into view. We were hungry, and I assured Christopher that I had never been to a Greek head village (as this was) where there was not, at the very least, a *magazi* (which means shop, but which often fulfils the role of numerous other public buildings too) with a bar offering minimal food. He never let me forget it. The shop in Amigdalia turned out to be a converted chicken hut selling tins of Spam and rat poison. There was nothing else. No one had piped water – none of the villages in the area did – and so the reservoir was the focal point of the community, as everyone arrived with their plastic containers strapped to donkeys and mules wearing brightly coloured *tagaria* (square shoulderbags) woven with the particular pattern of the village. The water had been brought by plastic hosepipe from miles up in the mountains ever since the wells dried up three years previously. The fountain always used to be the social centre of the village, as Greek literature testifies, and it was amusing to see how quickly everyone had reverted.

It was my first experience of an entirely Albanian-speaking community. They had spoken it since the fifteenth century without any contact with what we now call Albania. In 1402, and on several subsequent occasions, southern Evia was extensively colonized by Albanian-speakers. They arrived in the first instance at the behest of the ruling Venetians to replenish the dwindling population. It was a package: full freedom in return for productivity and help with the defence of the island. People known as Albanians have steadily filtered into Greece and spread themselves around over the centuries, and if you travel around the mainland you frequently come across a village where at least some of the old people speak Albanian. (Greece is not unique in this respect: there are so-called Albanian communities scattered over half of the earth. Many strains of the language come under the blanket heading 'Albanian', too: Norman Douglas cites 30 alphabets.)

Although many people still speak Albanian on Evia from Aliveri downwards, it is there on the eastern slice of Kavodoro that the language is still the true *lingua franca* of whole communities (although they all know Greek too). It is probably the purest Albanian settlement in the country. 'Half of Greece speaks Albanian,' a shepherd from Vrestides told me, although he had never been further afield than Karistos, thus revealing the trait born of insularity of perceiving your own community as the yardstick for all things.

Although everyone stared at us and shouted to each other, 'Where did they spring from?', they were open and friendly, perhaps because they saw us as a bit of a joke. A family called us into their yard and offered bread and *raki*. The grandfather was a hale type who said he drank two kilos of his own homemade wine each day for his health but refused to touch beer because it was harmful. We quickly realized that there was no hope of renting a room as the houses were so small, so we reconciled ourselves to kipping on the beach a mile or so further on, and wound our way down. It was the beach where Kirios Bouyoukas had dropped the rods and pipe. Some fishermen put in and we bought a kilo of their catch and cooked it on a fire. We had managed to purchase a kilo and a half of retsina from a barrel (local Greek wine is purchased by the kilo not the litre) which made the prospect of sleep more likely; to call the wine rough would be an abuse of the word, but it seemed appropriate enough for the occasion. Once we had put on all the clothes we had with us and lain down we were disturbed twice: once by a man who warned us that we were sleeping on the spot where rocks tumbled down from the mountain, for which we were grateful and moved, and once by a marauding goatherd who was either drunk or mad. (He probably thought the same about us.)

Next day we washed in the sea and were about to set off to find Kallianou when the family who had befriended us the previous day turned up *en masse* with flasks of hot goats' milk for our breakfast. It was dramatically windy, and they told us that their grandparents used to perform special rituals to soften the north wind involving throwing salt on fires and cutting up marrows. During our days in Kavodoro we spent half our time scrambling down shale slopes rescuing the sunhats we had bought in Karistos. At Vrestides a couple were winnowing wheat on a circular threshing floor. Each Kavodorian village had at least one, and often a house had its own. Wheat has always been a staple subsistence crop on the island. Rice has disappeared over the past century or so, and so has cotton.

In order to see the cape itself I persuaded Christopher that we should turn off the road at Prinia, and we continued along a path until we could see it. Way down below the coastline curled and uncurled, edged by a fraying ribbon of foam and the glittering surface of the azure Aegean. Six soaring hawks and a white-bellied osprey circled above us. A lighthouse on a bare wedge of brown rock marked Cape Kafireas, the furthest tip. King Nauplius the Argive, the son of Poseidon, was standing exactly where we were when he lit torches to confuse and shipwreck the Greek triremes on their way home from the Trojan War in order to avenge the murder of his son Palamedes. The sailors thought they were being guided into shelter. Euripides wrote a moving chorus speech about it in *Helen*, and both he and Sophocles wrote whole plays on the subject – but they are lost. Nauplius certainly didn't do things by halves. As his son's murderers were away fighting in Troy he had already dropped in on all their wives to tell each in turn that her husband was bringing back a Trojan concubine as his new queen. He was ultimately punished years later when Zeus arranged for him to be killed by false torches himself.

The returning triremes were not the only victims of the cape. The Greeks named it Xilofagos (wood-eating) because it ate wooden vessels, and the villagers used to make furniture and roofs from bits of washed-up boat. Dio Chrysostom (sometimes called Dio of Prusa) was marooned in a storm near Kafireas and used his experience with the locals as the basis of his Seventh Discourse, delivered some time during the first century AD. He met a hunter who took him back to his isolated home, told him his life story and lavished the usual Greek hospitality upon him. Dio extols the natural abundance and humble, spontaneous joy of the hunter's life – the rural idyll – in order to make the point that poverty is a greater facilitator of happiness than wealth. (He goes on making the point, in fact, again and again, obviously working on the principle that if you say it often enough people believe you.) Both Greeks and Romans often told stories about the corrupting influence of money. I wondered if the shepherds and hunters of 1990 were 'happier' than Athenians. Dio, keen on the idea of a long Hellenic tradition, would certainly be foxed if he came back to update his Discourse and heard them all talking Albanian.

Back on the road we continued to Schizali, which clung to the steep mountainside like tufts of goathair on a barbed wire fence. The road ended there and we resolved to find Kallianou by path. We proceeded down through terraced slopes and on to a coastal track, the huge, glaring blue bay west of the Kavodoro headland stretching below. After crossing a ravine we walked along a dried-up riverbed, climbed up another mountainside, got completely lost and six hours later were forced by approaching darkness and very little water to return to Schizali, exhausted and bleeding. To add to our distress there was no shop of any kind, so we had to go right back to Prinia which, despite boasting only 10 houses, had a school with a leaking roof and a bar. We followed a shepherd to the bar, which was someone's back yard.

Six more shepherds sat around on the stone terrace, cradling their tall shiny crooks with scorchmarks under the curve. They had blue eyes and didn't look remotely Greek. The family whose house we sat outside comprised two old people, their son, who was drunk, daughter-in-law and seven grandchildren. Displaying the rural talent for appropriating modern goods, the old woman was wearing shoes made out of tyres. She had somehow sewn the leather forming the top of the shoe onto a section of tread. At first they were all taciturn, but the men soon began talking to us, or rather to Christopher, altogether more worthy of attention because he was a man. It was not the first time we had enjoyed that experience. They were thwarted in their endeavour by Christopher's 10 words of Greek, however, and so in the end were forced to address me anyway, *faute de mieux*. The women were silent and the children hid behind them: they hadn't seen foreigners before.

By now my Albanian vocabulary was up to about 25 words, and with the excitement of the exotic I was keen to use it. For some reason I was constantly frustrated as no one would teach me any verbs. I never found out why. They would reel off lists of nouns as fast as my pen could take them down, but as soon as I asked how you say 'is', for example, they would claim it was the same as in Greek. So although the nouns were easy to learn – largely monosyllables with a satisfying Anglo-Saxon brutality to them like *book* (bread), *verr* (wine), *boor* (man), *goor* (stone) – I ended up with nothing but a string of them which I either had to supplement with idiotic gestures or with Greek verbs.

Plates of delicious food began appearing: fried marrow flowers, bits of pork belly, tiny fried fish only an inch long, bread, tomatoes and olives. They offered us the floor of the yard as a bed for the night and we gratefully accepted, mindful of the shelter it offered from the lacerations of the wind. When the drunken son had passed out, everyone drifted away. I woke in the middle of the night, freezing cold, and became obsessed with the sound of a frog which I convinced myself was trying to insinuate itself under the blanket. The next morning I realized it was a squeaking wire attached to a basket. We drank some tea and said our goodbyes, slipping some money into the old man's pocket 'for the children'.

Determined not to be frustrated in our endeavours to cross over to Kallianou on foot, we found a flinty track south of Amigdalia which went over the mountain spur. A wiry woman was driving 30 sheep a thousand feet up to drink. She was a model of temporal ergonomy, as while driving the sheep she was spinning thread from a ball of wool onto a wooden distaff. She had to take the sheep up there twice a day as there was no water below. '*Afta ine kaka chronia*' (these are bad years) she said of the drought, which was the worst Greece had experienced for a hundred years. The grapes were tiny and the olives had failed. They even had to cut food for the goats, as there wasn't enough shrub left. Her plastic shoes were badly split. She said she had five children, and one had gone off to Canada 13 years ago. 'He married a foreign woman, I think she's Dutch, I'm not sure. I'd like to go and visit, but, you know, it's expensive and, well, I've never learnt to read ...'

We climbed higher and higher until we were almost level with the naked and fissured jags of rock lunging through the sky. The sun was like brass. Clouds condensed around the top of the highest peak like turbans and then dissolved, swept away by the wind. An ancient man came past on a mule and got off to talk to us. He was on his way to light a candle at the church of the prophet Elijah right up on the top of the nearest rock face. Elijah always qualifies for mountaintop shrines, presumably because of all the instruction he got from God on Mount Horeb and his eventual assumption: the churches are symbols of his proximity to heaven. As many writers on Greece have observed, in this role he handily took over the mountain temples to the sun god Helios, to whose name his own, in Greek, bears a striking resemblance.

'I'm lighting a candle for my wife. She died on 31 May exactly 10 years ago today. We must pray for her,' said the old man.

'But it's 13 June,' I said unhelpfully.

'*Palaioimerologitis imai*'. He was a follower of the Old Calendar, which meant he was 13 days behind the regular date. There is a sizeable contingent of these people in Greece, even though they are officially excommunicated. It's a peculiar business which began in 1924, when it was decided that the

Orthodox Churches of Constantinople, Greece and others were to switch from the Old, or Julian Calendar, to the New, or Gregorian Calendar used in the west. Some people didn't like it and seem to have accorded the issue a rather disproportionate importance. Their objection was partly based on the fact that the decision had been taken by several autocephalous churches acting off their own bats (though the Ecumenical Patriarch had started it by convening a conference in 1923 at which the proposal was put forward) rather than as a single, unified gesture of the whole Orthodox Church. They had to be excommunicated, of course, because Orthodoxy cannot tolerate splinter groups.

The extraordinary thing is that the Old Calendarists keep going, still maintaining churches (the most well-known on Evia is Evangelistria in Chalkis), monasteries and even the odd bishop. The Church doesn't seem to take any action to resolve the problem. The main difference between the Old Calendarists and the rest, besides the matter of the date, appears to be the former's absolute insistence on the letter of the Bible and other theological texts rather than an interpretation of their spirit. What I found most interesting was how public perception of the issue varied, and the degree to which it was misunderstood. An uneducated, devout woman in Paradisi told me in no uncertain terms that the Old Calendarists worship the devil. Three middle-class widows on retreat at a monastery said that the only difference between the two groups was the date they use. An Athenian intellectual dismissed the Old Calendarists as a fringe bunch of old loonies, and the editor of a heavyweight Orthodox journal said the issue was a very serious one indeed for the Church.

The entire population of Kavodoro used to be Old Calendarists, but now only a few dozen families remain adherents. The clergy did at one time try to bully them into submission. The story goes that the Bishop (more correctly, following a decision by the Greek Orthodox Church in 1922, called the Metropolitan) ordered the people of Platanistos to liturgize according to the New Calendar, and sent a priest to conduct the service. The result was an empty church. Our old man concluded the conversation (during which he had occasionally lapsed into Albanian) by saying that it didn't matter if you were Old or New, as long as you felt the power of God within you. This sounded like something Christ might have said. It had little in common with the dogmatic exclusivity of theologians I had spoken with. The man's religion was priestless now (the last Old Calendar priest disappeared from the area long ago) but this, climbing up a mountain to light a candle at the age of 80, was faith indeed.

During the Turkish Occupation, many moons before the Calendar controversy, there were reports of a peculiar crypto-christianity in some of these isolated villages. Hawkins describes the perpetrators as Albanian-speaking men of Christian origin who professed Islam in order to avoid taxation, even going to the length of having two names. 'With the exception of a few superstitious practices of the Greek church, which they have retained,' he continues, 'they are considered as appertaining to neither religion.' Cryptochristianity was widespread among Greek-speakers under Ottoman rule, particularly in Pontus on the Black Sea. They simply pretended to be Muslims.

The old man was the last person we met on the east side of the mountains. Although there was a good deal of foot traffic between villages in any given area, there was little movement over the mountain – the woman with the distaff had lived all her life in Amigdalia, for example, but had never been to Kallianou, although she knew it was a long way (six miles as the crow flies). The ledge which took us from one side of the mountain to another marked a transformation in the landscape. The hillsides of the lavish valley we descended into were greener, the curves gentler and the wind softer. After two hours we hadn't seen a single sign of life in the huge space, and only a ruined house and two dirt roads to indicate that life had ever existed. Herbs and shrubs proliferated; one variety, allegedly not found anywhere else, was famous in Turkish times for the honey the bees made from it. It shared with mastic from Chios the distinction of being reserved for the sultan's harem. There seemed little hope of finding any, as the French scholar Jules Girard wrote that the pure stuff was already scarce in 1852.

One of the roads descended and turned the corner to Kallianou, a head village with no centre, straggling up and down the slopes and extending its incorporeal tentacles to the Aegean. They say that when Constantinople was taken by the Turks a ship decorated with the royal colours was wrecked near Kallianou and gold coins from its hold were found among the rocks. It was a relatively affluent village with piped water, handsome houses and time enough for exuberant displays of geraniums in oil drums. Even the river on the valley floor was flowing – a rare sight in Greece in 1990. But they were still threshing their own corn. We met the postman, who was driving from house to house and stopping at each for a cup of coffee. It hardly seemed worth asking him if there was anywhere to stay, as we hadn't come across anyone even with a spare room so far, let alone anything more formal, but I did, and he gave me a peach from the back of his van and said there was a taverna on the beach with rooms to rent. This sounded highly unlikely, but we pressed forward for a further mile and found a largeish building which looked closed. By this time we were not only filthy with dust and dirt, but also had feasted on wild mulberries which had dyed our t-shirts, arms, legs and faces with a spattering of rich red, with the result that we looked as though we had just ripped a sheep apart. Trying to think of a way of blaming Christopher for the fact that we were without food and shelter after a seven-hour sweaty hike, and that we hadn't seen a shower for three days, I had a look around the back just in case, and there was palpable deliverance. An old couple were pottering around on a vine-roofed terrace with a large kichen behind it. They said they had a spare room and that there was cold beer, and asked if we were interested in freshly-baked stuffed aubergines. Nothing can equal the joy of unforeseen respite: expectation tempers pleasure.

We spent a happy two days either on the taverna terrace or on the empty beach, where the sea was continually foaming. That section of Aegean coastline is probably the Hollows, where a rough sea wrecked a Persian squadron sailing round the island immediately prior to the Battle of Artemisium in 481 BC. There is a literary tradition, put about by Lucan and others, that during the first century BC a Roman consul (possibly Appius Claudius Pulcher) went to the Hollows as a result of an utterance by the Delphic oracle.

Within hours of our arrival my freckles were verbally assaulted by the barefooted taverna owner. Were they, she was keen to know, the result of a skin disease? She went on to say that it was a tragic abnormality that I had so much white hair as it made me look 40 despite the fact that I had such a young face.

On the second evening two entertaining couples arrived from Athens and we had a jolly time involving several vats of retsina and a charcoal grill. This solved what had hitherto been for me one of the great mysteries of Greek rural life: the function of the hairdrier plugged in in the kitchen of almost every taverna. It was hard to believe that people who washed in cold water and got up at four to milk the goats were keen blowdriers, and in the unlikely event that this was so, I wondered why they did it in the kitchen. I got my answer when the proprietor, Barba Yannis, aimed a few blasts at the wood and charcoal to get the grill going.

The conversation turned to the forest fires ravaging the north of the island. The papers were full of shock-horror pictures – perhaps the first time Evia has ever made the front page. There had been so many fires – even for a year of drought – that there was talk of arson. Everyone was convinced that this was the Turkish method of destroying the Greek tourist industry so as to siphon off foreign currency to their own resorts, thus increasing their chances of joining the EC. I felt that Evia was an unusual island to choose for such an attack as there were virtually no foreign tourists on it, but I kept quiet lest they should take me for a spy.

I resolved many years ago in Greece not to be inhibited by the fact that women rarely drink much. Whilst wanting to avoid cultural *faux pas* you have to weigh up the personal cost against the net benefit. Still, I was amused to hear Barba Yannis confiding to a crony that 'Foreign women do drink a lot of wine, I've noticed.' I was less amused when his wife, who had been silent for about an hour, suddenly chirped up, 'Can't you get rid of them with chemicals of any kind?'

Early the next morning (though not as early as we had planned because our heads hurt too much) we took the coast road westwards. At first it climbed the mountain, overlooking the sheer, beachless cliffs that characterize the whole east coast, and then turned south down a wild valley. We were aiming for Agios Dimitrios, a head village on the lower slopes of the east side, and after a couple of painful hours we reached it. Strong-armed women were washing clothes at the row of communal stone troughs at the river. We drank some water in the shop and bought provisions; the owner's wife served us while the man himself played the *kavodoritiko* on a three-stringed walnut lyre of his own creation.

As we couldn't find anywhere to stay we left, heading south-west past flocks of goats wearing huge bells, and shortly took a detour to look at a church near the site of the old village. It was a tiny crumbling building with two tiled ridged roofs forming a cross, frail and dwarfed by the hillside. There was a settlement there before the tenth century which was famous for its work with the purple dye they extracted from a type of mollusc. The church was probably late thirteenth century, and a roughly hewn white font shaped like a baby's bath lay on the uneven flagstone floor. The villagers say that once they had their new church they put this font outside for use as a water trough for the animals. But a cow died, which they interpreted as punishment for their disrespect, so they brought the font back in again.

After another hour and a half, walking mainly along flat land which opened out to a plain ahead, we saw a sign to a village irresistibly called Paradisi. It used to be called Bezani, a Turkish-Albanian name, but that was changed some years ago as part of a campaign to expunge evidence of the Turkish Occupation. Places in Greece often have a new name and an old name, like traps on a board game for travellers. They chose Paradisi as the area was so verdant; this was ironic, as during our stay the water supply was cut off for 18 hours a day. The spring was still in full spate, however, so we filled up our water bottles, and while doing so we met a woman called Ourania who had lived in America and spoke English, which pleased Christopher who was beginning to feel like a ventriloquist's dummy. She insisted that we accept coffee at her home, and it turned into a long indulgent lunch. It emerged that the whole family were Jehovah's Witnesses. There are around 25,000 Witnesses in Greece, spread among some 300 Kingdom Halls. They have a hard time from the Orthodox Church, and Ourania had actually been physically attacked when living on the mainland. (Amnesty International have supported several imprisoned Jehovah's Witnesses in Greece.) Ourania was not a proselytizer. She was relaxed, natural and witty, and I always think of her now when the doorbell rings on a Sunday morning, and sometimes the memory makes me less cross.

There happened to be a big party scheduled in Paradisi that

night laid on by the *Sillogos* (Village Association). By the time we got to the valley floor they were industriously arranging tables in the street (which had been closed off), organizing a stage and fixing lights. It was already 6.00 pm, and it was irresistible. We asked around and eventually found a couple who were prepared to rent us their front room.

It was one of the best parties I've ever been to. About 250 people (more than twice the village population) had made up their minds to have a good time. Food and unlimited retsina were included in the price of the ticket. As soon as the eight-piece band began everyone rushed to the dance floor. It wasn't long before we were dragged up, and Australia would have been proud of Christopher's efforts as his previous experience of Greek dancing had been confined to seedy restaurants in Perth. After midnight the *Proedros* (Chairman of the *kinotita*, a small administrative group of villages, like a district) made a speech welcoming deputations from the neighbouring Associations of Yiannitsi and of Katsarori (great cheers) and reading out a list of benefactors (applause). He then conducted a spirited raffle, the main prizes of which were goats. I quite fancied a goat, but I won 25 flagstones (stones from Karistos are famous). After inspecting my prize and making admiring noises I donated it to the construction of the new village spring. Serious drinking commenced, interrupted only by ever more vigorous dancing and plate-smashing. At 3.00 am we snuck home, but the band played on until beyond dawn, finishing at 6.15.

And so once again we walked held in the vice-like grip of a hangover. I had read about a castle on a hill called Filagra (anciently Filakra) about 12 miles away by road, so we started out in the cruel sunlight and turned right down a long valley. Neither of us was admitting how bad we felt to the other, but we tacitly agreed to jump into the back of an open truck which stopped to give us a lift. It was wild country. The owner of the truck, obviously a rally driver in a previous incarnation, dropped us at Pothio, and we walked down to Lower Yiannitsi, where we could barely extract details on how to reach the castle as the locals were so convinced that we would never make it. People constantly told me I 'couldn't' go somewhere, either because it was too far or too difficult. When I tried to establish just how far 'too far' was they never knew. Occasionally a shepherd measured the distance in cigarettes (the number smoked on the journey) but this was useless information unless I monitored his nicotine consumption rate for several hours. Someone told me once that they use the same system in Nigeria.

At the saddle of the mountain a path led to a plateau hundreds of feet above the bay. The oldest of the two churches up there, a Lower Yiannitsian had told me, was dedicated to St Filagra. As no such person has ever been canonized this just goes to show that people are quite capable of unilaterally moulding their religion to their immediate environment – and why not? The indefatigable Evian chronicler Yannis Gikas (Greeks are passionate local historians) writes about semi-pagan prayers to natural phenomena which are said in the church, and until relatively recently around Easter the locals held a liturgy for the appeasement of the north wind.

The castle itself was on the headland just beyond the peak, but what was left of it turned out to be rather a disappointment. It was built by the Catalans, who were obliged to abandon it as a result of one of Alfonso Fadrique's peace treaties with the Venetians.

By the time we had climbed down I was feeling appalling, and it was more than the hangover. I limped along, snivelling behind Christopher until Pothio, where I sat at the shop and refused to walk any further. Eventually a truck came through and took us back to Paradisi, where I beat off a plate of goat's testicles (a local delicacy) proffered by our hosts and went to bed. I had a fever. Being ill when you are on the road is horrendous: no doctor, no Heinz tomato soup, no hot-water bottle and no television to move into the bedroom. I couldn't even concentrate on any of the books I had with me. We decamped to Karistos. In town, after a reunion with the beaming Litsa and her high-ceilinged room, Christopher sniffed out a copy of last week's *Sunday Times*. The only piece in it I was able to read was a long extract from a book about the Queen Mother, which was an indication of how ill I was, and which alarmed Christopher. A pharmacist confirmed a high temperature and I retired to bed once more, ably ministered to by the long-suffering Christopher, who did make friends with some locals on his solo taverna forays. The inability to communicate verbally seemed to mean that he drank even more than usual, to compensate.

After a few days of rest and aspirins we decided I was well, and, sensibly enough, the first day's activity was climbing a mountain. Ochi is over 4000 feet, which makes it second only to Dirfis on the whole island. Zeus and Hera liaised on it, apparently, and the name may derive from an ancient word for sex. We established that a dirt road was bulldozed in 1982 from Metochi, a couple of miles east of Karistos, leading to the chestnut forest about three-quarters of the way up. At this point we made a very serious mistake. We decided to rent a motorbike to cover the first few miles. Anyone who has ever rented a motorbike in Greece knows the machine is generally 'unroadworthy', as your solicitor might say as she pursued your compensation claim for multiple injuries. This would certainly be an appropriate description for the two bikes we took out, one after the other, and brought back to the shop again. The first was so slow that a goat trotting up a hill overtook us. The second had successfully carried us a mile or so when the throttle handle seized up and we had to push the bike back. In neither case did the man in the shop put up the least resistance; he accepted immediately that the bikes were fundamentally flawed as if he had known all along, and meekly gave us our money back. After this promising start we walked to Metochi, whence it took four hours to climb to the top of the mountain. Most of the lower slopes had been burnt out and consisted of black stumps on a grey eroded surface. Occasional oleander bushes and plane trees had survived in the gullies, but higher up the landscape was desolate, except for the one exuberant chestnut forest. Above it we emerged into a clearing occupied by Evia's highest goatherd, overlooked by the Refuge. The latter was a large building put up by one of the national mountaineering clubs and now obviously used by more sheep than people.

The rocky ascent to the summit had been marked with splodges of red paint. The wind was so fierce I could barely breathe. The inevitable prophet Elijah church on top was surrounded by a quantity of dwellings that I later read were once – incredibly – the cells of a small monastery. After a good deal of scrambling we were rewarded by a full frontal view of what we most wanted to see – the enigmatically named Dragon House of Ochi. The four walls, with two windows, were intact, as was most of the corbelled roof except a narrow central panel. The edges of the stones were carefully shaped, and the lintel was a single stone three yards long. Without any particular aesthetic qualities it possessed a dogged beauty, perhaps because of its bijou neatness against the wild and vast mountains that dwarfed it. Positioned there, out of kilter with its surroundings, it brought to mind a stellar Portakabin on an uninhabited planet.

There is one other intact Dragon House site on the island (near Stira) and several questionable ruins (notably at Filagra and Archampolis). They are among the most delicious secrets of Evia. The stones used are so enormous, the tradition goes, that they can't have been lifted by mortals, and must have been carried up the hill by the dragon creatures, mythological half-human, half-animal monsters. The age and function of the Dragon Houses have been a topic of debate since the early nineteenth century. They have been put down as dwellings, storehouses, shelters for signal-fire watchmen, Dryope palaces, quarry buildings and temples, especially to Hera. The problem with the temple suggestion is of course that the Dragon Houses bear no resemblance whatsoever to any other Greek temples. People used to say the buildings were prehistoric, and someone came up with the idea that they were temples to Hera built by the Pelasgians before the Trojan War. Then there was a strong contender ascribing the style to Carians or Carian influence in the third or second century BC. The Ochi site was excavated in 1959 and, partially as a result of the dig, the most credible theory yet emerged, continuing the Carian connection, and argued most convincingly by Professor E. Vranopoulos.

It goes as follows. The dig revealed a number of vessels, bones and ashes indicating sacrifices and thus endorsing the temple explanation. The slit along the top of the roof was probably an escape route for smoke. The Houses in Stira and Ochi are near ancient marble quarries, and a similar building on Mount Hymettus on the mainland is also near a quarry site. In southwestern Asia Minor, near Halicarnassus, a local tradition of the same architectural style has been shown to be the work of Carians and Lelegians during a period of several hundred years from about the sixth century BC. These peoples came over to work in the quarries of southern Evia on several occasions from the fourth century onwards, and it seems likely that the Dragon Houses were built as temples by migrant workers or slaves from Asia Minor. How they managed to get the vast stones up a mountain remains a mystery.

Hawkins claims to have discovered the building. He went up the mountain on a mule, and got terrifically excited when he found what he originally assumed was a temple, '... of a most ancient and peculiar construction'. He must have been a Latin at heart, as he concludes that it was probably dedicated to Neptune.

There is of course a rich store of local mythology on this

strange building constructed by giants on the top of the mountain. The dragon, the story goes, was in love with a girl from a local village, and he used to visit her at night, leaving his horse outside with exactly enough hay to last until just before daybreak. When there was no hay left he knew it was time to leave. But the girl did not love the dragon, and she tried to think of a way of getting rid of him. She asked him what he was frightened of, and he said nothing, except her brother's sheepdog. So the cunning girl asked her brother to bring the dog to her house the following dawn, and in order to prolong the dragon's stay she put sand in his horse's hay. The dragon fell for it, and the dog attacked him and chased him all the way up the mountain, where the dragon managed to get into his house through an underground passage. But the dog sniffed him out, and the dragon escaped through the hole in the roof, but the dog eventually killed him. His sister heard his death cries but arrived too late, and buried him. In the old days shepherds could show you footprints of the dog and the dragon, and two stones, one on top of the other, which they said were his tomb.

The surrounding regions were a collage of browns and yellows interrupted by dark green cypress groves and the white boxes of Karistos. The huge bay gleamed and melted into the paler blue of the Evian Gulf which, to the east, curled round towards Kavodoro and vaporized. As we descended, some of the villages at the back of the plain behind Karistos appeared in the shadow of the mountain. There was a marble quarry above Mili once, and five enormous columns still lay there, endlessly waiting to be shipped off to Rome. The marble is green and white with a veined appearance, which is why it is one of the ones they now call cipollino, after the Italian word for onion.

Before we left Karistos I visited St Mavra, both a monastery and the only working Old Calendar church in the south of the island. It was a pale blue and white confection on the northern outskirts of town, and the ironwork gate revealed that it was also dedicated to St Timothy, an early Egyptian martyr like Mavra. I was warmly received by the old priest, although my attempts to question him were consistently foiled by his interrogation about every detail of my life. I established that the monastery had two nuns (in Greece the word 'monastery' applies both to monkeries and nunneries) who were, he said, young and fresh. This turned out to be a piece of ecclesiastical irony as the pair shortly shuffled into the cloister and didn't look much short of 90. He showed me round the church, which was built in 1915, nine years before the split caused by the Calendar controversy. It had a double-headed Byzantine eagle in marble on the floor. Before we left the priest took a swipe at Protestantism and gripped my arm. 'Let's make you Orthodox,' he breathed, peering into my face. I already found this denominational exclusivity, which was to become a recurrent feature of my trip, mildly irritating. It was just as Robert Louis Stevenson said in *Travels with a Donkey*, when the Catholics at the monastery of Our Lady of the Snows dismissed his religion and zealously urged him to convert or lose his soul: '... it is not always the most faithful believer who makes the cunningest apostle.'

Chapter Two

The process of the world's impoverishment in the things that really matter to most of us rushes forward at an ever-increasing tempo, although the full extent of post-war disasters has yet to be appreciated.

NORMAN LEWIS, To Run across the Sea

Christopher was despatched back to Athens on a boat after a raucous farewell lunch, and the next morning I caught the 6.30 am bus to Stira. Litsa and her parents waved me off even at that hour, rushing to buy hoops of sesame bread which they thrust through the grimy bus window. I felt increasingly reluctant to leave a corner of the island that had become so familiar. I wondered if I could find what I was looking for by simply staying on in the high-ceilinged room.

We arrived at Stira after less than two hours. The village was grouped around a somnolent square with a clump of pine trees in the middle, overlooked by a tall church. It opened one eye when the bus arrived, and closed it once it had clocked the handful of people who straggled off and disappeared down the motley streets. I found a room with an old Macedonian man in pyjamas: the house seemed to have a curious interchangeable system of bedrooms, as he offered me first the room he had been sleeping in. I chose a room upstairs, overlooking a valley with the chapped textured surface of a thousand olive trees.

I set out to find the Stira Dragon Houses. After a valley filled with purple thyme I passed a goatherd's hut in a clearing. An old man and his prospective son-in-law greeted me, leaning on enormously tall smooth olivewood crooks and staring in mystified amazement. Patrick Leigh Fermor ponders the role of the solitary foreign traveller in Greece in *Roumeli*, and concludes that he (obviously the notion of it being a she was beyond the bounds even of conjecture) is regarded as (a) an omniscient sage, (b) a millionaire, (c) a lunatic, (d) a spy. Being female I was ruled out of the first category. I usually looked fairly wrecked, so it stretched even their imaginations to put me in the second, certain as they are that all foreigners are loaded. As there is precious little in Evia to spy on there was only one conclusion to draw, and I always got the impression that they drew it pretty fast.

They pointed out the Dragon Houses, shimmering in a heat haze, and I made my way along the vermicular path pushing through the dense undergrowth. There were three of them, close together. Having seen the Ochi building these were instantly recognizable as Dragon Houses, although I wondered for how much longer. They may have lasted 2000 years but the branches propping the roofs up didn't look as though they would survive the next winter. I wasn't surprised to see them at Stira. Like Karistos it is one of the oldest Evian settlements, probably also founded by Dryopes. Later on Karistos and Eretria took turns to subjugate it.

On my way back the family sent out a representative to invite me over for lunch. We had an earnest conversation about the giants responsible for building the Dragon Houses before moving on to the more serious business of eating and drinking. The father, Dinos, who was shearing a sheep with a huge pair of scissors, had deep-set blue eyes and a heart-stopping smile, and his daughter, Vangelitsa, had long naturally blonde hair. They owned a donkey, two mules, three dogs, 50 sheep and 300 longhorned black goats. Their hut was a dry-stone cube, with toothpaste, soap and numerous other items jammed in between the stones on the outside and a large mattress on the ground in front of the door. Vangelitsa and her fiancé, Dimitris, had been engaged for a month, and over the meal they discussed the dowry and wedding arrangements. The whole village was invited, and several neighbouring villages too. They asked me if I was married, and claiming that I was at least engaged seemed to offer the only opportunity of being upgraded out of the lunatic category.

The table was set – a board placed on three stones under a huge tree – and we sat around it on more stones. They crossed themselves and poured generous glasses of their own retsina. It tasted of mountains. We ate *youvarlakia*, calf meatballs mixed with rice in a viscous soup of lemon, egg, garlic, onions and potato, with homemade bread and *kefalotiri*, their own goats' cheese, set in a wicker basket. During the meal all four of them constantly accused me of not eating enough. Greek *filoxenia* (hospitality towards strangers) insists on guests leaving at the very least sated but preferably bilious. After a thimbleful of syrupy coffee I set off for the top of the mountain. Vangelitsa ran after me.

'Look, we'd really like you to come to our wedding in the autumn. Do say you will.'

An hour later, wondering where western society managed to dispose so successfully of that kind of spontaneity, I reached the top of the mountain beyond, the site of the acropolis of ancient Stira. Three huge stones forming the entrance gate were still standing, and inside I went up some steps and climbed around the rocks. On one side the Aegean rose into the sky in a blue haze, and on the other the Evian Gulf shimmered bright sapphire, three small islands floating on the surface like decorations on a cake. The mainland, as ever, wasn't far behind. It was the first time I had seen both coasts from one spot. On the valley floor irregular fields were bordered by olive groves and spired with cypresses. The landscape throbbed with the buzz of bees and wasps, punctuated occasionally by goat bells. Lizards zoomed away from my feet.

I could see why the mountains had come to play such an important role in the folklore of southern Evia: they were a natural spur to the imagination. The coast-dwellers used to live in terror of the mountaineers, to the extent that the men became identified with *kallikantzari*, savage and frenzied creatures who indulged in an orgy of wild behaviour in the 12 days between Christmas and Epiphany. The concept almost certainly evolved from the half-man-half-horse centaurs of ancient Greek mythology, or, similarly, the satyrs and goatish *sileni* who were Dionysus' companions. Although the 12-day period has Christian significance now, certain pagan festivals used to take place between what we call Christmas and Epiphany, and many things were absorbed from the old religion into the new, as they always are when a people changes its religion. The *kallikantzari* of folklore couldn't transmogrify at will, but were generally described as therianthropic, and varied in form from region to region. In some areas they were a type of demon who lived in the underworld and only came up for 12 days. On most Aegean islands they tended to be portrayed as human beings, and in southern Evia they merged into the mountaineers, who were allegedly seized by a wild and bestial frenzy during the 12 days, reaching such a pitch that even their appearance altered and became more animal-like. It must have started with some very Dionysian revels on the part of the mountaineers. It's all very understandable. I used to think that after the Christmas party at college the rugby team might be about to turn into a pack of wild animals.

Homer depicts the centaurs as representations of the basic

male desires such as womanizing, drinking and fighting. He really makes you think about how far 3000 or so years have brought us.

On the other side the mountain sloped sharply down to a lush valley, peaks receding into the steaming background until Ochi. Further around the mountain I came to a dry-stone church – no spot, it seems, has ever been too remote for the Greeks to offer a token of their devotion. Beyond it I discovered ruined battlements from the Lombard-Venetian period – almost certainly the important stronghold of Larmena. Like Castel Rosso, it was built by the Lombards, and changed hands many times before the Venetians finally secured it in 1334. Almost half a millennium later it was again the object of bitter dispute, when, at a critical stage of the War of Independence, Elias Mavromichalis was brought over to join the Evian troops. He was the son of the legendary Petros, the last Bey of the Mani in the Peloponnese, the cradle of the Greek revolution. The Greeks decided to attack the fortress at Stira as the Turks had a large grain store within it, but then did so without waiting for reinforcements, and in the drubbing that ensued Elias was shot dead. The Turks shifted the grain over to Castel Rosso, then under the command of Omer Bey, and the Greeks promptly besieged that too, but were forced to withdraw after another failed mission. The Evian army was thus dispersed for a period, giving the Turks freedom to rule much as before. There were still outbreaks of fighting, of course: the following year a gruesome episode took place at Karistos when the Greek commander Odysseus defeated a group of Turks and sent 50 decapitated heads and three intact Turks off to Athens. The three probably thought they had had a lucky escape until they arrived, when they were stoned to death.

Back on the east side they had built a cave church into the sheer rock; it was marked by a small white wooden cross perching on one corner. I had to climb up to it on all fours. My legs and arms were crisscrossed with scratches from the intractable sharp-pronged bushes growing among the loose stones. The descent was equally precarious, as the stones were liable to slip away under my feet, and I began to think that perhaps I really was a lunatic. After a couple of fallen columns (in the late nineteenth century the Stira marble quarries were partially owned by Marmor Ltd of Finsbury Square in London) the hut reappeared. The old man was asleep under an olive tree, but the dogs woke him and he beckoned me over. We talked for a while, and he questioned me closely about my family. (Greeks like you to have a family; it reassures them. The family is the foundation stone upon which the entire social structure rests.) He told me that he wanted to buy a house for his other daughter, who lived in a rented flat in Athens with her husband. 'He stole her from us,' he said benignly. In other words, they married in secret because one or the other set of parents didn't approve of the match or had arranged another marriage. This used to be a frequent occurrence; if you ask an old person about it he or she will reel off the names of the people in the village who married in secret. Usually the couple would sneak off to a nearby village and an obliging priest, and a rapprochement generally followed sooner or later. The 'stealing' of brides still goes on a good deal, but only in the least westernized communities, where marriage is still perceived more or less as an essential social act rather than a matter of individual preference. The old man was trying to sell some of his grazing land, but it was difficult to see how he was going to manage to buy a house in the city on the proceeds, even with his revenues from goats' cheese, wool and olive oil, particularly with the wedding coming up, at which he said he intended to roast 30 goats on a spit. But his commitment to the concept of family meant that he was still going to break his back to buy his recalcitrant daughter a home.

Just before I left he asked me what the spots on my skin were. He was another one who didn't know about freckles. I explained and he said, 'Well, don't worry, it doesn't matter. They don't show from a distance.'

The track led eventually to the houses at the back of the village, interlaced with cobbled lanes, whitewashed walls and apricot trees. This is the village that is dismissed in four words in Franklin P. Johnson's long article on the Dragon Houses in the 1925 *American Journal of Archaeology*. 'The wretched Euboean village' is the most illuminating remark in the whole piece, as it sums up his contemptuous attitude towards the modern Greece he regrettably came across in his ardent pursuit of antiquity. A woman shouted after me bearing a glass of water; at the bottom was a dollop of *vanillitsa*, thick, sticky and very horrible sugar mastic. She asked me how I liked 'Stoura'. The alternative version is not uncommon. It's an archaic phenomenon frequently heard in the dialect of Kimi on the east coast, which is similar to what is known to dialectologists as Old Athenian, formerly spoken in Athens and Aegina and still heard around and in the Mani. On Evia the so-called Old Athenian dialect is usually associated with Kimi, an idiosyncratic linguistic pocket where 'Koumi' is still regularly heard, but people now think it was spoken throughout the southern half of Evia, as well as in Attica, the islands of the Saronic Gulf, and much of the eastern Peloponnese. This huge, continuous dialect area was gradually broken up by the arrival of the Albanian settlers from the fourteenth century onwards, and in southern Evia the regular southern Greek dialect emerged, but pockets and vestiges of Old Athenian or the Kimi dialect remain, such as this use of 'Stoura'.

The old man's house only had a sink in the kitchen, and when I went down to clean my teeth the next morning there was a sheep's head in it. He said he was going to boil it. I left and got the bus down to Nea Stira, the new village, only two or three miles up the coast but it could be a world away. It's not really new at all, and may have been the site of the first settlement of Stira, but New is an appropriate adjective now. It is a foreign tourist centre catering for German groups, and its real life has drained out of it with every new shop offering suntan lotions, T-shirts and priapic postcards.

One of the islands I could see from the beach was presumably Aigilea, now called Stira Island, where, according to Herodotus, Hippias dumped the Eretrian prisoners on his way to Marathon. It might not be that at all, but for my purpose this didn't matter much; what interested me was that the island cropped up in a really odd little chunk of Book Six where Herodotus says Hippias dreamt that he was sleeping with his mother, which he interpreted as evidence that he would return to Athens and recover power, but then sneezed so hard that a tooth shot out on the beach and he couldn't find it, which was a sign to the contrary. I wondered if such an aleatory approach to their own destinies had made their lives easier than ours. Pondering this question I went down to swim, but the water's edge was thick with jellyfish, so I skipped it, for only the second day of the trip. Besides, I felt like a twofold alien – neither a Greek villager nor a German grouper. A surprisingly good taverna on a little promontory offered palliation of other local inadequacies, but in the end Nea Stira was a resort moulded to fit the foreign tourist machine. So, normally the first to be tempted by the sybaritic life, early the next morning I headed for Aliveri, the next stopping-off point on my meander northwards.

'Take my octopus, dear,' said the wrinkled crone in black scrambling up onto the bus. At 6.30 am, at least, Nea Stira belonged to the Greeks. We rattled off north along the seahorse's spine with the sea visible alternately on left and right and Venetian towers sprouting in abundance out of the fertile plain of Distos. At Lepoura we turned on to what Evians, in a quaint example of conceptual relativity, call the 'national road'. It isn't a national road at all, but it is a major island artery, and one of the few roads in a half-decent condition.

Approximately 6000 people live in Aliveri, but to me, having been for a while in remote spots, it felt like New York. A huge thermoelectric power station fuelled by locally mined lignite belched away in the port and a continuous stream of juggernauts thundered through the narrow streets. It was hot, noisy, crowded and frenetic. I found a scrofulous 'hotel' overlooking a square where someone was selling black cherries out of the back of a van, and a polite wall-eyed man checked me in. Its insalubrity was impressive. There was a dead mouse under the bed, so I went downstairs.

'I'm afraid there's a mouse in the room.'

'Dead?'

'Yes.'

'Well, I don't suppose it will bother you then.'

Eventually he came and took it away, and I went off in search of a more edifying experience at the Panayitsa.

The most impressive piece of history in Aliveri (the name comes from a local Turkish estate-owner, Ali Veros) is the Byzantine church of the Dormition of the Virgin, known locally as the Panayitsa. I found it on a hill, next to a bulldozer demolishing a row of houses and overlooked by whitewashed cottages and a lemon tree. An old woman was sitting outside one of the cottages slicing beetroot. She said she went into the church every morning and evening to light a candle, and delivered the standard speech about Turkish barbarity. Chunks of an earlier church were wedged in the gaps in the uneven exterior walls of the tiny building. There was an inscription in it once which said that it was built in 1393 by a priest called Stamatios and his wife. Inside I could see what had prompted the diatribe against the Turks: they had tried to set fire to the church after scratching out the eyes on the frescos. What they left behind had been assaulted further by damp. One of the best preserved of a line of tenebrous figures, eyes looking right down the centuries, was St Vlasios. The inscription he carried talked about the 'unpicturable' power of God, which was paradoxical seeing as what they were trying to do was picture it.

The ancient settlement called Tamunai or Tamuna must have been near modern Aliveri, if not actually on the same spot. It is written about in connection with its temple to Apollo (but now nobody knows where it was), the venue of an annual festival called the Tamunaiai, and with a battle in the middle of the fourth century BC, the culmination of deliberate build-up of tension on the island by Philip II of Macedonia, who had his eye on it. The only proper source of information about the battle is Plutarch and he isn't comprehensive – he was writing a biography of Phocion, who led the Athenian expedition against Evia at that time.

Fifteen years ago I visited St Luke's Byzantine church (Osios Loukas in Greek) in Phocis on the mainland, and near Aliveri there was a dependency. It was destroyed in 1874, but replaced, and as my visit to Phocis had made a big impression I set out to find the Evian version. A village called Agios Loukas had grown up around the church and developed into a thriving community of about 1500 people only three miles north of Aliveri. Why the nomenclature accorded Luke the title *Agios* in the case of the village and *Osios* in the case of the church was baffling. Both are translated as 'saint', and the very approximate distinction is that generally *osios* refers to a monastic saint who did not die a violent death while an *agios* is a martyr-saint or a hierarch-saint. There are various exceptions for certain married saints and it's all terribly confusing – and then just when you think you've sorted it out you come across both used simultaneously, for example *O Agios Loukas o Osios.*

On the bus I asked a woman if she could tell me where to get off for the church, and her face lit up. 'My father witnessed a miracle there. There was a boy, from Avlonari, and on his way to school he saw a vision and was struck dumb. They tried everything to recover his voice, but they couldn't. One day the boy met an old man who took him up into the mountains. Later the boy's father brought him to our church, and as soon as the boy saw the icon of St Luke he said "That's the old man I met. It's the same face." The next day he could speak. St Luke cured him.'

She was full of miracles. Her aunt saw an olive branch grow out of a bottle of holy water from the church, and she herself had heard heavenly singing at midnight in Gremastos. The icon in the church, she said, was fished out of a well.

The bus stopped in a square dominated by the huge nineteenth-century church, the colour of English sand. The Byzantine scholar Anastasios Orlandos described it as *akalaisthitos* (tasteless) in his 1951 essay on its predecessor. It was locked. I was walking aimlessly around it when a widow appeared. She was the caretaker. But she had seen my notebook. 'You're not a journalist from Athens are you?' she barked. 'Which side?' (Greek newspapers are very politically aligned.) It was clear the door would not be opened if the side wasn't the correct one, but thankfully I was foreign, and therefore exempt. The church turned out to be full of uninteresting glossy modern icons.

Katina, my friend from the bus, had invited me back to her family home (she herself lived in Chalkis) and insisted that I stay for a meal. *Yaya* (granny), a sprightly 87, was fidgeting around the stove tugging at her yellow and black headscarf. Various other members of the family strolled in and out - nephews, nieces, cousins, sisters-in-law, uncles – and ate, sat, lay down, or just stood around. Homes are fluid units in a Greek village. Eventually four builders fixing the roof pitched up as well, and we all ate spaghetti. The builders were young, tall and muscular, with broad backs as smooth as the inside of an almond and the colour of toasted caramel. They ate silently, wiping their mouths with the backs of their hands when they had finished, and they looked like Greek gods, except for the gold chains around their necks.

The road west out of Aliveri hugged the coast in precarious zigzags. After seven miles we left the province of Karistia and Skiros for that of Chalkis and arrived at the coastal village of Vathia, also known as Amarinthos. I had telephoned the monastery hidden way up in the hills to ask if I could stay, and heard the faint voice of the Abbess crackle. 'Come whenever you like.' So I got off the bus in the middle of the main street at Vathia and simply headed inland. It was hard work – six miles uphill, until I was almost at the top of Mount Kotileo – but it was worth it. Within two hours I felt as though I had been cocooned in St Nicholas for years, and spent most of the day doing nothing at all except helping the Sisters with a few small jobs and browsing in their library. We soon got used to each other, and they called cheerily if they saw me stalking the cloisters, and chatted away, although I didn't eat with them (guests never do) – they brought me food in a 32-seater refectory where I sat in solitary splendour. There were no mirrors anywhere, which I found very refreshing; I couldn't even catch a glimpse of myself in the bathroom first thing in the morning. I thought I might introduce the same system at home. (There were also no baths or showers, and this was less appealing.) The nine nuns, with their two dogs, a cat, chickens and a goat, were almost self-sufficient, growing olives and a wide range of fruit, nuts and vegetables, and although not plugged into the electricity grid they did have a generator which ran for an hour or so in the evening. The Abbess took me to see what they called *to ergostasio* (the factory): two young nuns were gluing icons of St John the Russian on to blocks of wood which would eventually be sent off to be sold at his church in Prokopi.

The fact that I was foreign caused quite a stir, and they all started talking about the German woman who had come to stay six years previously. By the end of the first day a string of texts had been brought over for me to translate, including, inexplicably, the operating instructions for a sunray lamp in Dutch. On my second day, over a glass of the ubiquitous *vissinada*, a cordial they made out of morello cherries, Sister Kalliopi and Sister Magdalini went for the jugular. They had spied a small Bible in my room, and it had given them an appetite for the fight. 'Why don't you become Orthodox?' And off they went in a spirited attempt to convert me. On this occasion they were deflected by the splash of the monastic cat falling into the reservoir (a regular occurrence) but subsequently I was not to be so fortunate.

The *katholikon*, or main church of the monastery, was a fine Byzantine building in excellent condition. Sister Magdalini was convinced that a church had existed there as far back as 1100. The monastery was founded by monks from Constantinople, and during the eighteenth and nineteenth centuries it flourished, materially, and built up an impressive dominion of land and property, but it appears that this diverted the brotherhood from more spiritual concerns. In the 1920s and 1930s much of the monastic land was confiscated by the state, and by then most of the monks were 'unfit for ascetical life', as the monastery's historian, Konstantinos Fouskas, coyly puts it. At the end of 1928 St Nicholas was all but dissolved, soon became a branch of the Makrimallis monastery instead of existing in its own right, and was inhabited only by a caretaker monk. In 1948 it was turned into a nunnery, but nothing much happened until 1963, when a handful of nuns arrived from Argolis and organized the construction of new buildings around the old Byzantine heart.

The modern St Nicholas consisted of a group of white stone buildings with reddish brown windows and shutters, a red-tiled roof, a small marble mausoleum where the previous Abbess was buried, and a row of balconies overlooking the valley, the Gulf and the mainland. The arched colonnades around the flagged courtyard were dominated by the most enormous plane tree, which Abbess Makrina claimed was a thousand years old. I wanted to measure the girth of its trunk with my armspan, but I thought the nuns might become suspicious if they saw me embracing a tree. It must have been at least 21 feet, and the church bell hung from one of its branches. On the upper levels there were two new churches, an ossuary full of heaped-up monks' bones, and a cemetery for the bishops of Chalkis, overlooked by a flowerbed. Roses, geraniums, fuchsias, hydrangeas and a pungent white gardenia bloomed all around the courtyard. The outside wall of the old church itself was inset with hundreds of marble and ceramic decorations, including a glossy plate, and a narrow stone bench ran along the front wall for people to sit and gossip after the service in the time-honoured tradition of almost every Christian culture. Inside, around two marble columns and three transversal arches, the exquisite frescos were mesmerizing, and I never tired of them through the many hours of services; on the contrary, my thoughts floated around them against the background of a nun's chant until what they represented became more real than the worldly reality outside the monastery. My eyes usually lingered longest on a fresco which covered one wall and looked like a Breughel in the dark. It depicted the 40 martyrs squashed together on the seashore, stripped to the waist and about to die.

The nuns' day was structured around their prayer routine. It began with the *proini akolouthia* at 4.30 am, which was 5.30 am in the rest of Greece (some monasteries refuse to accept the concept of summer time, and so for half the year are an hour out of step with everyone else). The service included the *orthros*, roughly the same as matins. It lasted about two and a half hours, and much of that time was spent crouched on the floor. After a day's work the nuns would change back into their best habits for the *esperinos* (like vespers or evensong), which went on for about an hour. The last service was the *apodipno* (literally, 'after dinner'), which they said immediately before going to bed. It would be difficult to imagine a more mystical experience of prayer than the nuns of St Nicholas at their *apodipno*. They stood in total darkness around the arched cloister, looking up at the top of the mountain and the expanse of sky like a tangible heaven.

They were terrific chatterboxes, and grew increasingly familiar. (Though they were disappointingly tactful about the Bishop, who, I already knew from elsewhere, was not at the top of anyone's popularity charts, except presumably those of the ex-junta, who appointed him.) Often the Abbess would beckon me over to sit with her on the white wooden bench in the cloister from which she bossed the Sisters around. They began teaching me *kalogerika*, the ecclesiastical language of the monasteries, and became ever more obsessed with my status *vis-à-vis* God. The cherry-lipped Sister Magdalini cornered me in the rose garden one day and said, brandishing a trowel, 'Heretics don't go to paradise, you know. Please convert, for the sake of your own soul.'

On Saturday a priest appeared from Chalkis to stay overnight and take the liturgy the following day. (Of course the nuns can only take communion when a priest turns up: if no one does they chant the *tipikon*, which is the liturgy without the sacerdotal elements.) We were sitting round a table cleaning a huge mound of spinach when we heard his car draw up in the gravel courtyard. He was early, and the imminent prospect of being caught off guard caused a tremendous panic. The nuns flew around the room like cornered birds, flapping spinach leaves from their habits, donning new layers of black fabric, lighting candles, hurriedly bundling vegetable debris into newspaper, squawking at each other and appealing to Christ and the Mother of God. I fled to my cell, whence I was summoned a few hours later and proudly presented to the Father like an archaeological find. My heart sank when he kicked off by asking disingenuously, 'What religion are you?'

'Protestant,' I gulped, as the Sisters drew nearer.

'Why?' That was a tricky one. I was feeling particularly ill-equipped to fulfil the role of apologist for the Anglican Church, as only that afternoon I had heard a programme on the World Service about how it was yet again disappearing up its own bottom in an attempt to stay on the fence. The priest was already on to Luther. My mind was spinning. I tried to summon up the familiar face of my vicar, Tom. It didn't work.

'What about the Anglican position on transubstantiation? Do you take communion?' I caught the eye of St Nicholas on an icon: not much help from that direction. I vaguely heard the priest quoting the dictum about worshipping the saints: 'A day without a saint's festival is like a road with nowhere to rest,' which always made me think of that other one about a meal without wine being like a day without sunshine.

'Did Christ leave us one church, or did he leave us many?'

It's not fair, I thought. *I didn't set up the Church of England.*

'Oh my child, we pity you.'

At that point I stopped listening.

At the liturgy itself the nuns got rather confused and made me sit outside the door for the eucharist (there is a reference in the service to non-baptized people leaving, though it shouldn't apply to Christians baptized in other Churches – but they meant well). After the service, however, I had to smile when over coffee a visitor brought up the subject of Father Maximus, an Athonite monk-priest who had just caused a scene by publishing a book in English exposing and protesting about the abuse of the traditional way of life on the Holy Mountain and the invidious Greek nationalism squeezing out monks from other parts of the Orthodox world. The title of the book was *Human Rights on Mount Athos. An Appeal to the Civilized World.* It was odd enough to use the term human rights about a place where entry is entirely voluntary. To use it in all seriousness to discuss at length the plight of men who are no longer welcome on the mountain, ignoring the fact that women cannot go there at all, as nothing short of a massive joke at the expense of the gynophobic culture that fostered the likes of Father Maximus.

I resented all the visitors, anyway; I liked it when the nuns and I were alone together. Unless you have grown up with nuns (I didn't) you don't really think of them as human beings, and certainly not as sisters under the skin. I remember reading somewhere that it was funny how shocking it was (for British people) to hear a nun speaking with an American accent. I thought of this one day as I sat reading in the sun while an ancient beak-nosed Sister whitewashed the rim of the terracotta flowerpots and asked me, for the umpteenth time, why my mother 'had let me go so far away from her'. It sounds like an absurd truism to say that each had a distinct personality of her own which slowly emerged, day by day; I had vaguely equated uniformity of dress and lifestyle with uniformity of character – a grave mistake. And they displayed, of course, such earthy humanity, like when they got the words wrong in church and had a brief pause to argue over the correct psalm, or when one Sister spotted me with a camera and said, 'Don't take me from the front – I look too fat.' It comforted me enormously to think of them there, following their rituals, every single day, and as I think of them now in the tranquillity of the study it comforts me further to know that they are there even as I write.

It occurred to me as I lived among the nuns and their few visitors that most people I know in London have no spiritual dimension to their lives at all. The more modernized and 'sophisticated' people become the less they acknowledge the spiritual world and their relationship with it. Progress, it would seem to a Martian, is the journey away from God.

On Sunday I escaped to Agios Loukas, where Yorgia, Katina's cousin, had invited me for lunch. We walked up to an area called Monastiri, where Yorgia and her sister taught me how to tell the age of an olive tree. Through fields of chickpeas, pears and aniseed-tasting amaranth they questioned me closely on what we do and do not grow in England. When I revealed that we do not have olive trees they stopped dead in their tracks. 'But how do you manage?'

Meanwhile the Sisters' familiarity grew to include mild rebukes. 'Didn't you hear the bells at 4.30?' Evgenia said to me one day when I caught only the last half an hour of morning prayers. There was also the problem of leg-crossing, which they told me was not permitted within monasteries. When I asked why they told me it was 'out of respect'. I found this notion difficult, as the nuns often belched loudly in church, which I would have thought showed far more disrespect, but I didn't pursue it. I was blissfully happy, and after a week was beginning to feel that I had crawled so far back into the womb that I might never descend again. So when 20 French tourists arrived in a bus I decided to hitch a lift on to Eretria with them. Two of the men were wearing shorts (strictly forbidden), and they were given pairs of trousers from the store of clothes kept by all monasteries for the purpose. The trousers were too small, and the men waddled around ridiculously with their flies undone.

When I left, the Abbess and nuns crowded round the entrance, pleading with me to take care, and to return soon. Leaving almost broke my heart.

Chapter Three

Greece is a secretive country: its most intense realities are usually the least visible.

KEVIN ANDREWS, Athens

Euboea ... surpassed all the other islands in goodness.

ISOCRATES, Panegyricus

When I reached Eretria six miles to the west I drank some beer and felt ridiculously guilty, as if the nuns could see. Everything outside the monastery felt tawdry, second-rate and superficial. Then I prowled around the streets looking for somewhere to stay, and eventually, after a good deal of confusion, rented a wonderful little flat with a concrete floor in a garden blooming with jasmine, bougainvillea and ox-eye daisies and framed by apricot, mandarin and orange trees. It was very cheap, and offered the rare and unexpected pleasure of hot water. The house opposite, a porcelain plaque revealed, was once the home of Konstantinos Kanaris, a nineteenth-century prime minister.

The modern town was hideous. Grouped around a small harbour, whence a ferryboat shuttled the four and a half nautical miles to the mainland, its grid of wide streets tailed off at the edges as if it had been rubbed out. It bore the soulless stamp of the town-planner, and it was difficult to believe that this was once among the great city-states of Greece, running a sophisticated mini-empire. But the ruins were there, scattered indiscriminately among the modern buildings, and each seemed to mock the other.

Refugees from Psara, an island near Chios, colonized Eretria in the nineteenth century to such an extent that its name was temporarily changed to Nea Psara. This was the only event of any significance to have occurred in modern Eretria. The history of the settlement was extraordinary: a thousand years in the vanguard of western civilization had been followed by 2000 as one of its most insignificant foot-soldiers. Its soul seemed to have died with its illustrious past, and its noble aspirations – cultural and political – had been reduced to rubble like its temples. If ever a place represented the transience of human achievement it was Eretria. Its achievement has been considerable, too. By the eighth century BC it was a major maritime power, establishing colonies first in Asia Minor and then in what we know as Italy. It frequently undertook joint missions with Chalkis, and also controlled, for a time, Andros and other Aegean islands. (The whole of Euboea was famous for its pioneering seafaring all over the Greek world; the eighth-century Homeric Hymn to Apollo refers to it as 'glorious at sea'.) The expansion eastwards is understandable, given the island's position. But westwards? Chalkis and Eretria went to Italy before any of the other Greek city-states – this was a significant achievement. Perhaps the psychological effect of the presence of the mainland on the horizon was a factor, and the mountains across the water induced a wanderlust, a need to go beyond them.

Eretrian domestic territory extended westwards as far as the rich Lelantine Plain on the way to Chalkis, and it is often suggested that it was a quarrel over this fertile land, famous for horse-breeding, that led to a punishing war between the two rival city-states which Thucydides claims 'half of Greece was dragged into' during the eighth and seventh centuries BC. It is one of the earliest documented Greek wars. Commercial rivalry is more likely to have been the cause. No one really knows who won, but Eretria still seems to have been functioning perfectly well when it ended – although the desire to export itself had withered.

It built up quantities of dependencies in the centre and south of the island, and owned an important sanctuary to Artemis, near what today is Vathia. When you see the lengthy lists and tables of its possessions in academic journals you realize just what an efficient and powerful machine Eretria was. It was also rich, and progressive. Around 500 BC Aristagoras of Miletus in Asia Minor appealed to the Eretrians as allies, and they fought for the Ionians in their revolt against the Persians. The Ionians lost, and retribution, when it eventually came 10 years later, was catastrophic: the Persians looted Eretria and took many of its inhabitants off as slaves.

The Eretrians who were left behind rebuilt their city, and a decade later they were able to send ships to the battles of Artemisium and Salamis. After the Persian War the whole island was slowly sucked into the Athenian orbit, and its attempt to get out of it again in 446 BC was foiled. Athens planted a settlement in Eretria, and the Eretrians fought on the Athenian side in the Peloponnesian Wars, though they were still keen to escape its clutches and in 411, after the Spartans had beaten the Athenians in a sea battle in the Eretrian harbour, the Eretrians destroyed some Athenian ships and killed the men trying to escape. The break had been made, and Eretria formed some kind of alliance with Sparta; it probably set up the Euboean League with Chalkis too. But the separation didn't last long. Eretria and Athens made a formal alliance in 394. The island was like a handful of little magnets ricocheting from one big magnet to another. Eretria formed another alliance with Athens in 378, but thought better of it before the decade was out when the Theban star was in the ascendant – they were so fickle. (The proximity of Thebes of course made it a handy ally for Eretria and Chalkis.) Some kind of Euboean civil war ensued, polarized into pro-Athenian and pro-Theban factions, and soon after Eretria, with the other city-states of the island, signed up with Athens again.

Philip II of Macedonia, who had already invaded Thessaly, now started softening Euboea up as, like everyone else before and after him, he badly wanted it. According to Demosthenes, in 351 he sent letters to the Euboean city-states warning them that they would be in trouble if they relied upon their alliances with Athens for safety, and further inducements followed. Eretria was ruled by a series of tyrants during this period, and the instability and tension exploded at the Battle of Tamunai in 349. Eventually Eretria made peace with Athens and in 341 democracy was restored.

Exactly what happened on the island around 338 is unclear, but the Macedonians appear to have exercised control over Eretria virtually continually until the Romans arrived. Some time in the 270s Eretria did break away from Macedonia, as much of Greece had already done, but it was soon retaken. During a brief interlude from about 253 to 249 or 248 Eretria was ruled by a king who rebelled from the Macedonians to establish the unlikely kingdom of Euboea and Corinth.

Eretria was taken by the Romans in 198 BC. Livy writes a moving description of its fall. During the Second Macedonian War at that time the Roman general Quinctius Flamininus sacked the city-state, but it was later granted nominal independence. A pattern evolved whereby Rome-supported oligarchies controlled the island. It was the beginning of the end for the once-great Eretria, and after Euboea was dragged into the First Mithridatic War of 87 BC it was destroyed and not rebuilt. To the Lombards and Venetians over a millennium later it was as nothing.

The ghostly outlines of all the buildings marking the rise and fall of this great power were visible in the archaeological sites of Eretria, most of which were overgrown with weeds and grazed by sheep, offering sustenance to the aesthetic sensibilities only of people like me whose imaginations feast best on decay. I stumbled upon the fourth-century theatre, seating 6000. It had a vaulted underground tunnel connecting the stage and the orchestra, facing the audience, whence emerged actors playing either the gods of the underworld or dead people or the *deus ex machina.* I had intended to seek out the person with the gate keys and crawl through the tunnel in search of an ancient experience, but shortly before I left London my friend Richard Holmes told me that he had done it and it stank of urine. In the museum there was a photograph of it being discovered in the 1890s which offered a microcosmic illustration of the story of the rediscovery of ancient Greece, at least until part way into this century. Two imperious western European men in hats, black suits, stiff white collars and cravats were looking very pleased with themselves next to the famous tunnel while three dark-skinned locals lolled about in ragged clothes and stared blankly at the camera. It reminded me of a conversion course from Ancient to Modern Greek I did years ago. It was originally put together for archaeologists wanting to learn Modern Greek to facilitate their digs, and the exercises consisted entirely of phrases such as, 'You have stolen my money! Give it back, you cad!' or, 'Carry these bags to our quarters,' or, 'You will be punished if you touch this.'

Just below the theatre six Greeks were jabbing away inside a complex mass of fenced-off ruins. In the museum later I saw graceful green bronze cauldrons found there, tucked in stone jackets and covered with lead lids. They found carbonized bones inside. In 1891 a tomb was discovered some way off to the east containing a sepulchral stone inscribed with the name of Biote, daughter of Aristotle, and it might have been the grave of the great man himself, too.

The houses along the west wall, where I was standing, dated from the fourth century and were enormous for that period, indicating a rich merchant population. In the declining years of the third and second centuries they were divided up into flats for less affluent families to live in, just like we do with our houses in similar times of social change.

I picked my way around the back of the town and came across several more sites, one of which was partially covered with a sheet of yellow corrugated plastic. Everything had such an abandoned air that I began to feel disenchanted. One site, next to a burnt-out lorry, was covered in rubbish, the once-circumjacent fence had collapsed and three noisy sheep were tied up on it. Suddenly, near the yellow plastic, I spotted three men with expensive equipment engaged in what was clearly painstaking reconstruction work under a brand new timber roof. The site was shut off, this time with proper railings, and as I couldn't make them hear me I climbed over the railings and signalled. Two of them signalled back, directing me in through one of three glass-panelled double doors built around mosaic floors. A bearded man appeared to be hoovering. He switched off his machine, and I diffidently told him that I was interested in the ruins. He turned out to be an Italian-speaking Swiss archaeologist called Gabriele who was an Eretrian expert. The house was built by Macedonians in 375 BC. We took off our shoes and he unlocked the doors. The mosaics were made of small, uncut stones and the colours – black, white, yellow and red – were natural. They were exceptionally beautiful. The principal mosaic had not been cleaned, and as Gabriele showed me each part he sprayed it gently with water and it sprang to life like a magic painting. One threshold was adorned with velvet-eyed sphinxes and panthers, and in the vestibule Thetis on a hippocampus brought arms to Achilles. In another room a Medusa's head lay like a patterned rug.

Gabriele was from the Ecole Suisse d'Archéologie, who had

been digging in Eretria for over 25 years. He was an inspirational figure, toiling away with his Swiss car parked under an olive tree. I thanked him, left him to his hoover and walked uphill a little to the Classical gym. I could still see the basins built into the walls of the baths, fed by pipes from the hill behind. It was overlooked by the older acropolis, on a hill which was itself overlooked by Evia's Mount Olympus. I climbed up to the ruins of the north tower through the ubiquitous olive groves and strip of cubist wooden beehives painted in bright blues, yellows and white. Mount Parnitha was positively shining over on the mainland.

On the way back into town I passed what was once the temple of Apollo the Laurel-Crowned, partially shaded by a huge eucalyptus. (He wore a laurel wreath, according to Apollodorous and Plutarch, because of an unhappy seduction attempt. He had pursued Daphne, a mountain nymph and priestess of Mother Earth, but Mother Earth whisked her off to Crete, leaving a laurel bush in her place. Apollo, a Don Giovanni prototype, made a wreath out of it to console himself.)

Individuals from Eretria crop up frequently in ancient history. One of the most famous is Menedemus, a philosopher born in 339 BC. He became leader of a school of philosophy in Elis founded by Phaedo, and brought it home, where it became known as the School of Eretria (Cicero mentions it). Nobody actually knows what Menedemus said or thought, which is rather a handicap to understanding his philosophy. It is known, however, that he was keen on the satire of his fellow Eretrian Achaeus, a fifth-century tragic poet (Aristophanes quotes him twice). Menedemus left the immortal diktat that his town was so unhealthy (he must have meant because of the mosquito-infested marsh to the east) that he had to spend every evening drinking to ward off noxious influences. He was extremely matey with the Macedonians, for which he was eventually exiled.

I idled away the following morning playing backgammon in the yard with the woman from next door. It led into a long lunch, of course, involving prodigious quantities of food and retsina. I had lost every single game of backgammon. In need of exercise I persuaded one of my new friend's extensive progeny to accompany me to the ruins of the Iseion. It quickly emerged that she hadn't the faintest idea where it was. Recourse to my books eventually steered us towards the coast. It was a temple to the Egyptian goddess Isis which probably belonged to a colony of Egyptian merchants in the third or second century BC. Near it the Circus California (from Italy, confusingly) was just setting up. The stoa (roofed colonnade) of the ancient market-place was squashed between a caravan and a group of dwarves. It was a sophisticated affair, built in the sixth century and substantially embellished 200 years later. Some of the coins found there were stamped with the image of an owl, the symbol of Pallas Athena. (The association gave rise to the saying 'an owl to Athens', the equivalent of our 'coals to Newcastle'; Aristophanes uses it in *The Birds.* They had a lot of sayings like that. My all-time favourite, now sadly fallen into disuse, except from my lips, is 'vampires to Santorini'.)

Up at the tiny museum the garden was strewn with a multitude of headless statues, amphorae and column fragments, all sprinkled with pine cones and eucalyptus leaves. Inside there were six glass cases, an exhibition put on by the Swiss and an unravaged urn alone in the corner. The second case contained a set of four miniature cups with handles, descending in size like matryoshkas, found in an infant's tomb, and a string of milky gold glass pearls left on the body by a grieving mother. In the grand fourth-century houses archaeologists recently unearthed a terracotta Medusa with wide, deep-set eyes and a full, sensuous mouth, originally painted white and gold and hanging on a wall in a banqueting room in the mosaic house. They had such style.

The next evening some acquaintances from Vathia whom I

had met at the monastery invited me out to dinner in the nearest thing in Eretria to a smart restaurant. Glad of the company, I was obliged to fish out the least crumpled frock and put it on back to front as there was a hole burnt in the front. Before dinner we walked around to the wooded island of Pezonisi, near the port. You get there by a bridge now, but previously it was accessible at low tide over the sand flats. It formed a natural mole for the ancient harbour. Now they call it the Island of Dreams after a hotel with an annexe of bungalows which has invaded the whole of it like a cancer. The bridge was lined with young trees called First of May.

The weather was glorious. One morning I took a bus out to Vasilika, a lively village on the 'main road' from Eretria to Chalkis sporting a handsome Lombard tower. As I walked a few miles north to the village of Filla other towers appeared on the hillsides. The medieval constructions are a feature of central Greece, but the 50-odd on Evia are unusual in that they are intervisible, once forming an effective signalling chain and now a skeleton of Latin power. Although generally referred to as Venetian, other western occupiers were responsible for some at least, and as such towers were widely used by the Byzantines, some may predate the Fourth Crusade.

Filla was a drowsy village which quickly began to irritate me when the first six people I asked claimed no knowledge of the Byzantine church of the Panayitsa which I knew was there. I eventually dragged directions out of an ancient man sitting outside the *kafeneio* (coffee-shop). As I made off he shouted, 'It's locked. The key's in the first olive tree on the right at the left fork of the track.'

The church was properly called Madonna below the Hill of

the Castle, and it was full of delicately painted saints. From it an arduous path took me up through territory liberally studded with goatherds' huts to a well preserved castle. The expanse of countryside all around it – virtually unchanged since the Middle Ages – gave me an idea of why those feudal westerners fought so hard to keep their little bits of territory. The view from the castle, best from the top of a precarious flight of steps up to the battlement, was full of the green bushiness at the heart of the Lelantine Plain. It wasn't just the ancient Greeks who cherished the plain. The historian J.B. Bury says that the Venetians called it, 'The life of this island, the eye and garden of Negroponte', and there was a special official called a potamarch whose job was to keep it irrigated. A pair of towers sat on top of the hill opposite, in the background the Evian Gulf narrowed to become the Straits of Aulis, and the sprawl of Chalkis seeped in to the west. It was at Aulis, almost exactly opposite, that the Greek triremes amassed on their way to Troy and Agamemnon sacrificed his daughter Iphigeneia.

Filla castle was the home of Likarios, an Evian knight whose strange and romantic story has ensured that he lives on in the Greek imagination. He is one of the island's favourite sons, but the funny thing is that he wasn't really Greek at all, and he was an appalling brute (not that the latter trait has ever stopped men becoming heroes). His story is a swashbuckling one of wounded pride and an overpowering lust for revenge, as he was driven by the ignorant pride of the Lombard lords into the service of the Greek emperor, and inflicted immense suffering upon his own kind.

Likarios, before he rose to fame, was the child of penniless immigrants living in Karistos in the second half of the thirteenth century. His family had come over from Vicenza in the early years of Lombard rule. He became a knight in the service of a Latin baron and secretly married a dalle Carceri widow, which went down so badly with her family and the feudal aristocracy in Evia in general that he had to go into hiding. The nobles were implacable, determined that the upstart should be put in his place. This bit so deep into his soul that he committed his life to the destruction of Lombard power on his native Evia – and to destruction in general. Gathering together a band of his own ilk he terrorized the villagers living near his stronghold, which was near Karistos. But he wanted to get the barons, not just the peasants, so he made overtures to Emperor Michael VIII Paleologos. This was good timing, as the Byzantines had only recently retaken Constantinople and were riding high to recapture what they could of their lost territories from the Latins. So Michael supplied the men, and they and Likarios (called L'Ikarios by Byzantine historians) waged a bitter war against the Latin lords. Likarios was an ace strategist, and immensely successful. His finest hour was probably when he took Castel Rosso from the Burgundian Othon after a long attack by land and sea in 1276. It was a great prize, and Michael, flushed with triumph, offered him the fiefdom of the whole island. Likarios took almost all the important castles before venturing beyond the island to continue his attacks elsewhere. He became Imperial Vice-Admiral, and very nearly succeeded in taking Chalkis too. After capturing Filla castle, built by the Lombards, he led his prisoners off to Constantinople in triumph, and returned to live in Filla, master of the whole island with the exception of the town of Chalkis. The Greek serfs must have looked up at the castle on the hill and felt a chill in their hearts. Likarios was appointed Admiral of the Byzantine fleet, captured almost all the Aegean islands from their western lords, then disappears from the records.

It was a magnificent spot to lie idle, and it was only thirst that eventually propelled me downwards. I drank at the village spring and continued on to the tiny fishing village of Lefkandi. It was sheltered in a small bay, and the air was as still and warm as an incubator. Six members of a Greek family were not swimming but standing neck-deep in the glassy sea, the grandmother still wearing her straw hat, their voices carrying up to the wide terrace of three tree-shaded cafés where a handful of people sat talking. Five brightly painted boats lay immobile on the water, and to the left an olive-clad promontory stretched into nowhere. I sat in one of the agreeable cafés and pulled out some material on the excavations in progress on the promontory for well over 20 years. A team from the British School of Archaeology in Athens initially arrived at the Xiropolis site to investigate a portion of the Geometric settlement, in existence from about 1100 BC to about 700 BC. But they discovered more, much more, going back as far as an Early Bronze Age community. In the site report they suggest that the first settlers arrived from the eastern Aegean in about 2100 BC. For some time it was without doubt one of the most important settlements on the island and, in the eighth century BC, among the first to embrace literacy by using the new Greek script culled from the Phoenicians. Its name, however, is not known. It may at one time have been the community called Chalkis, or Lelanton; some of the preceding generation of archaeologists thought it was Old Eretria. There is also a maverick theory that it was the forgotten city actually called Euboea, referred to by Strabo and others (the poets liked the idea of a forgotten and perhaps drowned city; Aeschylus latches on to it and says it was swallowed by tidal waves). It was probably overwhelmed in the great war between Eretria and Chalkis, or the inhabitants were simply forced to flee Eretrian hostility. In about 700 BC it was sacked and soon became the dry and abandoned shell that its modern name Xiropolis implies.

As the sun was setting I joined an old man at the bus stop. During the course of the afternoon I had noticed that buses rarely appeared: the system was to stand at the stop and flag down any passing car to take you up to the main road. The old man was soon successful and we both piled into the front seat of a van. The driver knew some English and was keen to practise it. 'I like very much your perfume. What is it please?' I didn't have the heart to tell him I wasn't wearing any.

High in the mountains northwest of Eretria I found St George's monastery, for centuries an important spiritual centre, balancing precariously on the fine line between existence and non-existence. Half a dozen people were living on the premises including a priest, who was watering his hydrangeas when I arrived. A sign outside warned me not to sing or dance. The priest answered a few questions and disappeared. The *katholikon* was right in the middle of the open courtyard. An inscription above the door which looked like ARMA but which was really 1141 written as letters had bestowed the meaningless name Arma upon the monastery. The church was the work of three different periods, and the priest told me they had found fragments of a temple to Apollo which originally occupied the site. Only the nave of the early church had been preserved, and in it scraps of frescos gleamed in the darkness. Richly-coloured zodiac signs arranged around the edge of the windowless dome of the seventeenth-century narthex were topped by a menagerie of strange creatures. In another section four women with breasts and arms like Indian fertility goddesses were dancing.

Blinking back into the sunlight I saw a woman with no teeth and a waist-length chestnut plait cutting up onions under a mulberry tree. The courtyard was full of walnut trees, pines and a mass of roses and fuchsias, as well as neat pots of basil and mint. The woman, Sophia, lived in Arma, and after asking me what my salary was she chatted away and brought me water, coffee and *loukoumi* (known in the west as Turkish delight). She wanted to know if I'd been to secondary school – by no means the first time I had been asked that question. It was, for her generation, the benchmark of progress.

I wanted to take a different route back, and as we walked to the entrance so she could point the way she suddenly stuck her head into a large terracotta amphora with a narrow neck and began talking inside it. Thinking this must be a local custom I observed with interest, but it subsequently emerged that the monastic cat had selected this uterine spot to have her kittens, one of whom was writhing around in the bottom.

What she did not tell me was that the path constantly offered forks and turnoffs, and after struggling through a stifling pine forest I soon became hopelessly lost on the rocky sides of mountains unvisited, apparently, by any flock. The sea continually came into view and disappeared again, and I resolved to keep it in sight at all costs and proceed towards it, but this got me into all sorts of trouble as I encountered gullies and escarpments. As ever it was blazing hot. An unfinished road finally materialized in the distance (there are unfinished roads all over the place in Evia which suddenly stop, without warning, at whatever point the money ran out) and I scrambled up to it, and an hour later reached some elegant villas, a village whose name I never found out, and then the coast road.

My landlady in Eretria lived in an old stone house painted red and white. She was one of those old Greeks who can't grasp the notion of a foreigner speaking their language, and during all our 'conversations' so far I had spoken normally and she had uttered only nouns, which she enunciated with grossly exaggerated precision whilst miming whatever she was trying to say. It reminded me of my dad on childhood holidays in France. On my sixth day, however, when I called on her to pay the rent she was so preoccupied with her chickens that she forgot about my special status and chatted away normally. She was 60 and unmarried, and on learning that I too was single she said, 'Well, you're young. You've still got a chance.'

She insisted on picking me a bag of mirabelle plums from her orchard, and gave me two eggs from her hens and a basin of sardines from a bucketful her brother had caught that morning. The next day she came to my quarters and saw me writing, and she began reciting poems she had written, then singing songs learnt from her parents, who were refugees from Asia Minor. In the end I couldn't get rid of her.

Most days I went for a swim. The beach was full of red bricks but the water was delicious. I met a perky Scotsman who had worked for the *Daily Telegraph* for 20 years and moved to Eretria 12 years ago, returning to the UK each winter to buy clothes in Regent Street. He part-owned a shop on the front, and on Friday evening we sat outside it and watched the ferry spewing out hordes of Athenians.

'I don't know where they all *go*,' he lamented. 'The island soaks them up like a sponge every Friday evening, and on Sunday afternoons someone wrings it out and they return to their hell-hole of a city.'

I had to leave the next morning to meet my friend Sarah Caygill in Chalkis, but before taking the bus I nipped up to a Macedonian tomb northwest of the theatre. There were four in the area, carved into the rock and vaulted. But when I found the steps leading down to the tomb, tucked into a bluff, there were six oleaginous snakes slithering around and it put me off. The expedition was a double failure as it meant I had no time to break the journey to Chalkis with a visit to Arethusa's Spring as I had intended. This spring, often referred to in ancient history and mythology, is beyond a hill shortly before Chalkis. It was the experience of two fellow travellers that impelled me there, my predecessors in the 1830s and 1840s. The first, Colonel William

Leake, was told that the spring didn't exist any more, and reports as much. He was an extraordinary man. One achievement of his distinguished career was that he rescued the Elgin Marbles by sending divers down for them in 1802 when the ship carrying them and him was wrecked. The second, Jean Alexandre Buchon, who found the spring, concludes that the Colonel was deliberately misled by Turkish disinformation. The business of recording what the locals say has always been tricky. Herodotus probably got it right, as his criteria for inclusion seem to be more to do with the intrinsic appeal of what people say rather than the veracity of it, like when he solemnly reports that the inscription on an obelisk records the number of sausages eaten by the workmen during construction.

Buchon's interpretation of Turkish nastiness is backed up by his assertion that the Evian Turks were the most intolerant in Greece, and the most generally ferocious. A lot of travellers mention this, such as the eminent British scientist Henry Holland, who visited in 1812, and, shortly before him, Byron's friend John Hobhouse – the Right Honourable Lord Broughton – who regarded the Turks with particular venom. Even Gibbon quotes a popular saying in Greece during the Turkish Occupation, 'From the Greeks of Athens, the Jews of Thessaloniki and the Turks of Negroponte, Good Lord deliver us', and there is a song in the Venetian dialect about a man escaping from 'the Turk of Negroponte'. Edward Dodwell, writing in the first decade of the nineteenth century and recounting his experiences with military precision, went further and said that the 'vicious and tyrannical character' of the Evian Turks rubbed off on the Greeks, 'who became more cruel and oppressive than the Turks themselves ... Indeed the bad conduct of those renegades', he goes on, 'has given rise to a Turkish proverb that a bad Christian can never become a good Musulman.'

Jean Alexandre Buchon became my companion on the bus journey to Chalkis and subsequently never left me for long. An urbane French intellectual of some literary distinction, he visited Evia three times, once very briefly, as recorded in his book on the mainland, *La Grèce continentale et la Morée*, and twice for his *Voyage dans l'Eubée, les îles Ioniennes et les Cyclades*. He was a committed traveller, and left no stone unturned: if he spotted a crusty old inscription high on a wall of a house when he was striding down a street he would call for a ladder, bucket and sponge and climb up to inspect it. His prose is a model of clarity, and the tone is relaxed; if a sense-of-humour failure is discernible at times, he is Rabelais himself compared with Colonel Leake. While prone to the odd romantic comment or philosophical flight of fancy, he is never pretentious. I got a real sense that he enjoyed his travels. He says he found the plain between Eretria and Chalkis intoxicating after the aridity of Attica and the nudity of the Boeotian mountains. I liked him. I was sorry he had missed the south, as he would have enjoyed it. Inclement weather kept him away.

Chapter Four

Grangrongrously magnificent!

EDWARD LEAR *describing a mountain pass in southern Evia in a letter to Chichester Fortescue dated July 1848*

The journey from Chalkis to Kimi was long and excursive: the road had to skirt the corpulent Dirfis mountain range in the centre of the island. Hugging the coast until just before Aliveri, it eventually veered north at Lepoura, a village known for its strategic location on the road grid rather than for any intrinsic features, rather like Crewe on the rail network in the UK. It was the gateway to the south and east.

I was travelling with Sarah, who had escaped from a Japanese bank for 10 days, and speaking English felt like being set free. The bus conductor organized us from the start, and we were to change at Avlonari. When we got there we went into a shop to buy some cold drinks, deliberated over which to choose, and Sarah remembered a vital piece of news from London she had omitted to tell me. It concerned our mutual friend Anne-Marie Barrett, a wonderful woman who for some time and for reasons known only to herself had been walking out with a person whose appeal we found difficult to locate. The tidings were that it was all over, and that the information had been delivered to

A-M over Charlie's carphone (Charlie was a bond dealer) which was proof of course that we had been right all along. When we came out we had missed the bus. We both started laughing, but the conductor, who had also got off the bus and must have come off duty, began shouting at us for our uselessness, consumed with fury that we had foiled his best efforts to get us to Kimi. We sat down at a *kafeneio* on the road to wait for the next bus, due in two and a half hours.

The second half of the journey took us through the configuration of villages around Kimi, with ubiquitous Dirfis behind and glaucous valleys sweeping to bays on the right. The change in the landscape was remarkable. It was greener, with a greater variety of flora, and more undulating. We threaded up through the villages and through Kimi itself, which stood on a high ridge, and descended on double hairpin bends to its port, called simply Kimi's Seashore – Paralia Kimis. It's the only port on the east coast where you can catch a ferry; in fact it is one of the very few spots where boats can safely land at all, as the coastline consists largely of sheer cliffs and unnavigable rock. If you sailed in a straight line eastwards you would skim the top of Chios and end up in Turkey, near the Gulf of Izmir. The ferries go to Skiros (which belongs administratively to Evia) and to the northern Sporades. The Paralia was small, with an easy atmosphere of quiet contentment, rare for a port. We found a room with a marble floor in a house next to a fig tree laden with fat fruit (though not fat enough, as it was not yet August). Elizabeth David says somewhere that the best figs in the world come from Evia, and she knew they were from Kimi, though she refused to say so in case everyone rushed off there to strip the trees bare – my revelation, I'm sure, will not have the effect she feared. They were originally brought over from Izmir (then Smyrna).

We swam at the sandy Tsoutsini beach. The sea was immaculate. Robert Byron knew about the special qualities of the

Aegean. In *The Byzantine Achievement* he wrote, 'As the sapphire and the aquamarine from the turquoise, so differ the waters of the Aegean from the flat blue of the Mediterranean whole', and like others before and after him he used the Aegean as a powerful metaphor for Greekness. Freya Stark begins her eulogy in *The Lycian Shore*, 'For what words can give even the ghost of the Aegean bathing? When the body is lost because the radiance and coolness of the world have become a part of it, and nothing seems oneself any longer ...' It was entirely different from the Evian Gulf. It was pellucid green, with a deep and ridged sand floor, all lit up with the phosphorescence of the water, clear and pure as a diamond. Stark ends by describing hours spent in the Aegean with a Romantic sentiment worthy of Coleridge: 'No life is wasted that can remember them, as I hope to do till I have to leave it all.'

On the subject of the Aegean, it is astonishing how any innocent truth can be laundered through the patriarchal myth. In *The Greek Islands*, first published in 1963, Ernle Bradford contends that the Greeks named the Aegean Sea after a male (the Athenian King Aegeus) and the Ionian Sea after a female (the priestess Io) because of their respective maleness and femaleness: the first clear and precise, the second hazy and sentimental. Warming to his theme, he goes on to suggest that the maleness of the first 'engenders an air in which woolly thinking is impossible'. This is an absurd and repellent theory which could of course only have been invented by a man. If we started taking the gender of proper nouns as the basis for epistemological theorizing we could recreate the world. People might consider why London's largest coach station was named after a woman but most famous square after a man. Even Freud didn't go that far.

Local predators were about. I only left Sarah alone for 10 minutes and a group of Kimian youths wrestled the trunks off one of their number in the water and dropped them next to her.

From a vantage point they laughed and clapped as the unfortunate victim steeled himself and approached Sarah, hitherto buried in a book and stoutly ignoring the gang, to recover them. She glanced up to see a naked man emerging from the sea and making for her, but she kept her cool, and he kept his trunks.

Along the beach a man caught a huge octopus with his hands. He turned the body inside out, tossed the guts away, shook it about a lot, repeatedly slapped it hard against a selection of rocks, swirled it around in the sea and hung it over the rowlock of his boat.

On the seafront we discovered a charming specimen of the lovable genus *pantopoleio*. (The word lingers in the formal and artificial *katharevousa*, a travesty of a language; it has an 'n' on the end if you want to be really pedantic.) These are Everything Shops and you frequently come across them in Greek villages, stacked higgledy-piggledy high on all sides with a multiplicity of goods, ancient and modern, filling every available space. In this one a small corridor no more than two feet wide constituted the only pass through a mountain of boxes, crates, sacks and stacks, Cyclopean spools of rope and fishing line, piles of footballs, pyramids of buckets, 200 filthy jars of mustard, 300 spray cans of cockroach killer, dust-caked bottles of dubious lurid liqueurs, a tray of lemons perched on an ironing board, a stand of plastic jewellery – and more, much more. Behind a fridge at the back three men were playing cards in a space about four feet square. The place was a triumph of *laissez-faire* on the part of the management over all modern concepts of stocktaking, marketing, hygiene or common sense.

Next to it a row of ouzeris lined the front, and we passed several happy evenings at the one which quickly became our favourite. Ouzeris are much rarer than they used to be in Greece, I suppose because they don't make much money, and because younger people want more western drinks like beer and whisky, but in the Paralia they were alive and well, with a little plate of tiny *meze* brought with each round: a morsel of octopus, a slice of fried courgette, a sliver of tomato and cucumber, an olive and a cube of cheese.

The coast to the west was mountainous and uninhabited, and we were determined to visit one or two of the tiny villages dotted on the map and get down to the shore on the other side of Mount Afroa. In the ouzeri we met an affable Kimian with time on his hands who suggested an expedition, so one morning Sarah and I packed a small bag between us and set off in his shiny red car.

Although a new 'road' had recently been opened through the mountains, it was largely unfinished and made for very hard driving. At the wheel Xenophon was unfazed. The car snaked along between mountains north of Vitala, of which we glimpsed only a mass of red roofs clustered on the hillside. (The village practises the extraordinary custom of marrying its daughters off at the age of 15 or younger, with the result that most of the women are grandmothers in their thirties and great-grandmothers in their fifties – and there are plenty of great-greats and even triple greats, too.) It was the oregano season, and we passed an old woman on a mule carrying bristly green sheaves of it. From the top of a peak Xenophon pointed out Ano and Kato Metochi. The villagers in the Upper (Ano) part had terraced the hills. The Lower (Kato) consisted of half a dozen huts on a long beach in a wide bay, and a scattering of little wooden boats lay on the sand like baby whales.

Xenophon, a committed smoker, needed to stock up, so we stopped at the higher village, where three generations of a family were sitting idly outside the taverna scrutinizing the strangers. The children of this remote place, of which there were about 10, used to have to walk to school in Kimi, before the road was made. It was a five-hour journey, so they would sleep in town from Monday to Friday. We set off again, and followed a hose carrying water to an isolated house for at least two miles. (On the way back we saw a tree up into which they had invisibly inserted a pipe and nozzle so that water sprang out at waist height.) At about 2500 feet we crossed Afroa, and meandered down to Chiliadou, where there were a string of beaches and half a dozen houses. We passed an old man sewing needles onto a *kalamariera*, the brutal-looking instrument used to catch certain types of squid (the needles are strung tightly round a lead weight like a hairbrush, and pierce the squid when they swim into them). The other type of local squidfishing involved a kind of open bag dragged along the seabed, and over the years this has yielded a rich crop of antiquities. The fishermen are required by law to offer them up to the state, but generally human nature prevails, and it is an indication of genuine intimacy with a fisherman's family to be shown such a catch. Most of the squid around Kimi are caught by professionals from Piraeus, the Athenian port, between October and May, and sent back through Evia to the fish market by truck. The Kimians, Xenophon told us, catch a lot of swordfish, and using the universal sign language of anglers he ranted about one he and his cronies had caught recently weighing 100 pounds.

We asked the squid man if there was anywhere to stay, and he pointed to a ramshackle taverna with a large terrace overlooking the sea. They had a room, with three beds, and an outside shower rigged up on the cliff face. Xenophon took it for granted that we were all going to share a room, which Sarah complained about, but under the circumstances we had little option. We spent the afternoon exploring. The next beach along was for nudists only, and there were about six of them on it. Before the nudists there were monks, living in a monastery long since dissolved.

Over dinner the taverna owner's wife was less than enchanted by rural life. She had three children. The building was not on the electricity grid, but a small generator supplied power for a few hours each evening, and this kept the block of ice brought from Kimi solid in the fridge. They had no animals, but grew a variety of fruit and vegetables, and she made her bread in a stone oven 50 yards away from the house. She spent most of the day washing clothes and dishes. In the corner of the taverna there was a stuffed flamingo that had flown to Chiliadou two winters in a row and then frozen to death.

We walked, swam and read, and two days later drove back to Kimi at sunset, reluctantly, but with some relief too on my part as I was finding the continual simultaneous translation between Xenophon and Sarah exhausting, particularly as they disagreed on virtually everything. The rocks absorbed the light and glowed red as the sun disappeared, and the sea faded to a gleaming opal. At Kimi we said goodbye to our new friend, his car now caked with orange dust, and thumbed a lift down to our room on the sea with the village electrician, who was shouting and shining a torch through the windscreen as he had no headlights.

The most recent census revealed that the population of Kimi was 4000 souls. This was quite a victory for the town council, as the real figure was not much more than half that: they had provided free buses from Athens to induce anyone with a vague Kimian connection to come over and register, thus increasing their per capita government grant. The modern town was founded in 1700 by nine families from the Oxi valley, and later they were joined by some Cretans and a large group from the island of Sifnos, who brought their rather beautiful style of pottery with them. A seafaring tradition developed, unsurprisingly given the advantageous position of the town, perched on the east coast with nothing but a clear sea and a couple of wealthy islands between it and Turkey. In the second half of the 1880s the port of Kimi had 45 ships and a team of 450 men. The region remained a micro-culture, isolated from north and south alike, and cut off too by the mountains from the fat and fertile quarter of the island that is central Evia. An unhappy result, inevitably, has been a small but endemic incidence of slow-wittedness resulting from inbreeding; for a short period not so long ago there was even a special remedial class at the local school to accommodate its unfortunate victims.

Architecturally there were two halves to the town, but they were shaken together like a cocktail. One half consisted of large and handsome stone houses with two storeys above a half-ground-floor half-basement affair which was originally a store-room for wine and oil, in traditional, symmetrical, vaguely neo-Classical style, with elaborate wrought-iron balconies and fancy carved stone flourishes. These were the heritage of a prosperous, more populous and very elegant nineteenth-century Kimi. The other half was made up of modern whitewashed concrete apartment blocks. These were the manifestation of an enfeebled, style-less twentieth-century Kimi which had lost touch with its roots.

The main square was named after Kimi's most famous son, the pioneering cytologist Yeorgios Papanikolaou, to whom all women who have smears should be grateful (they don't call it the Pap test for nothing) and who spent most of his career in the US, dying in 1962. His father was mayor of Kimi. There was a solemn bronze bust of him in the square, and a whole room dedicated to him in the museum. St Athanasios' cathedral dominated the square. A rather complicated diocesan history has led to the odd situation of the Bishop (or Metropolitan) of Karistia and Skiros having his see not in either of those places but in Kimi. (The diocese was suppressed altogether in 1896 when the island was stripped of its archbishop and reduced to a single bishopric.) The Bishop of the other diocese on the island has his see in Chalkis, and his territory extends to the west and north and includes the northern Sporades (which don't belong to Evia). But while the island has two bishops, the *nomos* (an administrative unit roughly equivalent to a British county) of Evia has three, as the *nomos* boundaries extend on to the mainland west of Chalkis almost as far as Schimatari, where the road leading off the island from the bridge meets the main Greek north-south highway. (The Turkish administrative division of the *sanjak* of Evia similarly incorporated a chunk of the mainland, though in that case a far larger chunk.) The third bishop is of Thebes and Livadia. It is a curious anomaly, and paradigmatic of the island's double life as a non-island.

I met a charming priest in the cathedral who showed me around and proudly explained its history. It was built in the late nineteenth century, and its *pièce de résistance* was a fourteenth-century *epitafios*, a woven sepulchre cloth showing the recumbent Christ after the Descent from the Cross. It was an exquisite object. The priest explained that it was one of only two depicting Christ with rejoicing angels. The other was on Mount Athos. In 1987 it was carried off to Athens to be exhibited. I later learnt from an English Orthodox deacon living in Kimi that this convincing and delightfully recounted story was entirely false. The cloth was a liturgical *epitafios*, used in the regular liturgy rather than for the Good Friday burial service (its use in the latter is a practice long since abandoned). But it was still very rare.

Down the road the Educational and Cultural Association of Kimi had founded the folklore museum in a typical old house. In the garden they had even built a small theatre, shaped like a segment of an amphitheatre. The museum had a wealth of Kimian memorabilia from 1800 to the 1930s: impossibly elaborate clothes, uniforms, kitchen utensils, furniture, stiffly posed photographs and daguerreotypes, coins, farm implements, silk embroideries (Kimi and the surrounding villages were renowned for the materials the women made from cloth from their own silkworms), looms, barnacled *pitharia* (earthenware storage jars) dragged from the sea, strange Russian pictures brought home by sailors, wine barrels, and more. They had a pair of shoes made out of tyre tread exactly like the woman in Kavodoro had worn. In an island so geographically fragmented by mountain ranges and with such a wide span of economic development, reality in one place is a museum piece in another.

The most moving exhibits were the tinted photographs. The women were wearing the traditional cream embroidered shirts with flowing sleeves, buttoned at the neck, with waisted silk dresses on top scooped away at the front, boleros, scarves, and, for special occasions, belts with elaborate metal buckles. Some of the men had on the *evzone* gear now only worn by embarrassed guards in Irodou Attikou in Athens and many millions of plastic dolls: stiff knee-length skirts, waistcoats with a high collar, pompommed shoes, thick tights, and the pillbox hat with waist-length tassel. One picture showed the annual expedition of the Pan-Evian Society. In 1940 they had made it, amazingly, to Fort Lee in New Jersey. (This organization actually has an American branch. In 1975 they held a ball in New York.) There were shots of local festivals with the entire town, dressed to the nines, gathered around a church. St Nektarios appeared in the centre of one taken in 1900. From 1891 to 1893 he was the Preacher (a state-funded role) for the whole island and wandered all over it on foot, though he spent a great deal of time in Kimi, and they think of him as their own. He was also a bishop (of Pentapolis in what is now Libya). He died in 1920 and was canonized in 1960. The priest in the cathedral told me that he was very popular (and he lives on in village consciousness – plans had been hatched locally to publish a volume of his letters). What you don't often hear said around Kimi, but what anti-Orthodox snipers like to bring up, is that he had something of a reputation. Stories are particularly plentiful about the convent he founded on Aegina in 1908. Cigarettes, alcohol and unpriestly activities with nuns are but three of the accusations levelled at him – and not only after the event, as in his own day the authorities launched some kind of official investigation. A few people still feel very strongly about it. An abbess wrote a book denouncing him only about 10 years ago, for which she was promptly excommunicated.

Kimi's major claim to fame in Greece today is probably its role as the Evian Evian. A medicinal spring, noted for its efficacy in eliminating gallstones and generally considered a good thing, rises at the nearby village of Choneftiko (which means digestive). The Greeks, not usually known for their marketing skills, lost no opportunity in this case, and bottles of water labelled Kimi are sold throughout the country. Close inspection of the bottle reveals that the water comes *topothesia Choneftikou* – from the region of Choneftiko, which is not the same thing as the medicinal water itself at all, but nobody seems to mind that. We went to have a look at it one day, and afterwards I dragged Sarah off to inspect a tiny Byzantine church somewhere near Pirgos (Tower), a small village about four miles south of Kimi named after the Lombard or Venetian stone cylinder still presiding over it on the hill above. Walking up to the village from the main road we saw the church, tucked away on a slope to the left, with a plain whitewashed exterior and a conservatory on one side overlooking the valley. It was locked, so we set about finding the keeper of the key, whom we discovered frying cheese for her grandchildren.

It was a narrow church built in the thirteenth or fourteenth century, and it had an arch halfway along supporting the vaulted roof. A candle held up in the sanctuary revealed fragments of the remaining frescos, including the *Melismos* (literally, the cutting up into pieces, or symbolic sacrifice of Christ), where Jesus, shone upon by a small star, was depicted as a child lying on a *diskario* (the liturgical object that holds the communion bread). It was difficult to imagine a more blatant image of transubstantiation.

When we returned the key the little family overwhelmed us with everything they had in the kitchen and garden: dried figs, peaches, green plums, *vissinada, saganaki* (fried goats' cheese) and bread. Sarah was astounded at this display of *filoxenia* (hospitality to strangers), which now seemed normal to me. I had lost count of the number of jugs of wine sent over to my taverna table by neighbouring groups who had noticed a new face. It is a feature of Greece discovered by all travellers, and while it might have withered with the onset of mass tourism and a different rhythm of life, in the untouched villages I found it as abundant as ever. Most writers on Greece have expounded upon it. Patrick Leigh Fermor describes in his book *Roumeli* the Greek capacity to relate, immediately, to others as '... one of the great and uncovenanted delights of Greece ... a direct and immediate link, friendly and equal on either side, between human beings, something which melts barriers of hierarchy and background and money ... it functions ... in almost prelapsarian unawareness of its existence ... all the gloomy factors which deoxygenise the air of Western Europe, are absent.' The stranger from that suffocating place, he adds, can cast off the armours his society has encased him in: 'Miraculous lightness takes their place.'

I don't think the phenomenon can be explained as simply (though it would be enough) springing from the joy of relating to other human beings. Ancient literature reveals a deeply-felt notion that failing to show kindness to a stranger invokes misfortune (and conversely it was because the laws of hospitality had been transgressed by the guest Paris that the Trojan War had to take place). In the same way there is a perception (subliminal perhaps) of the efficacy of *filoxenia* in the spiritual world. In other words the actions of hospitality are related, on a higher level, to the inner world, and the stranger is thus a kind of redeemer, offering the giver the opportunity to do right in the eyes of God rather than wallowing in the misery of the human condition. If this is an example of another pagan idea grafted on to a Christian culture, it put down deep roots in the new soil; the concepts it embodies of spiritual existence and worldly existence are more meaningful than almost anything else in the Greek village consciousness.

Right in the middle of the east coast, where the island turns a right angle, there was a monastery high in the hills to the Transfiguration of the Saviour, known simply as Sotira (Saviour). On the way up we checked our route with an old woman who asked us how long we had been staying in 'Koumi'. I don't suppose there are many people around who still speak the full Kimi dialect, though it is not extinct. It used to have some archaic characteristics, like the pronunciation of double consonants and stresses in the wrong places, and k pronounced as ts before i or e: thus, traditionally, the town was called Tsoumi. Later in the summer, in Athens, I went to see a woman whose mother was the schoolmistress in Kimi for many years. The daughter was passionate on the subject of the Kimi dialect. She had moved to a grey suburb of Athens where rubbish was eddying across the street when I visited her. She pulled out a heavy, bound typescript and showed me her translation of Aristophanes' *Plutus* into the dialect.

At the monastery we were greeted by a statuesque Sister with a remarkable sculpted face and a shy manner who towered over the other nuns. She was French, had converted to Orthodoxy during her Russian studies and was sent over from France not knowing a word of Greek. We trailed around behind her as she showed us the monastery, which was destroyed several times during the War of Independence. The star attraction in the church was an icon to the Panagia Odigitria (Virgin as Guide). (There is a famous icon of her in this role at Constantinople. The Emperor Leo III walked among the troops with it in the early eighth century when the city was besieged by Saracens.)

When the last monks died off in 1968 Sotira closed down for eight years, whereupon three nuns arrived and set about reviving it as a nunnery. (This frequently happened, nationwide, as the number of recruits declined and the majority of monks chose to go to Mount Athos.) New buildings were added, and at the time of our visit it had 16 nuns and was still growing. Being cenobitic, like the majority of Greek monasteries, the nuns lived communally. Under the second observance, called idiorrhythmic, the monks or nuns live in a collection of groups of two or three, each under a spiritual leader. Both observances belong to the same order, which is often referred to in non-Orthodox circles as Basilian. This is an incorrect term, though St Basil was involved in the evolution of the order. In the middle of the fourth century, a few decades after the persecution of the Christian Church had ended, St Basil did form a kind of active order (a group of monks working in a community but withdrawing to the 'monastery' at sunset). At roughly the same time a number of Christians went off to live virtually alone in the desert. Thus these two strands of asceticism developed at around the same time and evolved to constitute two of the three observances of monastic Orthodoxy. The third, the hermetic, also appeared in Egypt in the fourth century. Now most hermits live on Mount Athos. It's trickier to be a hermit in

Greece these days, with a proliferating road network and intrepid tourists.

Sotira kept time with the rest of Greece. (There are whole villages which never bother to change their clocks in spring and autumn, and this attitude towards time is an example of the introspective nature of the traditional Greek village.) Sisters marched in and out of the serene central courtyard with its cypress and peach tree and canorous spring, organizing icon-making and woodchopping while the young nephews of one nun played with the monastic cat outside the nasty concrete belltower. After a lunch of macaroni cheese (strict Orthodox observance forbids oil on a Wednesday and Friday, and as olive oil is such a staple of the Greek diet this is severe fasting indeed) we set out from the back of the monastery for the ruined Latin castle on the top of the hill. It was a steep climb, past a church covered in stained concrete. The Greeks can be delightfully pragmatic when they name things: the two blobs out in the Aegean were called Big Island and Little Island. An eagle wheeled overhead. A minor military installation they comically call a Nato base was hidden by a hill, thank God, and only the tips of the wind-powered electricity generators were visible (needless to say they had functioned only for a very short period and then broken down, never to be repaired). A peculiar factory was hidden in the hills, built to manufacture Artemis ballistic weapons. The site was chosen for dubious reasons involving government connections, and it was swiftly pointed out that eastern Evia was perhaps not the choicest spot for an arms factory as it was the first place a Turkish plane would fly over, so, amidst much ridicule in the national press, it was turned into a manufacturing plant for military uniforms. Thus against all the odds the vista from the top of the hill was just as the Latins would have seen it as they scanned the horizon anxiously for pirates, or Turks, or an opposing faction of victorious Fourth Crusaders.

*

After Sotira, our next visit to a monastery came as something of a culture shock. We arrived at Manzari, on a hill about six miles south of Kimi, in the early evening, and were auspiciously greeted by two dogs barking maniacally. Two nuns and two women visitors sat us down with a plate of syrupy cherries to be interrogated. On learning we were Protestant, the Abbess turned to one of the women.

'What exactly is Protestantism?'

'Heresy,' came the swift reply. It wasn't the first time that I had been called a heretic. It annoyed me intensely. But they were right, according to Orthodox doctrine. Heretics are people who aren't baptized into the Orthodox Church.

The nuns grew confused when they learnt that we both had the same name, supposing that this was the foreign system. When I revealed that I knew Sara was Abraham's wife they visibly cheered up about us (this subsequently became my ice-breaking monastic party piece). Manzari was a depressing place, redolent of decay. A local later summed it up thus: 'You don't get any sense of a spiritual life. It's a collection of women who happen to live under the same roof.' The most recent addition to the ranks joined a mere 30 years ago, and several of the nuns had been there half a century – the record holder, now 84, had notched up 58 years, and she shuffled about the courtyard in her stockinged feet, squinting at us and tripping over the dogs.

Our room had a plumbed-in sink but no taps, just a grey tin above it half-filled with water and twigs, with a rusty spout which could once be turned on and off. The stiff cotton sheets were intricately hand-embroidered, and planks stuck out from the ends of the hospital-style beds. The window overlooked the mountains, and the door led on to the uneven courtyard filled with lemon trees. The whitewashed church had a blackened interior and the nuns had hung icons over the ghostly frescos. Nailed to a tree outside, next to a line of washing, was a poster exhorting the public not to blaspheme, asserting first that it was not Christian, and then, lest this were not discouragement enough, that it was not Greek.

We stayed one night and Sister Filothei, suffering badly from arthritis, took us under her wing. I taught her the word for chick-peas (which we ate a lot) in English, and she struggled about the monastery chirping 'Tsikpeece, tsikpeece,' and asked me if we have dogs in England.

There was nothing to keep us there, so we headed towards a steep hill called Oxilithos (Sharp Stone) and found the eponymous village on its slopes. The extinct volcano at the top of the hill was, the locals assured us, a hundred million years old; there were other volcanos on surrounding hills, and most of the land was formed of some kind of volcanic petrifaction. We picked our way down to the eastern end of the village, past a straggle of houses, huts and chickens, and found the tiny Byzantine church of St Nicholas, crouching above an ancient, clotted-barked olive tree. Pushing the door ajar we crept in, inhaling the familiar rich, musty and decadent fragrance. An inscription revealed that it had been renovated early in the fourteenth century. Less than half a mile away we found its approximate contemporary, the fragile and equally fine St Anna. The central portion of the island, around the Aliveri-Kimi axis, has the richest Byzantine heritage, and in Oxilithos of all places you couldn't fail to be struck by it.

Our only other experience in Oxilithos was of the Kastello Nightclub, which we visited with some Greek boys we had met in a beach bar down the hill. It got going at about midnight, and at 3.00 am, after three hours of frenetic dancing to imported western music under strobe lights, traditional Greek music was played, and as if relieved from a terrific ordeal they all seemed to grow six feet in height and launched into a statuesque *sirto*.

Their pink stretch miniskirts and Levi 501s melted before our eyes and they became their grandmothers and grandfathers. We left at 4.30, and hitched a lift home in the pitch darkness with a confectioner called Euripides.

Perhaps the greatest joy of my visit to Kimi was the afternoon I spent with Father Meliton, an English orthodox deacon living in Greece since the sixties. He was a gimlet-eyed man with a black ponytail, long pointy beard and an infectiously enthusiastic manner. I visited him at his home, an anachronistic collection of buildings on the slope from Kimi to the waterfront, built in the 1920s by the first bishop of the newly reconstituted diocese of Karistia and Skiros, Panteleimon Fostinis, who was quite a character. In his previous job, in Athens, Fostinis had made some useful connections, and the complex was funded by a wealthy goldsmith from Piraeus. Now largely defunct, it included an orphanage, a school, a small hospital, the diocesan centre and several churches (one open-air), a belltower, courtyards and gardens. In the school playground a pond had an island intricately carved in the shape of Evia, even including a little Skiros opposite. The churches were full of the paintings of Konstantinos Artemis, a mawkish twentieth-century Greek artist of modest fame.

Papous, as Fostinis was known locally (literally, grandad), had to make a quick exit as he was shopped for harbouring Allied soldiers during the Occupation (in a room next to the church a false wall drew back behind a cupboard to reveal a long corridor). He skipped off to Turkey, later became Bishop of the Greek Armed Forces in the Middle East, and ended up as Bishop of Chios.

Father Meliton was an engaging companion, and something of an expert on local ecclesiastical history. The following Sunday it was on his advice that I went to the liturgy at St George's, the church in the Paralia consecrated by St Nektarios in 1893. Orthodox churches require women and men to stand separately, and I had thought that it was always women on the left, on the side of the Virgin's icon, and there I went, quite near the front. But it turned out that the geographical divide varies from church to church. Sometimes it's women at the back and men at the front, as it was there, and my mistake was obviously one of the major events of the year amongst the tiny congregation. I expect they still mention it from time to time.

Whilst Sarah went windsurfing I set off from the coastal village of Platana uphill to Ano Potamia. Discoveries there have begun to explain the mystery of ancient Kimi, which may have co-founded and given its name to the very first Greek colony in Italy, established around the middle of the eighth century BC. The cultural and technical contribution of these early pioneers to the development of western civilization was incalculable. The Roman alphabet probably evolved from the Greek one taken west by the Euboean colonists, for example, and you can't get a more significant cultural import than that.

It was, however, tantalizingly difficult to reconstruct any kind of past for Kimi. There was almost certainly a neolithic settlement and a Classical Kimi at Ano Potamia, but the latter was probably only a dependency of Eretria, and one of a group of towns that collectively formed what is thought of as ancient Kimi, together responsible for the civilization of the central east coast. One of the problems was orthographic. An Ancient Greek word very similar to 'Kimi' means 'a whole load of little towns', and this is probably how the name originated. The site was not actually in Ano Potamia, but on a hill called Kastri to the right before the village. A couple of signs sent me off on the right track, but as usual let me down once I was stranded halfway up a mountain miles from anywhere being barked at by a killer sheepdog. By the time I located the ruins I was in such a bad temper that I wished I were windsurfing.

The neolithic settlement appears to have come to a halt some time before 3200 BC, whereupon the hill was uninhabited for perhaps as long as 1700 years, until the Classical period. The remains of this later community included what looked like a kiln. The ruins were very overgrown, and the modern church nestled right up to them, united as evidence of humanity in spite of the 2000-odd years separating them. People lived there until the end of the first century, when the settlement disappeared again, and apart from a short Byzantine occupancy the hill has been empty ever since. The fourth-century fortress remained largely intact for centuries, only to be destroyed by the great Francesco Morosini, leader of the Venetian-inspired Forces of the Holy League, a kind of revived Crusade. His claim to fame was that he blew up the Parthenon in 1687.

An eminent Greek archaeologist at the turn of the century thought that the Kastri site was Oechalia, a Euboean city-state which crops up in ancient literature, but the theory has been rejected. I never did find out where Oechalia was. I was surprised to see it turning up on the map at the back of Robert Graves' *The Greek Myths* at the spot where Chalkis is. Greek experts seem to think it's down near Avlonari. It might, in fact, be one and the same thing as the 'Kimi' of the ninth or eighth centuries; nobody really knows where that was.

Did the Euboean Kimi found its once-powerful Aeolian namesake (usually transliterated as Cyme) in Asia Minor, or, more to the point, the hugely important colony of Cumae west of Naples and opposite Sardinia? The contemporary Kimians think of Cumae as their own, and to prove it have twinned themselves with Bacoli, the municipality which includes Cuma, as it now spells itself. Eusebius says the ancient Cumae was a colony of the Euboean Kimi, but Thucydides claims it was founded by Chalkis and Eretria. Strabo refers to colonial collaboration between Kimi and Chalkis, and the most plausible explanation is that Cumae owed its existence to the ancient equivalent of a Joint Venture, and that the name came from one partner in it (the similarity between the names is diminished by the transliteration of Kimi, of which the first vowel in Greek is u). The Romans actually called all Greeks Chalkidians then, so far was Euboea in the vanguard of territorial expansion westwards.

Regarding the alphabet, it is almost certain that the letters arranged on this page have evolved from the Greek script the Euboean (and perhaps Kimian) colonists took to Cumae. Exactly when, how and where the Euboeans got it in the first place is not clear – except for the fact that they adapted it from Phoenician traders. The settlers at Xiropolis over on the other coast were writing with it in the eighth century. The very first place it was used may have been the trading settlement of Al Mina in what is now southern Turkey. Once the Euboeans had taken it to Italy the Etruscans almost certainly evolved their script from it, and that in turn became the Roman alphabet used now throughout the west. Later, the island was one of the few regions of eastern Greece to use the form of the alphabet that Kirchhoff categorized as 'red'.

The most interesting question is not how, or where, or when the Greeks created their alphabet, however – it is why. Some academics say that Greek writing was invented to record business accounts, but I do not allow the most exquisite handmaid of language such a squalid birth. Six months after I returned from my trip, Cambridge University Press published a book by Barry P. Powell, concluding that a single man from Euboea invented the Greek alphabet in order to record the *Iliad* and the *Odyssey*. (It is often said that the poems reached their present form on the island.) I suspect that this highly scholarly thesis was not taken up by many classicists in the field, but I thought it was wonderful.

I climbed down from the site and went into Ano Potamia. It was tiny (population of 200 but it used to be double that) and crisscrossed with the narrowest streets; they could take a bubble car or a tiny Fiat, but nothing bigger. I thought this was quaint, but later I met a man from the village who had made his fortune in Athens, and now he had two cars specially, one microscopic Fiat and one enormous Mercedes. It was just like Athens, where the pollution laws stipulate that you can drive on a Monday, Wednesday and Friday if your registration plate ends in an odd number, and on a Tuesday and Thursday if it's even, and then you swap weeks. The only natural Greek response to this of course is to have two cars, and that is what people with money do. I remember years ago they tried to thwart them by changing it to numbers below and above five, and then to some other system, which resulted in an article in *To Pondiki*, the Greek answer to *Private Eye* or *Le Canard Enchaîné*, announcing that drivers should take the square root of their registrations and divide by *pi* to ascertain if they could circulate on a Tuesday afternoon.

I located the *oinopoleio* (wine shop, but in this instance the only shop too, so it sold a number of things besides wine) and inquired if anyone knew anything about the excavations. The owner insisted on standing me a cold Nescafé, which was particularly generous seeing as I was his only customer of the afternoon, and telephoned the Village Chairman. 'There's an English girl here. Speaks Greek. You'd better come over.'

Even in a country richly endowed with local historians Nikos Tsekouras was exceptional. An electrician with little formal education, he had taught himself as much as he could about Greek archaeology and together with some other villagers funded a dig with personal savings. The Karamanlis government sponsored the restoration of the derelict school at Ano Potamia, and the upper floor had become an exhibition hall for the finds.

We went to the hall, where piles of crusted ancient vessels dredged up by local fisherman formed lithic mounds in the corner. Wooden-framed glass cases held loom weights and other items and explanatory diagrams were pinned on the wall.

Back at the wine shop Kirios Nikos spoke of Asia Minor and the remains of ancient Kimian colonies, and lamented that the

Turks were making money from a culture they claim is their own, but which is inalienably Greek: an old story among Turkophobes. He told me that he had written a piece on dying traditions in Ano Potamia.

I left and met Sarah, who was about to leave for Athens, to say goodbye. That evening I had agreed to meet up with a Greek man I had been talking to in the nightclub. This is almost always an extremely bad idea, but you get strange feelings about being on your own again and I felt like filling the time. Besides, there is something grimly enjoyable about not learning from your mistakes. In my history of disastrous dates this was spectacular. It was even better than the time in London when the man I had met at a party and agreed to have dinner with picked me up in a milk-float. On this occasion, when I pitched up at the appointed hour the man was waiting, immaculately dressed. He explained that it had taken him an hour to get there on his Vespa, and that he was due to start his nightshift at the cement factory in 55 minutes, so had to leave immediately and, immediately, he left.

My friends Aris and Monica Berlis and their four-year-old daughter Sophia had escaped from Athens for the summer to a borrowed cottage in Zarka, on the narrow southern spine of the island, and they had simply told me to appear whenever I wanted. We had known each other for years; we were neighbours once in Athens. The trip meant a deviation from my steady journey northwards, and I had to double back on myself. When I arrived Aris was simultaneously painting a window, smoking, and talking about *Northanger Abbey*. He was almost always smoking and talking about books, but I was surprised about the painting. My crumbling room overlooked a valley and had a huge chimney in one corner. The circle of mulberry trees outside the door once caused a major squabble between two neighbours who wanted leaf rights when the cottage was unoccupied. Mulberry leaves are the best goat fodder, and by September there is nothing else left for the animals to eat.

After lounging around for two days we went on an excursion in the car. About 20 minutes north of Zarka we passed Krieza, where General Nikolaos Kriezotis grew up. He led the Resistance fighters of the mountains and fought all over the island, besieging Karistos twice (without success), and he was also at the siege of the Acropolis in Athens in December 1826. Hundreds of Evians went over to help out on the mainland; the other Greeks called them *Evripaii* after the Euripos channel.

Shortly before Avlonari (where I had missed the bus with Sarah) we got out to look at St Dimitrios' church, probably fourteenth-century and unique among Evian Byzantine churches on account of its large size. On one side you can see foundations of an even earlier church; Avlonari was the see of a bishop as early as the sixth century, and continued as such for about a thousand years. The urbane modern village was off to the right and we all liked it a great deal, especially Aris, who began making plans to go and live there. Sophisticated houses wound up a hill and the streets became lanes, ending in a tall Lombard or Venetian tower which people rather inconveniently used to enter by a rope ladder slung from a high window. In the square a sinuous black man was moving from café to café selling radios out of a plastic sports bag. This was the first black person I had seen all summer. Until recently you very rarely saw anything except white skins even in Athens, presumably because Greece owned no colonies, and has not, in recent times, had a particularly attractive economy – or indeed a particularly hospitable attitude towards immigrants. I really noticed the physiognomic homogeneity; it was like watching black-and-white television.

Back on the main road we took the left fork and shortly turned off to a tiny village called Agia Thekla. Abandoning the car, we walked down a lane into a lush grove and found the church from which the village took its name. Thekla lived in Iconium in Asia Minor and decided to become a disciple of St Paul when she heard him outside her window preaching. She was persecuted relentlessly, and finally retired to a cave near Seleucia. This church too was probably fourteenth-century, and a hundred years ago a maverick American scholar suggested that it was built by Catalans. Thekla was, after all, the patron saint of Tarragona. (I couldn't recall seeing anything like it in Catalonia though.) It was full of heartbreaking frescos. They could convey more emotion and pathos, and more of a sense of the transcendental in their depiction of human beings than oceans of realism could even aspire to.

Next we left the asphalt and took a wide swing through the remote and rangy mountain villages to the east. Only in one had the influence of Athens and the west been powerful enough to stimulate the advent of *kafeteria*, so prevalent throughout Greece. Young people, rejecting the *kafeneia* of their fathers and grandfathers – patriarchal bastions of coffee and ouzo sipping, backgammon playing and arguing about politics – have built western-style café bars where they drink *Nescafé frappé* and eat pizzas. Athenian intellectuals deplore this cultural infiltration, and when the phenomenon is discussed I've often suggested that at least there is a space for women in this new environment. It usually sets off a cataract of proselytizing on the fragmentation of traditional society and loss of national identity. There is of course a very real and troubling dilemma here. If you recognize the inadequacies and impoverished nature of the vacuum that is replacing traditional structures, that is to say of the materialist, 'progressive' culture, you can find yourself tacitly endorsing an overtly gynophobic system. People who have grappled with this usually resort to the argument that at least the traditional culture was shaped around a coherent system with a place and therefore a meaning for everyone, and that the female role, in spite of its subjugated nature, was invested with deep significance and importance. This is true but inadequate. You could use it to justify almost any kind of ritualized subordination. You can't lament the demise of the old way while deploring a cornerstone of its value base; that would be intellectual escapism.

In the afternoon we descended to swim and eat fish at Petries, a small village with a sandy beach in a cove below. There was an ancient Eretrian dependency of the same name, but whether it was actually on the site of the modern village is another matter. Contemporary toponymy often exists solely to foil the western classicist: Greek revenge at last. The ubiquitous J. Hawkins claims to have been the first western European in Petries. He stopped in the cove for a couple of days in 1797 on a trip down the east coast, and wrote an irritatingly pompous piece about it. The Greeks of 1990, blissfully unaware of his existence, were engaged in their two favourite beach occupations: shouting (a national pastime) and playing 'racket' as near to other people as possible.

Zarka, where I was staying with Aris and Monica, was probably Plutarch's Zaretra, and also the Eretrian dependency referred to on inscriptions as Zarex. In the more recent past it was once important enough to have its own bishop. Up until a few decades ago the village was located down in the valley, but when the new road was built the inhabitants gravitated towards it, abandoning their electricity- and water-less stone houses for an easier, concrete life a few hundred yards away. Consequently the present community consisted of a long row of featureless modern houses on either side of a relatively busy road. A village without a square tends to be a village without a heart. The abandoned valley, however, was delicious, like a secret garden full of ghostly house shells. There had never been an electricity supply there, but this had not deterred the villagers from installing in one of the churches on the hill opposite a massive crystal chandelier with about 50 lightbulbs, dolefully dangling its redundant wire stumps.

A dirt track led tantalizingly up into the mountain east of Zarka, so one day I got up at sunrise and headed off. After half an hour I met a goatherd coaxing his hundred animals home for milking. He had a flat face and blue eyes, and spoke Albanian with his weatherbeaten wife. He insisted that I stay a while, and over a bottle of his own retsina (even I had trouble with it before 8 am), bread from his wheat and sharp cheese from his goats, sitting around an upturned wooden crate outside his hut, we discussed the differences between farming in Zarka and abroad. His grapes grew on short bushes, brushing the ground: 'I've heard that in Australia grapes hang in the air from branches like crystals from a church chandelier,' he said. He'd heard about it happening in Australia, but not all over the rest of Greece.

We went in to milk the goats. In April and May the two of them milked all hundred goats twice a day. Besides making their own cheese they sold milk to the local cheesemaker for 90 drachmas a kilo (sheep's milk fetched 40 drachs more). They strained a warm bottleful through muslin and gave it to me, poured the rest into metal churns which were strapped on to the side of a donkey, and the woman and I walked into the valley and up to the village.

Later in the week Aris had some business in Aliveri so I went with him, and afterwards we went down to Karavos, the port, bounded on one side by the power station and a huge cement factory. Over our coffee at a very old *kafeneio* we noticed a commotion at the bakery on the other side of the street. It was lunchtime, and people were collecting their *tapsia* (baking tins), which they had carried to the shop earlier to be cooked in the oven. Someone had taken the wrong one home, with the result that someone else was without her stuffed tomatoes. The culprit soon returned with the missing *tapsi* and the crisis was over. In the hard years of the fifties, after the Civil War, the ritual of carrying the family dinner to the bakery acquired a social function, especially in the towns (in villages there were often public or private outdoor ovens). Ordinary people – neither the very rich nor the very poor – would eat meat twice a week, on Thursday and Sunday. On Thursday they had stew, which didn't require an oven, and on Sunday a joint. It was the father's role, having put on his black suit for church, to carry the *tapsi* to the bakery before going to the service. It was the job of the head of the household because being able to afford meat conferred status and so the all-important Greek concept of honour was at stake. (If the meat were burnt or undercooked, however, it was the mother who had to complain to the baker the next day: a neat paradigm of the infrastructure of patriarchy.) Modern Greek literature is full of stories about the importance of maintaining your position through showing the neighbours you have food. Kostas Tachtsis, a prominent post-war writer, describes a boy going to buy onions instructed by his mother to say they were cooking *stifado* (beef and onion stew). Of course, they only had onions.

On every map of Evia I have ever seen, a large blob of blue indicates a lake just above Zarka. This is curious, since Lake Distos hasn't existed for a long time, and even the swamps that succeeded it have dried up. Old habits obviously die hard with cartographers. The ancients founded a settlement on a limestone hill in the middle of what was the lake but is now a plain; if it was the Dryopes it probably marked the northern limit of their territory. A later community built a fort or acropolis on the hill, and by at least the middle of the fourth century BC Distos had become an Eretrian dependency. The Venetians, or perhaps the Lombards, came and put up fortifications on the same site, as they usually did, and their jagged tower was still balancing on the top. Modern farmers have slowly been draining the swamp, chopping down the reeds and reclaiming the land, with disastrous environmental consequences as the area is a natural bird sanctuary and many rare species are being deprived of their habitat. Illegal hunting exacerbates the problem, as do the marble quarries on the west side – and all this despite the fact that the plain has already been designated a protected zone. The very day I climbed up to find ancient Distos, *Kathimerini*, a leading quality newspaper, ran a front-page story on a letter from Brussels expressing strong EC concern over Greece's environmental record and citing the drainage of the Distos swamps as a particularly unfortunate example of abuse.

We drove to the quarries through dusty modern Distos. It was an extraordinary, almost surreal scene, particularly as there was no sign of life: a massive hole in the ground, half a mountain sliced away and a thousand discarded boulders. I wondered if it would be like that after the bomb, and Aris suggested that it would make a good setting for the staging of an ancient tragedy, remembering Peter Brook's production of the Indian epic *Bhagavad Gita* in a disused quarry in Athens a few years previously.

The next day Monica and I crossed what used to be the lake, avoiding any lingering swampland, and tried to climb to the ancient site. The lakebed and surrounding mountains formed an extraordinary landscape unique in Greece: the plain, as flat as if created with a spirit level and squared in bright yellow and green, abruptly came to an end on every side and rose steeply into mountains. It was a huge flat-bottomed dish. We walked down a path through fields of vine and corn feeling as though we were in Kansas. Near the foot of the hill in the middle we found a cluster of abandoned houses, a church and clouds of orange butterflies. The area was malarial for generations. It's difficult to remember that before the advent of prophylactics the mosquito was the cruellest killer in the Mediterranean.

We only managed to get halfway up the hill, as the thorny and snake-infested scrub inflicted grievous bodily harm, and was full of concealed boulders. On the south flank, near an abandoned marble quarry, I saw my first Evian cow. The name of the island means 'land rich in cattle', and so I was always expecting to see enormous herds of them, but I never did. A young cow was once the symbol of Eretria, and they stamped her image on the side of coins struck by the Euboean League. That was probably a reference to the myth of the beautiful Io, a delicate white cow living in a cave on Euboea. She was the daughter of Inachus and had been turned into a cow by Zeus, who loved her, in order to deceive Hera, who was jealous. It continues in a variety of ways, according to whom you read; one story is that Io gave birth to Zeus' son Epaphus in the cave and subsequently died there from a sting of the gadfly set on her by Hera. (The Argives once worshipped the moon as a cow called Io and Argive colonists in Euboea may have brought the idea over with them.) Alternatively, some ancient writers claim that a woman called Euboea was one of the 12 or 20 daughters of the river god Asopus – and so it goes on.

There were plenty of other names for the island, too – sometimes I think that each author made up whichever name he felt like. One of the most common, and perhaps the oldest, was Makra or Makris, from the adjective 'long'. Poets were keen on Asopus. This plethora of names were not restricted to the island as a whole – there was not a river, hillock or headland in Evia about which I didn't unearth a tangle of conflicting names, explanations of names, myths and folk tales. Each stone, it seemed, was invested with a mysterious significance by its long and shadowy past. There were many Euboean locations, too, mentioned in the ancient books of the famous and the obscure alike, which had never been identified, and this, it seemed to me, was a happy state of affairs, as if mythology is reduced to a

The Dragon House on the summit of Mount Ochi - probably a temple built by migrant mine workers from Asia Minor some time during or after the fourth century BC. Nobody knows how they carried the huge stones up the mountain. *(James Lloyd)*

Two Sisters standing in the doorway of their Byzantine church at the Monastery of St Nicholas, hidden up in the hills behind Vathia.

(Author)

The tower of the maverick 'orphanage' complex between Kimi and the sea. *(Author)*

Musicians. *(Yannis Fafoutis)*

The church of St Nicholas in Oxilithos, built before the thirteenth century. The central slice of the island has a particularly rich Byzantine heritage. *(Author)*

A neoclassical town house in Avlonari. Sophia escapes past the oleander bush. *(Author)*

The famous bridge connecting Evia with the mainland, seen from the island side. *(Lefteris Monastiriotis)*

The heart of the island. *(Author)*

The Noel-Baker house in Prokopi. *(Author)*

Mizithra goats' cheeses hanging from the rafters in Sarakiniko, the village where everyone has the same surname. *(Author)*

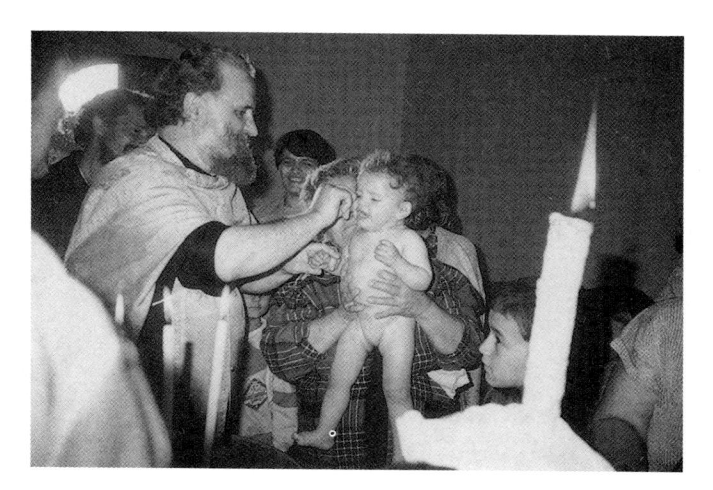

Stella is anointed. *(Author)*

Stella, looking rather happier, with her uncle. *(Author)*

Kokkinomilia in the Xiro mountains. *(Author)*

Struggling up the hill in Limni with the famous icon of the Virgin. She is taken up to her mother's church as a special treat on her birthday, and the task of carrying the icon is ceremoniously auctioned off by a local priest. *(Yannis Fafoutis)*

An ouzeri in Limni, with the ubiquitous octopus strung up across it to dry. *(Author)*

Limni. *(Yannis Fafoutis)*

View from the road between Limni and Galataki. *(Author)*

The polygonal dome of the church at Galataki monastery, taken from my bedroom window with Mount Kandili in the background. *(Author)*

The bride's parents dance next to the dowry while Vangelitsa has her hair curled just before the ceremony. *(Author)*

science it loses its appeal. The abundance of place names and their contradictory explanations is indicative of the jumble of mythological and historical theories about the island's first inhabitants. I liked the earliest, which were chaotic earthquake stories involving giants fighting and causing the island to separate from the mainland. There was an appallingly confusing fable about the Curetes, a mythological Cretan colony who pitched up (some sources say the first ones were the nymph Euboea's children). What it all came down to was that in Euboean pre-history a handful of tribes settled on various parts of the island at different times – notably Dryopes, Abantes, Ellopians and Perraibians – and that Ionians were ultimately both physically and culturally dominant.

The cow was enormous, with huge horns, and someone had tied it up with a long tether. An old man suddenly appeared, sitting side-saddle on one donkey and towing another, his booted feet resting on a loop of rope. We shuffled past the cow and all walked through the plain together. The man was 78, and when he learnt where I was from he said, 'Why are you so dark? You look like a Greek. I thought all English people were ugly,' and somehow it didn't quite come out as a compliment. Then he asked if I was married, and the diatribe that ensued made me think that he had been carrying it round in his head ready to deliver to the first appropriate person who appeared. He was not at all happy about the concept of single 29-year-olds running around. Marriage was the thing, and he obviously felt very strongly about it. '*Pethaini o anthropos*,' he kept repeating, which means that life doesn't go on forever. The crux of the matter seemed to be that offspring give life meaning, and if you haven't got any kids to leave your worldly goods to and to remember you it's all rather a waste of time. Reproduction is an essential component of tradition, and anything that doesn't conform to tradition is a dangerous threat that may upset the natural order and unleash chaos. If I had found this line irritating at the beginning of my journey, by now it made me wild, and I quickly got him on to the subject of his own descendants, of whom there were many, which kept him going until we parted company.

We liked swimming south of Zarka, slowly winding down to Mesochoria, a tiny crisscross of narrow lanes and skewed houses, and on along a dried-up riverbed in an otherwise lush narrow valley to the sand and marble chip beach. It was one of the finest on the island, and the fact that it was surrounded by privately owned land meant that people couldn't build ghastly breezeblock beach huts all over it as the Zarkans had done on their beach. There was a good taverna, too, specializing in fried potato omelette.

Across on the other coast the little resort of Panagia, more commonly known as Almiropotamos (Salty River), ran a ferry service to Agia Marina on the mainland. It was a strange, slovenly village with a thin sandy beach and lots of ugly buildings. Right in the middle of it literally hundreds of mines were piled in the menacing yard of a naval armaments store. They were probably obsolete, but that was hardly the point. The village was at the end of a wide fjord, and this was its redeeming feature. Kavalliani island squatted directly in front of the other end of the fjord. The island was still a naval base; the Greek navy mined the Gulf between Almiropotamos and the mainland during the war. With this and the slopes of Attica so close behind, it felt like a basin of water at the foot of a huge circle of mountains.

A dirt road led around a small promontory to the village of Agios Dimitrios, which was scruffy and full of fishing boats. The road linking the two was bulging with Athenians camping out for a month for their summer holidays: tents, caravans, plastic bags of water hanging on trees serving as showers and Almiropotamos close at hand for maximum consumption. These were consumers America would be proud of, except of course for one fatal flaw: Greeks don't produce enough for it to make any sense. They are in mid-leap between donkey and Mercedes without any of the interim development normally accompanying radical social change.

Greek literature has always been replete with images of the sea, typically in the twentieth-century poetry of George Seferis and Odysseus Elitis. (You could say the same about much of English literature, but although the image is the same the meaning is very different. It's a different sea.) The language is littered with idioms drawn from the sea: *ta kaname thalassa* – we made a sea of it, means we made a mess of it, and *thalassonome*, I am sad, appears in folk songs meaning I am very worried. You wouldn't realize the significance of it if you saw Greeks at the beach, though. They all stand stock still up to their necks in water, hats on, in little groups. At Almiropotamos I saw a man sitting on a chair up to his chest in water. His wife kept bringing him drinks, and I thought of my friend Mike Mackenzie-Smith who once brought a glass of wine to me in a bank queue in San Gimignano.

The escape route from Agios Dimitrios was one of the most beautiful journeys I made all summer. A dirt track climbed north up the slopes of Pirgaki, away from the wriggling coastline of the bay and a setting sun like a blood orange. We saw a patchwork of corn and wheat with a donkey like an embroidered motif on each patch, fringed at one end by a large red-roofed village sloping upwards. It was Argiro, enclosed by mountains and brooding obsessively over its plain. Shortly afterwards a track turned left and ran alongside what must have been another lake: a break in the peaks between the two revealed the perfectly framed Distos hill and its fragile tower. The ex-lake was another absolutely flat plate of cultivated land, so un-Greek in its aspect, and from the still-high road the extra elevation gave it the appearance of the wild west rather than Kansas. A string of cowboys could have galloped through at that moment.

The track led down to a tiny village rejoicing in the name of Porto Boufalo. The taverna owner in Zarka, a Boufalian, told me that the name came from the village's former role as a livestock port when the island used to send buffalo and other animals over to Attica. Bernard Randolph – the only traveller to mention it – was there in the 1670s, and says they also did a lively trade in dried acorns. Modern commerce seemed to be confined to shellfish, as there was a lone prawn farm raft floating on the water. It was entirely closed in by mountains, prostrate at the end of a small channel, and so had no horizon; it was oppressive, still and blank.

The barter economy has not quite died in Greece: it still gives the occasional kick. One evening a van drove through Zarka driven by a man drawling through a microphone, offering to exchange washing powder for olive oil dregs. He would, presumably, make soap with the dregs, and who knows where the washing powder came from.

Chapter Five

I have Euboea, I have Greece.

PHILIP II OF MACEDONIA

Aris and Monica were driving to Patras, and I decided to go as far as Chalkis with them. Before saying goodbye for the summer we had to go into a church so Aris could light a candle to mark the anniversary of his miraculous escape from a bad car accident exactly 10 years previously. It was an annual ritual. As he is not a believer I challenged him on the significance of his gesture (there were no sacred topics between us), and he accused me sharply of being 'a real Protestant there'. We often argued about the concept of a personal religion, but dramatic socio-cultural differences meant that we were irredeemably unreconciled. He squashed me by insisting that Orthodoxy is an utterly unremovable part of a Greek, and so whether you practise or even believe is irrelevant. I simply couldn't imagine how anything other than spiritual conviction could be the starting point for a meaningful personal religion. He did make me feel like such a bloody Protestant.

We heard on the radio that a boat had crashed into the bridge at Chalkis, and that it would be closed for some time. Aris and Monica decided to catch the car ferry at Eretria instead, along with everyone else who had planned to leave the island over Chalkis bridge. I left them steaming in the queue and eventually reached Chalkis by bus, where hundreds of people were crowded around each end of the bridge monitoring the progress of the workmen trying to fix it. It was a potent symbol of the crucial role the bridge has played in the life of the island ever since the first one was built at the end of the fifth century BC, when the Euboeans tried to obstruct the passage of Athenian ships through the channel and narrowed it so that there was just enough room for a single ship to pass through. It was a big job which was probably only possible with considerable help from the Boeotians, the Euboeans' neighbours on the mainland, for whom this was the ultimate case of having your cake and eating it, as Diodorus Siculus explains: '... it was in [the Boeotians'] general interest that [Euboea] should be an island to everybody else but part of the mainland to them.' The work was undertaken cooperatively by Chalkis and Eretria under the auspices of the Euboean League, and possibly other Euboeans helped out, so it probably constituted the first federal act ever accomplished on the island.

At Chalkis the Evian Gulf narrows to a strait less than 50 yards wide called the Euripus, and this proximity to the mainland has been the single most significant factor in the history of the island. Fifty yards is not a great deal. If you were to lay six London buses end to end, for example, they would take up more room than the distance from Evia to continental Greece at this one point. (If a seahorse had little clawed legs like a bird, the bridge would represent them, perching on the mainland.) By the time of Alexander the Great there was a bridge of a sort allowing a proper sea passage, and towers were built at each end. The Romans put up a more complicated affair which slid open and closed, and in the thirteenth century a Flemish Crusader, Jacques d'Avesnes, had a tiny fortress built in the middle of the Euripus, thus creating two bridges. It was a four-turreted square edifice called a *castello*. By the end of the seventeenth century a bridge with five stone arches linked mainland and fortress, and a wooden drawbridge joined fortress and island. At one time there were mills under the arches worked by the current. John Hobhouse describes his passage over the bridge in *Travels in Albania and Other Provinces of Turkey in 1809 and 1810*. 'We dismounted, and led our horses over a narrow bridge, about 15 paces in length, and then over a drawbridge to a stone tower in the middle of the strait, of an odd circular shape, like a dice-box, large at bottom and top, and small in the middle; the mouths of immense cannon appearing through round embrasures, about the upper rim. Going through an arch in this tower, we passed on to a bridge of wood, a third part longer than the other, standing over the principal stream.'

Buchon, in 1841, described the bridge as 'abominable'. In the 1880s the *castello* was destroyed, and in 1896 the whole channel was widened and an iron swingbridge went up. The one that had just been dented was an unspectacular specimen built in 1962 which opened by lowering and then retracting into the banks. A second bridge was begun in 1984, scheduled for completion in 1987 with the customary glorious Greek disregard for the practical realities of construction.

The rapid alternation of the currents of the Euripus constitutes a globally unique phenomenon which has attracted copious scientific enquiry for thousands of years. It has been known for the current to change direction 14 times in 24 hours, and it flows fast (the name means 'fast current'). Between changes it goes quiet for a few minutes. Nobody quite knows why. Sir George Wheler, travelling in 1675 in the company of a Dr Spon of Lyon (together they were pioneers of the topographical Greek travel book), calls it 'One of the great wonders of the world'. As you might imagine it makes the channel difficult to navigate: a nineteenth-century traveller noted that it was not unusual for a sailing ship to wait six weeks for a passage. The crash the day I arrived in Chalkis indicated that technology hadn't yet come up with a solution. Masses of authors have written about the current, from Aeschylus through Pliny to modern Ph.D. students, and it sank deeply enough into the consciousness of the Ancient Greeks to acquire the status of metaphor: 'Euripus' was used to describe a person of some volatility. The story goes that Aristotle got so worked up at the impenetrable nature of the tidal conundrum that he threw himself in (he definitely died in Chalkis, but probably of something less conceptual). Hobhouse reports an explanation offered him by a Turkish guard in the *castello*. 'Not a great many years ago this water was like any other part of the sea, and did not flow at all, but a Hadji (that is, a holy Turk, who had been to Mecca), being a prisoner in that tower when the infidels had the place, and confined in a dark cell, where he could see nothing but the water below through a hole in his dungeon, begged of God to send him some sign by which he might know when to pray. His request was granted by the change which immediately took place in the flowing and reflowing of the stream; and since that time the current has altered its course at each of the five seasons of prayer.'

This amusing little tale irritates Hobhouse considerably, and he dismisses it with a snipe about true devotion being more about propagation than examination. My favourite account remains that of the archetypal Brit abroad, Henry Raikes, who took one look at the water and with a spectacular feat of imagination commented in his journal, ... the current was at this moment falling with nearly as much rapidity as [the one below] London Bridge.

The rapid flow has been the only thing to save the Evian Gulf from being neutered by large-scale industrial waste pollution. Previously super-rich in fish, its stocks have been radically depleted, and the need to clean up and protect the waters – not least because so many villagers' lives depend on them – has become a hot political issue. Despite the intervention of the EC, the Greek record on environmental protection is far from exemplary so it remains to be seen if measures are actually enforced.

When I set about finding a place to stay all the hoteliers were surly and rude, as if furious at the prospect of having to take my money, and as most of their establishments were full I didn't have the pleasure of telling them I had decided to take my custom elsewhere. The hotel I had intended to stay in had been commandeered by the right-wing New Democracy Party: one of the hazards of travelling in Greece in an election year. (The other hazards are aesthetic rather than practical. Every building, every wall and every carvable field and mountainside scream with graffiti.) I ended up in the poshest hotel in town (these things are relative) and bargained the management down to an acceptable price.

As capital of the island, or, more correctly, capital of the nomarchy of Evia, Chalkis is an important administrative centre, and its geographical position means that it is and always has been a vital commercial centre too. The august British botanist Dr John Sibthorp, in Chalkis in 1787, goes as far as to say, 'No place in the world seems, from its situation, to lay so fair a claim to commercial advantages.' Further, control of the straits means control of the only alternative to the dangerous Aegean passage. This strategic position was so crucial in ancient times that it was made clear to the Roman Senate that if Chalkis was held, along with Corinth and with Demetrias in Thessaly, 'Greece could not be free' – or so Livy recounts in *The History of Rome*. At that time Philip V of Macedonia declared that Chalkis was one of the three 'fetters' of Greece for the same reason – he knew that if he controlled it he could control half the country. Christopher Wordsworth, the hymn-writing Bishop of Lincoln who came to Evia early in the nineteenth century, called the straits the Dardanelles of Greece, and said that they 'changed the character of the island'. It's not surprising that there has been continuous settlement in the area for thousands of years.

The importance of Chalkis and of the island in general to the ancient world was without doubt what drew so many travellers from the west from the seventeenth century onwards (some came earlier, too, but they left no journals). The intrepid ones ventured beyond the capital into the unknown interior of the island. I was working my way through their books, and I found myself thinking of this heteroclite bundle of diarists as my travelling companions, particularly once the personality of each rose from the pages. It was like being stranded on a desert island with fellow-passengers after a plane crash and having to make the most of it. I started to work out who would get on with whom, who would start bossing the rest around and what each would make of me. I had initially held out high hopes for Richard Chandler, in Evia in 1765, simply because he was funded by the promisingly named Society of Dilettanti, but I was soon crushed beneath the weight of his dead-pan delivery, and he got all his south-coast geography wrong. It didn't help that they were all men. (I had actually tracked down two nineteenth-century British women travellers who mention Evia, but as neither bothered to alight as she sailed past they had little to offer.) But I grew quite fond of one or two, such as James Caulfield, the fourth Viscount Charlemont, who was despatched on a Grand Tour by his mother in 1746 for mixing with the wrong crowd in Dublin. He wasn't quite 18, and he was so rich that he was able to charter frigates without batting an eyelid, which is a pretty cool way to travel; he was also lively and genuinely interested in what he saw, observant and idiosyncratic, and he loved the Greek islands, especially those on the eastern seaboard. Travelling doesn't seem to have stimulated his conversation, however, according to a comment in Boswell's *Life of Johnson*. In order to dismiss Charlemont as a fool Johnson says that the only remark he ever made about his voyages was that he had seen a large serpent in one of the Pyramids.

It is difficult to imagine, in the provincial ambience of the scruffy modern Chalkis, how illustrious its reputation once was. As the Aegean world entered the Iron Age in the eighth century BC, Chalkis was one of the most prominent city-states in Greece. At this time it sent out its first wave of colonists, founding so many settlements in the Macedonian peninsula east of Thessaloniki that the area became known as Chalkidiki, as it still is. It is also likely that Chalkis had already established the Greek settlement at the trading post of Al Mina, near what is now the border between Turkey and Syria. By the seventh century it had well-established colonies in the west, such as Pithekoussai near the Bay of Naples, Rhegion, now Reggio di Calabria, and almost certainly Cumae, as well as various Aegean sites. The mission undertaken by those Chalkidian pioneers is unimaginable now; it must have seemed like going to the end of the world. Like their fellow-islanders from Eretria and Kimi, the culture they took with them was hugely influential in western development. Chalkis was among the first cities in what has become Europe to develop coinage, and the colonists took it to Italy, along with the Euboean system of weights and measures.

The Lelantine War with Eretria had begun, however, and as it dragged on the drain of war diminished trading. Although Chalkis seems to have gained control of the plain, the psychological implications of such a drawn-out period of military aggression must have been considerable. There is a story in Plutarch about the population of Chalkis during the war. A man called Cleomachus of Pharsalus came over with Thessalian troops to help Chalkis out. His display of passion for another young man was, they said, all part of his military prowess, which led the previously homophobic Chalkidians to hold homosexuality in great esteem. With the zeal of new converts they acquired quite a reputation in the Greek-speaking world, to the extent that the verb 'to be Chalkided' was coined and in frequent usage;

they became a kind of alternative equivalent to the unfortunate Roger of the English language.

In 506 BC the city-state was forced to cede part of its territory to Athenian settlers as punishment for its support of the Boeotian League, an Athenian enemy. Coupled with considerable internal political dissent, this meant that by 480 BC Chalkis was so weak that it had no fleet of its own to send to the Persian War, and it was obliged to despatch men in Athenian ships. Although it was on the same side as Athens in this war against Xerxes, like Eretria and Karistos it had a curiously volatile relationship with the powerful city-state, and in 446 led a Euboean revolt against it. There is no doubt that despite significant Athenian cultural influence on the island (evident in pottery, amongst other things) the Euboeans couldn't stomach the way Athens was empire-building in central Greece. The revolt was defeated, however, and Chalkis became a tributary ally when the great Athenian general Pericles marched in. The crumbling democracy was restored and the relationship with Athens, master of the divide-and-rule tactic, lasted until 411, when Chalkis revolted again and declared its independence, on this occasion with more success. Athens had evacuated a good deal of livestock to Euboea during the Peloponnesian Wars (431–404) and the loss of the island (which was now receiving help from the Spartan enemy) was a deadly blow, both practically and psychologically.

Although an informal truce was swiftly established, relations between Chalkis and Athens were cooler than between Athens and Eretria down the coast, and Chalkis didn't make an official alliance with Athens until 378. Like the Eretrians, the Chalkidians later allied themselves with the Thebans, and then went back again to the Athenians. Soon the Macedonians were insinuating themselves into the city-state's affairs. In about 340 BC Chalkis seems to have presided over a reviviscence of the Euboean League, and it quickly turned away from Athens towards

Macedonia, and the power of the latter on the island increased. Chalkis was one of the powerbases of Demetrius Poliorcetes, the King of Macedonia who controlled Euboea (and much of Greece) from 294 to 287. Chalkis enjoyed a considerable degree of independence from the Macedonians – but then they had the Romans to contend with.

The first Roman attack failed, but the second, in 200 BC, succeeded; the city was burnt and the inhabitants massacred. When the Romans withdrew enough was left behind for Chalkis to reappear like the proverbial phoenix – and not for the last time in its history. It soon officially surrendered to the Romans, who despatched a garrison; this was removed in 194 when Chalkis, like the other Euboean city-states, was freed. Only two years later the Syrian King Antiochus the Great took Chalkis and made it his base, but he was soon beaten by the Romans; the Chalkidians fought on the Syrian side in that battle but escaped retribution. Next time they were not so lucky, and the Romans partly destroyed Chalkis after its citizens fought for the Achaean League in 147 BC.

In the middle of the first century AD St Paul sailed down the west coast of the island and through the Euripus en route to Attica on his second missionary journey. There is no evidence that he stopped, but after he had spoken in Athens a group of disciples brought the word, and the transition from paganism to Christianity began, like new stock grafted on to an old plant.

In 330 the new Roman Empire was dedicated in Constantinople and Byzantium began its long, glorious and weary course. Although it was to be over 300 years before Greek became the official language of the Empire, its heart and soul had shifted eastwards. Chalkis was absorbed into the Byzantine administrative system and fortified by Justinian during the fifth century. Attila the Hun came perilously close (he had begun his assault on the east in 441) but did not bring his hordes through Evia. Whether the island managed to escape the appalling internal strife occasioned by the monophysite heresy is largely unknown. (Byzantium was almost continually riven with theological rows, and the really heavy number was the matter of the nature of Christ.) Despite the fact that in those days the person on the street was deeply involved in such things (doctrinal issues playing a role similar to that of football on contemporary Merseyside), there is little written evidence of much percolating through to Evia, outside of the monasteries at least.

The Vandals and Ostrogoths came and went without touching the Aegean, and even the Slavs, who began working their way through the Balkans in the sixth century, don't appear to have left their mark on Evia. But once the spectre of Islam loomed at the beginning of the seventh century, life was never to be the same again for the islanders. Mohammed died in 632, and bits of the Empire were gradually lopped off by his advancing armies. The deadly combination of Charlemagne and the Pope did little to strengthen the Christian side when the latter crowned the former Emperor of the Romans in 800; it was, after all, supposed to be an indivisible Empire, but now it was split into east and west. The African Saracens embarked upon a series of particularly daring raids throughout the Mediterranean, and in 800 or 881, under the Emir of Tarsus, they laid siege to Chalkis with 30 large ships. They were unsuccessful, and the Evians repulsed them with the special oil-based substance developed a couple of centuries previously called Greek fire. It was shot or sprayed flaming through metal tubes from the back of ships to destroy enemy craft, and allegedly stayed alight under water.

Chalkis continued as an important trading post under Byzantium. In the later centuries western ships began appearing in its sheltered harbour, and it eventually became relatively affluent: Chalkis was richer than Athens, for example, and in 1169, 35 years before the Fourth Crusade, it was required to equip six ships for the imperial fleet when the emperor levied ship-money.

Many of the foreign traders who stopped there were Venetian. Venice was extremely familiar with the ports of the east long before the Latin conquest of Byzantium which was the culmination of the unspeakable Fourth Crusade. When its armada brought the Doge to Evia in 1171 to sort out a disagreement with the Byzantine Emperor it must have travelled a well-worn Venetian route. Evia was a natural target for a powerful maritime republic expanding eastwards, and Venice soon had its mercenary sights upon it. The Doge signed a treaty with Emperor Alexius III in 1199 granting the Republic free trade in Evia (and in many other islands and ports) in return for assistance against the troublesome Normans.

Clearly, when the Crusaders and their Venetian allies sat down to carve up the Byzantine Empire between them after sacking Constantinople in 1204, Evia was a rich picking. But its passage as a western possession was not a straightforward one. The history of Evia under Latin occupation has been called, in E.A. Freeman's *Historical Geography*, 'the most perplexed part of the perplexed Greek history of the time' – although it is a fascinating part, which sheds light on the nature of the Venetian Republic and on the mobile physiognomy of medieval Europe. Without the painstaking reconstruction work of the likes of Karl Hopf, John Bury and William Miller it might have remained obscure. The starting point, however, is clear: the Partition Treaty stated that a quarter of the Byzantine Empire was to be converted into the new Latin Empire of Romania, headed by Baldwin, Count of Flanders, and the rest was, on paper, divided equally between the Venetian Republic and the Crusaders – the latter led by Bonifacio, Marquis of Montferrat and shortly to be King of Thessaloniki. The Venetians were not likely to be short-changed in a deal of that kind, particularly with the horrendous Enrico Dandolo as Doge; they wanted trade routes, and sure enough they got all the best harbours and islands – including that of Negroponte, as both Evia and Chalkis were called at that time.

The Crusaders, however, were anxious to take possession of their new fiefdoms, and the ambitious Bonifacio marched them into Greece. It was a Fleming, Jacques d'Avesnes, who went over to Evia in 1205 and quickly gained control. He fortified it and then went off to the Peloponnese, allowing Bonifacio to divide the island into three parts, granting each to a Veronese who took the title of triarch (*terzieri*). This marked the entry of the dalle Carceri family onto the Evian stage; they were to be on it, or in the wings, for some while. Ravano dalle Carceri took the southern third, his kinsman Gilberto de Verona the centre, and the enviably named Pegoraro dei Pegorari the north. D'Avesnes died without heirs and the triarchs were left reporting directly to the new Latin Emperor. In early 1209 Pegoraro returned home, Gilberto died, and Ravano became the lord of the whole island.

So where did Venice fit in? There were other important territories of its new off-the-peg empire to which it was legally entitled that it was ignoring, not least the Peloponnese. If it was biding its time, the strategy paid off, but it might have been that it was too preoccupied elsewhere, or unable to raise an army. Ravano realized that he was isolated, and in 1209 offered the overlordship of the island to Venice, promising money and a silken garment woven with gold for the Doge and an altarcloth for St Mark's, plus free trading rights for the Venetians and their own church and warehouse in every Evian town. The treaty was concluded in 1211. Thus Venice played a sort of overlord role while Ravano still came under the Emperor's control. At some point between 1211 and 1216 the first governor (*bailo*) arrived on Evia from Venice. The foot was in the door, and only the Turks were going to push it out again.

Two hundred and sixty years is a long time, and it is perhaps surprising how little evidence of the great Venetian Empire remains on Evia. But they were not interested in creating little Venices everywhere; their empire-building motives were purely commercial. They did leave their stamp on Crete, another vital possession – but there was no Lombard presence on Crete to temper Venetian imperial instincts.

In 1216, when the colourful Ravano died, Venice saw the opportunity to insinuate itself into the actual running of the island, and the governor divided it into six, ruled by Veronese hexarchs, all sharing Chalkis as the capital. (Almost all the lords had their palaces built in Chalkis.) But the governor made sure he was in charge and, significantly, it was at this time that Venetian weights and measures were introduced. As always when an empire extends its tentacles overseas, settlers arrived from home in search of a new life, and, similarly, Veronese compatriots of the feudal lords poured in. The historical complexity of the period emanates partly from its appallingly labyrinthine genealogical background, as members of Veronese extended families married each other apparently *ad infinitum.* The way out of any kind of scrape seems to have been to get hitched to a second cousin.

The Venetians and Lombards got on reasonably well, and there were plenty of balls and other manifestations of aristocratic high life in Chalkis. There were disputes, of course, especially in later years when Venetian influence and intervention increased to the extent that a curious kind of double government was in operation – a recipe for disaster in any country in any age. Given the difficulties inherent in such a situation, the Venetians and the Lombards in Evia didn't do so badly.

But in 1236 a cloud blew onto the horizon. Baldwin II saw fit to bestow the suzerainty of Evia on Geoffrey II de Villehardouin, Prince of Achaea, in return for services rendered. Thus it became a fief of the principality of Achaea. Prolonged squabbling ensued, largely provoked by the personal ambitions of William,

Geoffrey's brother and successor and the villain of the piece. The upshot was that hostages were taken, war broke out, Chalkis changed hands three times and then in 1256 the Venetians and supporters of the Evian Lombard barons laid siege to the capital against William for 13 months. Chalkis capitulated, and eventually William concluded a peace treaty at Thebes with the Venetians and the triarchs. There was a strong feeling in Venice that their policy in Evia had not turned out entirely to their advantage, and they prohibited future Evian governors from interfering in feudal rights.

Meanwhile all the Latins were nervous as Constantinople was lost to the Greeks – though Byzantium was never to be the same again. Baldwin, their Emperor, had fled, stopping off in Evia in 1261. The Venetians were fretting about Genoese inroads into their trading monopoly in Evia, as their old rivals had struck a commercial deal with the Greek Emperor. This latter, Michael VIII Paleologos, recognized the advantage of setting Venice and Genoa against each other, and, more significantly for Evia, he signed a deal with the Venetians in 1265 promising peace as long as they didn't assist the Lombard barons of Evia (or a list of other potential attackers, including, peculiarly, the English) in attempts against the Greeks. The Venetians would have stitched up anyone for their own ends.

Relations between the Evian Lombards and the Greek Emperor deteriorated, culminating in a sea battle in 1275 which became sufficiently serious for the Venetians to abandon their neutrality, at least unofficially, and come to the aid of the Lombards lest they should lose the colony. At the same time Likarios went from strength to strength, united with the Emperor against the Lombards. Michael gave the knight the whole island as a fief in reward for his victories, but the truce between the Emperor and the Venetians was nonetheless renewed, with amendments, in 1277.

Likarios gained control of much of the island, and very nearly captured Chalkis itself. The Venetians, however, were not going to give it up easily: since the Latin loss of Constantinople Evia had become even more strategically important to them. Even Likarios could not go on forever. He disappeared and Venice asserted itself on the island, beginning, with Lombard help, to claw back territory held by the Emperor's representatives. A peace of a kind was established between the Emperor Andronikos II and the Republic in 1285, but minor hostilities continued in Evia, which was again a particular bone of contention. By 1295 the Venetians and Lombards had most of Likarios' fortresses back. Venice enjoyed a remarkably palatable excuse for interfering still further with Lombard authority as all the baronies were held by women at that time, which meant that they were fair game for any kind of exploitation and intrusion. Anyway, Venice was a world power by then, and could do what it liked.

War broke out between Venice and Genoa in 1294, and then between Venice and Emperor Andronikos. Truces were signed, but no sooner were the Greeks temporarily at bay than the Grand Company of Catalans – once a Greek ally – sailed into the Evian Gulf. The Catalans were only around for a decade or two but the havoc they caused on the island percolated even into the language: a proverb was still in use in the nineteenth century which translated as, 'Not even the Catalans would do that.' (When Gibbon wrote about their expedition to Greece he didn't have the benefit of a translation of the wonderful *Chronicle of Muntaner*, written in the 1320s in the Catalan language by an influential participant with a philosophical turn of mind. Lady Goodenough translated it into English in 1920.) For the Venetians in the first decade of the fourteenth century there was much to fear from a Catalan invasion of Evia, not least the danger that they might join forces with the Lombards, as the two ruling parties of Evia were going through one of the most difficult periods of their relationship. The powerful Baron of Karistos, Bonifacio da Verona, looked in particular as though it might have crossed his mind to overpower the Venetian quasi-overlord, and was very matey with the Catalans.

The Catalan expedition was actually on course for Evia, but Venetian ships happened to be in the area and attacked it (Ramon Muntaner was taken prisoner). The Catalans took Attica, Evia's neighbour. Venice cranked itself up for war, but the relationship with its supposed ally Bonifacio deteriorated. In 1317 Alfonso Fadrique, the son of the King of Sicily (who was the sort of overlord of the Catalan company), arrived in Attica and married Bonifacio's daughter, and hostilities between Catalans and the Venetian-Lombard coalition began in the same year. Fadrique got into Chalkis, forced the Venetians to sign a peace treaty and actually took possession of the town, but Venice shortly won it back. In dealing with the Catalan problem Venice had become more powerful still on the island, and the Doge decreed that it would occupy all the towns and fortresses.

After further hostilities the Catalans and Venetians made peace in 1318, and the truce was twice renewed, but there was still trouble between the Venetians and the Lombards. Then in 1328 the second Catalan-Venetian war began, complicated by the fact that at this time there were only two Lombard triarchs, and both were anti-Venetian. Furthermore, the Catalans allied themselves with the Turks, and both parties hammered the island with piratical raids. The war came to an end, more or less, with a truce in 1331 (in which the Lombards were included) which was subsequently renewed; Fadrique agreed to desist and make reparations. The Turks, however, continued to raid.

The Catalan problem was solved and the official suzerainty of Achaea had been forgotten, but the Genoese loomed large, and in the conflict between these two maritime trading nations with important possessions in the Levant it was clear that Evia would be a major consideration, as it was the chief Aegean base of the Venetian fleet. In 1350 hostilities broke out and culminated in a Genoese raid on Chalkis, half of which was burnt down. Peace was concluded between the two republics in 1355. The Venetian administrators soon repaired Chalkis and in 1356 took further steps to pull the island up from the state of decay it had fallen into, including the institution of repopulation measures. It often bestowed Venetian citizenship upon its subjects, sometimes as a reward for bravery in the frequent wars, and in 1353 everyone in Negroponte except the Jews had been granted the privilege – with certain conditions attached.

In 1363 the governor declared war on the Catalans again, but the matter was swiftly resolved. Enter, in 1380, the Navarrese Company, another band of mercenaries supposedly out to recover the dominions of the titular Emperor of Romania. Everybody panicked when they took Corfu and Attica, and it seemed likely that they would proceed to Evia, as all the others had; but they were diverted.

The Lombards staggered on as triarchs until Nicolo dalle Carceri, a powerful baron who controlled two-thirds of the island, died without heirs in 1383. Besides being an Evian baron he was ruler of the Duchy of the Archipelago (which chiefly consisted of the central Aegean islands), but he lived in Evia because it was nicer than Naxos. While a regent took care of his ducal responsibilities he schemed to extend his Evian territory, and in 1380, while Venice was at war with Genoa again, he colluded with the Navarrese, and even hatched a plot to capture Chalkis. Nobody seems to have been very keen on him, not least his subjects, and he was murdered. Seven years later the holder of the other third of the island, Giorgio Ghisi, bequeathed it to the Republic. The Venetian hold over Evia had already strengthened considerably, but nonetheless the disappearance of these last two barons was highly significant, and Venice now appointed the triarchs (or, in the case of the southern third, collection of fief-holders) itself as its vassals. It came as no surprise that they were all from within its own camp – though the independent Lombard barons were still lurking. The last titular Latin Emperor of Constantinople had gone, so the feudal tie between him and the Lombard lords – still a strong factor, despite its insignificance on a practical level for years – was conveniently removed.

In the last decade of the fourteenth century and the first of the fifteenth there was trouble between the Venetians and the Athenian Acciajuoli in which the governor of Negroponte was heavily involved (this was hardly surprising, as the disputed territory of Attica was on his doorstep). It was resolved, but the Turkish problem was not, and that was becoming an increasingly important factor in the Republic's attitude towards its eastern colonies. Turkey was the great scourge of what was itself a great empire – an empire at its height when it was haunted by the potential loss of Negroponte. The Venetians, who had been busy leasing out portions of Evian land to noblemen, started being much nicer to the Greeks, whom they would need to help them defend themselves. All the islanders except the Jews were awarded fiscal and other privileges, and the barons armed their serfs with bows and arrows.

The problem with Evia during the fifteenth century was that not enough people lived on it and it didn't make the Venetians enough cash. Indeed it didn't make them any cash at all; it ran at a loss. The population, already depleted by Turkish raids, shrank further to about 14,000 families, according to William Miller's estimate. The Greeks were miserable and poor, and the Turks reappeared with monotonous regularity to make them even more miserable and much poorer. They even appealed to the Venetians to let them become tributaries of the Turks, a totally wasted effort on their part but a measure of their desperation. On top of all that there was an appalling plague in about 1416 and a serious earthquake soon afterwards. It's not surprising they left in droves; who wouldn't have?

Venice had a big problem on its hands in Evia now. It was the frontier of its empire, and it was going down the tubes. Nobody wanted to go out there any more, and they had to keep putting up the governor's salary; it was what the Foreign Office would call a hardship post. The unfortunate incumbents appealed continually to the Treasury at home, and instructions came back to fortify like mad and try to get people to live inside the strongholds (so many Greeks were being taken captive by Turkish raiders that the Venetians were afraid of losing their workers). Someone even came up with the bright idea of restricting the sale of wine to inside the fortresses to induce people in. The Albanian immigration programme was initiated. Privileges were introduced, for example the hearth tax was abolished, although this was something of a poisoned chalice as it was replaced by military service for all men over 18. But the conclusion was inexorable. Thessaloniki, which Venice had held for seven years, was taken in 1430, and Constantinople 23 years later. The Byzantine Empire had been struggling for breath for over two centuries, but still this moment of extinction was significant. Perhaps the Venetians felt a pang of guilt, as there can be no doubt that the death blow had been dealt by their forefathers, and they were to suffer now the retribution as one by one the jewels in their crown were picked off by the Turks. It was ironic that in 1452 the first official judicial code, containing special reference to the administration of Evia, was confirmed in the Venetian Senate. It had taken 31 years to draw up, and the Republic had just 18 years left.

But it wasn't over quite yet. A treaty was signed with Sultan Mohammed II in 1454. He arrived in Athens in 1458. The Turks were taking over Greece, gaining the whole of the Peloponnese, with the exception of Venetian possessions, by 1460. When they took Limnos in 1465 the wretched inhabitants came over to Evia, which must have been a textbook case of frying pans and fires. The Venetians were fighting for their eastern life, and for the lives of their Greek subjects, whose vassalage was but a luxury compared with what was to follow.

*

Mohammed had already been on an official inspection visit of Chalkis in 1458, so he knew what he had to contend with. When it became clear early in 1470 that he was on his way back, and for more than an inspection, Venice appealed to its allies for support, but precious little was forthcoming. Historians are wont to accuse the Republic of itself failing to supply adequate help to the colony in its hour of direst need. 'The princes of Christendom looked on as if in a theatre' is their favourite quotation when they write of the famous siege of Chalkis. If Venice was culpable, it would be typical of its behaviour in Greece. In the Mani it continually encouraged the Greeks to rise and then left them in the lurch whenever they did.

Venetian responsibility for the fall of Evia is attributable to one man: the Admiral, Nicolo Canale, who was on the spot with a fleet of 71 ships. He went chasing off to intercept the approaching Turks, and when he returned Chalkis was under siege, so he dropped anchor and waited, inexplicably failing to seize any opportunity to relieve his countrymen. For this he was sent to prison back at home, and subsequently exiled. His name lingers on in Venetian archives as the paradigm of shame and disgrace.

The attackers came by land and sea. The fleet, with about 300 ships and carrying a staggering load of over 60,000 men, proceeded northwards up the Evian Gulf, sacking Stira and Vasilika en route, and formed a bridge of boats across the channel at Chalkis for the waiting land forces to step over. There were somewhere between 100,000 and 300,000 soldiers in addition to the sailors, and when you consider that the population of Chalkis was about 2500, strengthened only by 700 soldiers from Crete and another 500 led by a Dalmatian, it was quite amazing that the siege, once Mohammed began his attack, lasted a whole month, even though the inhabitants had prepared themselves for a long one.

A sea-captain's clerk by the name of Giacomo Rizzardo left a detailed account of the whole episode which was published in Venice in 1844. He says that when the Turks offered generous terms in return for submission they were told to 'go and drown themselves and eat pork'. From this point on it was clear that punishment would be bloody, and it was. Besides incessant artillery fire into the town, Turkish horsemen ran all over the centre of the island and north as far as Orei, killing indiscriminately. The most vivid account of the siege in English is in the enormous leatherbound tomes of the seventeenth-century historian Richard Knolles. The Turkish army was so vast, he said, that when a load were slaughtered it didn't matter as there were always more, 'as if new Men had sprung out of the Bodies of the dead'. Forty thousand of them died during a hellish assault for a whole day and night without intermission. When Chalkis fell in mid-July Mohammed ordered all the men found alive to be killed, and upon the Italians 'he shewed his Tyranny with most exquisite and horrible Torments ... The horrible and monstrous Cruelty,' concludes Knolles, 'with the filthy Outrages by that beastly and barbarous people committed, at the taking of that city, passeth all credit.'

The Dalmatian, it turned out, was a traitor, and an elaborate plot was uncovered implicating other Dalmatian soldiers and an Albanian working in the governor's palace. But the plot was probably foiled and not the cause of Turkish entry into the town. What really gave Mohammed victory was the failure of Canale to break the boat bridges and so trap the Turks on the island.

Once the Turks were in, having filled the ditches with corpses of horses and men, the inhabitants continued to fight them off, with quicklime, with boiling water – with their bare hands, if necessary. Eventually the invaders reached the main square. The

Governor, Paolo Erizzo, fled to the fortress in the middle of the channel and pulled up the drawbridge, but they got him out, he was sawn in half, and Mohammed washed his hands in his blood. Besides all the males over eight, many of the women and children were killed; those who survived were shipped off to Turkey.

The rest of the island surrendered. Thousands and thousands of both Christians and Muslims had died. Canale made a feeble attempt to recover Chalkis, during which time he was arrested by his replacement, who had been rushed out from home.

There was wailing on the canals of Venice over the loss of Evia. It was said that it was the Republic's 'Right Eye', and it was one of the few flags that flew in St Mark's on special occasions. This is how Jan Morris puts it in *The Venetian Empire* (as opposed to her far longer and weightier *Venice*): 'For as the fall of Singapore was to the British in 1941, the fall of Evia was to the Venetians in 1470 – the first grim warning that empires never last.' They still had some Greek trading posts, and they still had Candia, which was the most valuable jewel in what was by now more of a tiara than a crown, and which we know as Crete – but it was not in the Aegean.

In January 1479 Venice ceded the island by treaty, thus according the Turks full legal possession. What had the Venetian Republic been to the island? At first a nominal, absentee landlord, little more than a concept. Then it had stealthily asserted its role of protector, insinuated itself ever further into the brittle infrastructure, and about 186 years after it had shipped the Fourth Crusade to the Levant it was resident overlord in the fullest sense of the word. But what had it meant to the people? How had it dented the collective consciousness? While there is no doubt that their lot was significantly improved for a period, the islanders on the whole were in a sorry state when the Latins arrived and in a similarly sorry state when the Turks kicked them out. Life under the Venetians must have been, by and large, one exhausting, adrenalin-charged trajectory from war to precarious peace and back to war, with, during certain periods, barely time to register the name of the enemy – unless of course you happened to be born at the start of one of the few stable periods. The Venetians were benevolent towards their foreign subjects, who were accorded privileges from time to time; most important of all, they were allowed to worship freely. The Evians seem to have fared better than the Cretans under the Republic, probably because the Cretans were more independent and fierce-spirited. But still, the Evian Greeks had no voice, like all oppressed peoples; there wasn't even an official interpreter till 1390. The archives of Venice are full of records of their dominion over Evia, a well-documented slice of a history shaped largely by the Venetians themselves. But what could the Evian Greeks document of those years? Their history is a passive one, buffeted from foreign rule to foreign rule with precious little control over their own destiny, like many millions of silent witnesses to history before and after. There were fortifications left in 1470, but most had been destroyed in the war or had already decayed, and anyway they meant little to the Greeks as they were to be taken over by another foreign power. There were the Albanians, introduced as a result of Venetian policy. But there wasn't much else. And it had all been for money.

Chalkis continued in its role of capital under the Turks, and by the sixteenth century, way before the foundation of the Greek state and thus before diplomatic representation was centralized, it was the base for various foreign missions covering the whole Aegean. Francesco Morosini, by now the Doge, attempted to take Chalkis from the Turks in 1688, but gave up after losing 1000 men in a disastrous siege. In the following century it became clear that the Turkish Empire was in serious decline, and the west, of course, looked to its own interests. One of the most spectacular pieces of cold-blooded political thuggery was a scheme put forward in the 1730s by the old-timer Cardinal Giulio Alberoni, whereby the Ottoman dominions were to be parcelled out willy-nilly. Evia, for some reason, was assigned to Prussia.

The islanders, unaware of these offstage political manoeuvrings, were living in economic and social chaos. At the beginning of the nineteenth century John Hobhouse was shocked to discover that there was 'no one representative of any Christian power' in Chalkis, not least because a westerner had recently been cut to pieces by a gang of Turks. The cells of vibrant intellectual activity that proliferated amongst the educated Greek minority in the two generations prior to independence certainly seem to have failed to materialize on Evia. After the mainland Greeks had won their independence and while they were arguing among themselves during a bitter period of internal strife, the Turkish flag continued to fly over Chalkis castle. Despite numerous treaties and protocols involving the Great Powers from 1827 to 1832, Hadji Ismail Bey refused to budge until the British warship carrying Bavarian soldiers and Neroulos arrived in the spring of 1833 (Ismail was acting on behalf of the Pasha Omer Bey, who had left the island shortly before the liberators appeared).

Evia was officially Greek at last, its national identity sanctioned by law after over half a millennium as the vassal state of a foreign empire. The government purchased large amounts of land from the Turks and some of the estates were broken up and bought piecemeal by private individuals. The island was designated a nomarchy and divided into eparchies in the administrative reorganization implemented by the three-man Bavarian regency (King Otto was only 17). Many Turks stayed on in Chalkis, and in the 1880s the venerable *Murray's Handbook for Travellers in Greece* recorded that it was the only part of the country where Muslims were still to be found, with the exception of Thessaly.

The name of the city reverted from Negroponte – or a list of variants of it – to the ancient Chalkis. (The more modern demotic version is Chalkida, but both names are widely used.) It was once received wisdom that the word derived from *chalkos* (bronze), which was worked extensively in the area. Despite the commonly accepted theory that it was mined by the ancients, metallurgical archaeologists now claim that there was virtually no bronze in Evia, but that it was imported and worked at the factories found at the site of the Early Bronze Age Chalkis. Another theory has it that the name comes from the mollusc called *chalke* in Phoenician from which a purple dye was extracted. (I am suspicious of this, however. Evelyn Waugh, in his irritatingly brilliant Mediterranean travel book *Labels*, says that 'Phoenician' is a term used to describe anything that happened before the Norman occupation.) A third theory, put about by Diodorus Siculus, is that Chalkida was one of the daughters of the river god Asopus – another name for the nymph Euboea. The Venetians and Crusaders called both the town and the island Negroponte, probably a corruption of Euripos, the name of the channel and itself on record referring to the island as a whole from the ninth century. This is not as unlikely a derivation as it sounds, as the u represents the Greek upsilon, which appears like a Roman Y in its upper case, thus Eyripus, Egripos, Negripon (the n came from the accusative form of the article placed immediately before the word in the phrase '*ston Egripon*'), which in turn became Negro Ponte (Black Bridge in Italian) because of the town's association with the bridge. The explanation often proffered that the Venetians named the town after the bridge in the first place is unlikely as the structure was never black (and the metaphorical interpretation of black as 'hard to negotiate' is a nonsense). The Turkish name was Egriboz, and the Albanians called it Grip.

*

The modern town was graceless and unkempt. The funnel system created by the bridge meant constant traffic congestion on both sides. The bay was clogged with industrial plants, notably Chalkis Cement, which employed 1500 people and produced cement from local limestone. The industrial triangle of Chalkis, Thiva (ancient Thebes) and Inofita is one of the most important in Greece. Its growth over the past 10 years has led to the doubling of the population of greater Chalkis, which, extending almost to Nea Artaki and including Lampsakos, in 1991 stood at 80,000: 45 per cent of the island's total. The industrial development also means that Evia overall is relatively prosperous – when indexed to the rest of the country, at least.

Even the meanest architectural sensibility would find the town dispiriting. The Lombard-Venetian period was little in evidence as the walls and fortifications of their large moated fortress, which they called *Città* and which the Turks used and adapted, were almost entirely destroyed in the 1880s, along with the mini-castle in the channel. The fortress was about two miles in circumference, and the 'new town' where the Greeks lived was a short distance outside it, with a burial ground between them. There was a Jesuit seminary there. It was only after the fortress was pulled down that the town outside the walls was properly developed; before the Turks left Colonel Leake found the Christian ghetto was 'in a wretched state of dilapidation'.

I wandered around the old Venetian and Turkish quarter, however, and I did find a warren of picturesque narrow streets of weathered stone houses with precarious verandas and exuberant gardens, and thin Tudoresque affairs with long arching wooden struts below narrow balconies. In a 'bookshop' I bought a pamphlet containing extracts from the diary of an unknown Englishman who had visited the town in the late nineteenth century. He had met a British navy captain who told him all about Chalkis, including the alarming frequency of earthquakes. The captain was Arthur Mansell, a Guernseyman buried in Chalkis in 1890. I never found out who the traveller was. A Greek found his diary in a bookshop in Athens, had it translated and published extracts.

Unusually for Evia, two of the most impressive buildings in Chalkis were Turkish. The first was the fortress of Kara-Baba, which is not on the island at all, but on the comparatively small mainland portion of Chalkis. Sultan Kara-Baba built it on a hill overlooking the streaked mountains of Attica in 1688, but by 1749 it was 'almost a ruin', according to Lord Charlemont. I though it had lasted rather well, particularly a configuration of vaulted chambers at the western end, and it included high walls, inner and outer staircases, slit windows, cannonports, a bell-tower, the remains of various rooms and storehouses, and, outside the walls, 10 water tanks sunk into the rock.

Near the entrance of Kara-Baba, in an unnamed grave marked by a simple stone carving of a cross, iron railings and a trailing geranium, I found Chalkis' most famous literary figure. Yannis Skaribas was a prose writer (and, less conspicuously, a poet and playwright) with a devoted following. His syntax and language, including a good dose of slang, were delightfully idiosyncratic. (He was also an ace Karagiozis shadow-theatre player.) If the truth be known he was not Evian at all, but from Agia Euthimia in Parnassida, but he lived in Chalkis from the age of 21 till his death at 91 in 1984. He refused to abandon it for the more fashionable Athens. He was a kind of eccentric leftist, a frugal man, and it was entirely characteristic that he elected to have an unnamed grave. It was entirely characteristic of life too that his wish was contravened by a blue and yellow signpost down the road pointing the visitor towards his grave. But he loved paradox.

The other notable Turkish building in Chalkis was the

mosque, in the old quarter, built between 1470 and 1600. The red-tiled roof and three-arched frontage were dirty stone, the three smaller domes above an arched colonnade had disappeared, and the tower for calling the faithful to prayer had been snapped off. But it had a certain appeal, and there was a nice seventeenth-century marble fountain outside bearing a delicately embroidered Arabic inscription. I later learnt that the fountain had been destroyed at the beginning of this century, and was painstakingly reconstructed by local craftsmen. The library had a book showing the original.

The building was owned by the state who were using it as a warehouse for Byzantine fragments. A civil servant was stationed in front of the door solely to tell people it was closed to the public. I would have thought a locked door would have been a cheaper way of doing the job, particularly as the public were patently not remotely interested. I was the first person for weeks, if not months, who had wanted to go in, and the man threw himself into his work with a keen sense of its vital importance; I had given him a purpose in life. If the rules were that no one should enter, that was final, he said, as if I were asking to enter the personal residence of the Patriarch. He had walked straight out of a Maupassant story. It was rare for me to empathize with the terrifying Colonel Leake, but on this occasion I did remember a remark he made when he was wandering around Chalkis over 150 years ago: But it is difficult to explore among these intolerant barbarians.

The episode was fortuitous, however, as a man who had observed the fracas approached and introduced himself as a member of the Evian Studies Association. He had been instrumental in setting up the folklore museum, and we went to open it up (it seemed to open to the public on a rather haphazard basis). It was housed in the only surviving portion of the Venetian fortress, occupying three parallel vaults next door to a huge barracks. Great care had been taken over the exhibits, which included costumes, maps, Venetian engravings, printing presses imported from America and wooden letterpress characters, a recreation of a turn-of-the-century town band and a mock-up village scene including a dried olive tree tied to a wall.

There was a fast-food joint nearby, no longer such a cultural anomaly in Chalkis (or any Greek town). But on top of the counters offering hamburgers and toasted sandwiches a sudden lack of confidence in the concept manifested itself in the shape of a heavy old glass cabinet containing *tiropittes*, leaf pastry cheese pies, the staple Greek snack food.

The Jewish settlement in Chalkis, so the local story goes, is the oldest in Europe, founded by Alexander the Great's prisoners of war. A rabbi called Benjamin of Tudela who travelled in Greece in the late twelfth century left records listing Negroponte as the fourth largest Jewish community in Greece, with 200 inhabitants. The Jews were heavily engaged in silk manufacturing, and later, once the Venetians were established, the business yielded considerable fiscal revenue. (Silkworm eggs had been brought west by monks in the sixth century, and under Byzantium the industry was a state monopoly. Silk was a most sought-after commodity.) They lived outside the town at first, but – unlike the Greeks – were assigned a ghetto within the walls for their own safety in 1355 (Genoese marauders had picked on the Jews in a raid in 1347). As the chief traders of the town the Venetians relied upon them, as they did in so many of their colonies, but that didn't stop them from consistently excluding the Jews from privileges accorded to other inhabitants. The public executioner was always selected from their ranks, and in 1304 they had to bear the cost of fortifying the Venetian district. When the Venetians were struggling to keep the island going at the beginning of the fifteenth century they were afraid of the power of the Jews and forbade them to buy land outside their own quarter. The Jewish population grew, and by 1440 the Venetians had to permit their ghetto to be enlarged – with the proviso that if they dared to live beyond a certain tower their property would be confiscated and they themselves banished. Occasionally the situation improved, for example towards the end of the fourteenth century Jewish taxes were reduced and the barbarous custom of shutting the Jews up in their quarter on Good Friday was abandoned. Then in 1452, doubtless to curry favour at a time of desperation over the impending Turkish invasion, the Jewish ghetto was repaired, the law was made equal for Christian and Jew alike, and the Jews' obligation to furnish a hangman was abolished.

It was said in Venice that it was a Jewish axeman who murdered the governor Paolo Erizzo when Chalkis fell, but that probably has more to do with the role of Jews in the Venetian imagination than with reality. Almost 600 years later, when the administration of another set of Italian occupiers capitulated, there were 325 Chalkidian Jews. The Nomarchial Committee of EAM, the Communist-dominated National Liberation Front, called on the Evians to help their Jews, and most of them obtained false passports and were taken to other parts of the island; those who weren't were swiftly rooted out for the death trains. A few were captured in the mountains. Sotiris Papastratis, an Evian who helped the evacuation, left an account of a Jewish teacher who was captured in Stropones, where people now go to ski. She was stripped naked, a piece of wood was stuck up her vagina and she was hung from the balcony in the main square. Greek collaborators took part. I would like to think that the episode was set down for the record in English somewhere. (The community was not among the worst affected in Greece in terms of loss of life: far from it. The huge Sephardic population of Thessaloniki was almost wiped out.) Many Jews escaped from Evia to Smyrna in fishing boats, and some made it to Tel Aviv. A number of families remained in Israel after the war, and the Evian Jewish population in 1980 stood at 170. I found the synagogue tucked away off a busy street in the old quarter, unrecognizable from the outside. The Jewish cemetery was up near the top of the town. As I walked up the frenetic urban atmosphere melted away and a quiet, flourishing community emerged. Two caretaking crones who lived on the edge of the cemetery were pottering around in their garden, and a cage containing four little birds was hanging from a tree.

Later in the week I met up with Katina, my friend from Agios Loukas, and her husband, Kostas. We crossed the bridge and drove around the mainland coast, stopping for a vastly over-priced coffee at an awful new hotel at Agios Minas. Shortly afterwards we stopped again to walk along a deserted beach, and Katina pointed to a small island ahead. 'We used to call it Englesonisi, after one of your compatriots who used to live on it. He was ... a strange one.'

The location was exactly right for Agios Nikolaos, the island fictionalized as St Gregory's by Christopher Isherwood in the book which can only loosely be described as a novel, *Down There on a Visit*. He spent the summer of 1932 there as a guest of an English archaeologist friend of Auden's, Francis Turville-Petre, who leased it from the villagers of Chalia (now Drosia), and who had the intention of excavating the hill opposite but never got round to it; from Isherwood's book you wouldn't think he was ever sober for long enough to make a start. He appears as Ambrose and presides over a kind of hedonistic and homo-sexual mini-fiefdom on the island. The experience represents, for the Christopher narrator, total cut-off, and the island functions as a symbol of mental alienation or disengagement compared with the viciously immediate involvement in the

European political ferment of the thirties also portrayed in *Down There on a Visit*. It is a brilliant book which nobody seems to read any more: Isherwood called it, at different times, one of his 'dynamic portrait novels', and a 'loosely constructed fictional autobiography'. The whole thing is a metaphor, to a certain extent, about a journey through an interior landscape: hardly an original device, but seldom handled as effectively.

We went to Katina's house, a lavish five-roomed affair just outside town. Every available inch of tabletop, sideboard and shelf was covered with the ubiquitous doilies, embroideries and tapestries *de rigueur* in all Greek houses except the most urbane and the most rural. It was like a museum of plastic flowers and gilded china. A cold drink was brought to me on an elaborate silver tray, and they continually insisted that I change armchair, lest I should not be sitting in the most comfortable seat.

I was glad to escape, claiming that I really had to visit St Paraskevi before dark, and was soon crossing the bridge back into town, surprised by a sprinkling of warm summer rain. Paraskevi, born in AD 117, is the patron saint of Chalkis. She was tortured for spreading the word, and is credited with the usual kind of sadomasochistic experience of early martyrs - thrown into boiling oil and bubbling tar and surviving, and so on. She performed a miracle and was freed, only to be beheaded by another group of persecutors. Her basilica-form church was in a quiet square in the oldest part of town, sunk in the architectural alloy of a crumbling single-storey cottage, concrete flats and an ochre stone neo-Classical house with an old piece of marble above the lintel carved with the winged lion of St Mark's. When I turned up a barefooted Turkish family comprising seven children, two young women and two grandparents were sprawled over the square, waiting for nothing in particular but eager to talk, and so we did, until the church opened half an hour later. Most of the 200-strong Muslim community in Chalkis arrived from western Thrace in the early eighties in search of work, and most too are very poor. There was a peculiar story in the newspaper one day about their representations to get the mosque back.

The church is often cited as an important example of what is commonly called Frankish architecture in Greece. The front wall was flat, unadorned and bright white, and the side walls bare stone. Two of the marble columns originally in the nave had been dumped outside the door. Going inside was rather like visiting a church in a dream, where bits of every church you have ever been in join together to form a whole. Everyone who has held power in the city had a go at it, and early Byzantine columns, Gothic extravagances and contemporary kitsch all swilled around together. Henry Raikes loved it, naturally, because it reminded him of England, 'in contrast with the wretched sameness of the round-ended Greek chapels'. The original structure was built somewhere between the fifth and eighth centuries, itself probably on the site of an ancient temple. In the early thirteenth century, according to Henri de Valenciennes, Emperor Henri, Baldwin's brother and successor, visited it when he was staying in Thebes, despite warnings that he risked a treacherous death if he did so. Ravano, once his enemy and certainly not the best friend the Roman Catholic Church has ever had, was now his host. There was constant conflict between the Latin barons and the clergy, and in Evia the Catholic Church was not held in high regard even after the Latin Patriarch had moved his see there in 1261 when the Greeks kicked the westerners out of Constantinople, thus making Evia the spiritual HQ of the Latin Empire in the Levant. In 1314 this office was combined with the see of Negroponte, in other words the titular Latin Patriarch of Constantinople was also Bishop of Negroponte. Once Venice had the island within its clutches in 1390 it relieved the Orthodox clergy there of a tax payable to the Latin Patriarch, which must have endeared it to Rome no end. They continued to coexist, however, and according to one source by 1426 the incumbent Patriarch owned a quarter of the island and had many serfs, but shirked his share of public duties.

The Lombards and Venetians made the church their own, then, and the latter dedicated it to St Mark and made it a dependency of San Giorgio Maggiore. It was partially knocked down and enlarged; there was an enormous Gothic shiny dark wood pulpit in the middle. The iconostasis was cool grey marble with narrow white Ionic-topped pillars, and sat ill with the warm raw brown stone walls. The Turks initially used it as a mosque, and then as some kind of warehouse and carriage garage. Earthquakes damaged it in 1854 and 1884. I saw an old photograph of the church once, taken on Easter Sunday. They used to make a Judas dummy out of green vegetables, hang it up outside the church and shoot at it.

One of my favourite spots in Chalkis was the covered market, right in the centre of town. It had been there for years and could scarcely have changed. In a narrow, busy street nearby, surrounded by houses and a flowery courtyard, the only surviving Venetian tower sported a concrete crenellation and served as a handy fixing point for electricity cables. It was once attached to a medieval mansion. During the war they used it as an air raid siren, and there was an ouzeri opposite called The Siren. A basil-festooned balcony jutted out to within a yard of the top of the tower, and the incumbent crone was pottering on it; she must have survived the experience – or perhaps she was deaf.

If there was one Evian expert I had to meet it was Diamantios Sampson, an archaeologist of note who, himself a Skopelot, had been excavating in Evia for 15 years and had written a number of excellent books on the subject. I had telephoned him to arrange a meeting at his offices in the museum (the museum itself was temporarily closed, as it had been for nine years) and was gloomily anticipating an awkward encounter trying to extract information from a crusty old relic who wouldn't take me seriously. His secretary explained that he had slipped out, and brought me a coffee. I was idly perusing a couple of archaeological journals when the door burst open and an extremely striking creature in his early forties strode in wearing shorts and a T-shirt, an emerald-green pullover slung over his broad shoulders. Thinking perhaps he was a passer-by looking for the tennis court I was just clocking the distinguished greying hair around the temples when the man put his hand on my shoulder and said, 'Hi, you must be Sara. I'm Diamantios.'

We spent the afternoon visiting the sites of ancient Chalkis; it would be hard to imagine a more enthusiastic guide. Listening to him made me think archaeology was the most fascinating subject on earth. I was mesmerized. His specialization was the neolithic period, and he once told me that he wasn't interested in a Classical temple because it was 'too modern'.

The city-state known as ancient Chalkis moved position several times. The first, where Diamantios had excavated extensively, was at Manika (Sleeve), a modern suburb named after the shape of the little peninsula it occupied. It was one of the biggest Greek city-states, prospering in the Early Bronze Age, from approximately 3000 to 2300 BC. During that period trading between communities became more extensive, and the Chalkidians controlled the straits. Manika was the principal Euboean repository of Cycladic artefacts, indicating close contact with the Early Bronze Age culture of the other Aegean islands (although Euboea had even closer links with the mainland). Besides streets, houses and two horseshoe-shaped granaries, which I saw, the diggers found bronze and obsidian workshops (there are masses of obsidian sites on the west coast, and quite a few elsewhere in the island too). The descendants of those early Chalkidians, however, had building of their own to get on with, and most of the largest Early Bronze Age site in Europe was slowly being covered in concrete.

A feature of Early Bronze Age cultures was an ability to deal with death, and thus the cemetery was right next to the town. (The Myceneans, in contrast, built their graveyards far away.) It was enormous, consisting of rows and rows (this is one of the earliest *organized* cemeteries to have been discovered in Greece) of large family tombs dug out of the rock. Diamantios had found markings on almost all the human bones, made of cuts and holes. Some were from snipping tendons in order to get the corpse into the burial position, but others (on the cranium, for example) must have constituted part of a burial ritual.

When this community crumbled the city-state rose elsewhere, and by Hellenistic times it found itself in an outlying district of the present town called Kamares. The acropolis, in all probability, was then on Vathrovounia hill, now owned by the army, who are reluctant to grant Greeks permission to enter, let alone foreigners. A few hundred yards away from the Hellenistic site (now covered either by buildings or by grass and huge reeds) we saw a magnificent aqueduct, almost certainly put up by the Turks, and a late Roman mosaic in a school playground. Then we went over to Nea Artaki and had dinner.

Political analysts in Athens often look to Evia as a microcosm of the country, as for years it has reflected national voting patterns almost exactly. Thus, in the recent past, it inclined to the right, until Pasok, the Socialist Party, came into its own in 1981 and held four of the six seats. That in turn began falling out of favour around 1986 or 1987, and in the 1990 general elections New Democracy, the right, won a majority, although it only had three seats: Pasok still held the other three. Again this distinguishes Evia from most of the other islands, which tend to have a more idiosyncratic political character, and is paradigmatic of the lack of a readily identifiable island culture. It has meant, though, a dramatic period of change in the political arena (which in Greece is, to a certain extent, also the social arena). The Pasok vote on the island rose from 14 per cent in 1974 to a huge 55 per cent seven years later and dropped back to 46 per cent in 1989. As the whole island is but one constituency, served by the six MPs, Chalkis is the nerve centre of all political activity pertaining to national government.

I grew to like the town in a perverse kind of way. I soon realized that although the complex of roaring streets created the illusion of a big town, it was really quite small. I could walk everywhere, to start with. After a week I had met a number of people, from the editor of the oldest local newspaper to the staff at the town hall, whom I had to bludgeon into letting me use the mayor's fax machine – I couldn't find another – to send off an overdue column to a paper. (The piece never arrived at the other end so I might as well not have bothered.)

Some afternoons I went swimming from the 'beach' on the mainland bank of the Euripus. It was really horrible, and seemed to consist of nothing but heat, but it would have been a shame not to swim. One day I went instead to get my broken tooth fixed by a dentist recommended by Diamantios. He was the man who had done the detective work on the neolithic teeth found at Manika. Perhaps teeth haven't changed so much.

My last day was a Sunday, so I went to the liturgy at the cathedral. Afterwards I looked into the adjacent church 'Spiritual Centre' where a small group of people were watching *Hawaii 5-0* on television. I had Sunday lunch *en famille* at the home of a young woman I had met at the monastery; we ate a mountain of overcooked pasta and pieces of meat as big as shoes. In the evening the town's white-suited brass band was playing on the front against a salmon-coloured sky, and all the Chalkidians strolled about in their best clothes. It felt like a nineteenth-century European spa town.

Chapter Six

The Romans and Greeks found everything human. Everything had a face, and a human voice. Men spoke, and their fountains piped an answer.

D.H. LAWRENCE, Fantasia of the Unconscious

La nature a tout fait ici pour l'homme, mais l'homme manque à l'Eubée.

JEAN ALEXANDRE BUCHON, Voyage dans l'Eubée, Les îles Ioniennes et les Cyclades en 1841

As I missed the bus I hitched up to Tharrounia, where I had arranged to join Diamantios on a dig. The trip involved doubling back on myself as far as Aliveri, and from there the road wove its way up the mountain, threading through three spindly villages before fanning out into a large *platia* at Tharrounia, a picturebook swathe of lopsided cottages draped around the curved end of a wide gully. The once 1500-strong community had thinned out dramatically. Only wizened crones, swaddled like mummies, crouched around the church in Democracy Square until late into the night.

I tracked Diamantios down to the disused school building, which he had commandeered for the sorting and labelling of the finds. After a rumbustious welcome he entrusted me to his eclectic band of archaeology students (mostly postgraduates and undergraduates from Athens University). At first they kept their distance, but they slowly came round, and after answering the same set of questions numerous times I became a member of the group, installed in one of the tumbledown rented houses they had converted into dormitories and party to their easily-revealed secrets, anxieties and opinions. I quickly adapted to their way of life, which I found very agreeable: the great thing was that due to my lack of archaeological training I wasn't expected to do any work. They were excavating in a cave, and we spent the mornings breathing its strange and clammy air. They indulged me shamelessly, calling me over to show me finds of special interest, letting me assemble pottery shards and explaining the rudiments of environmental archaeology. In the afternoons they either worked on their shards in the school or drove off in crowded convoy looking for surface finds. On these occasions I would run about with my notebook, learn to distinguish a worthless bit of rock from a prehistoric tool, steal figs and walnuts, and eventually sit under an olive tree with a book.

They worked very hard, and were often still in the schoolroom at 10 pm, but they certainly knew how to play hard, too: they partied till 5 am almost every morning. On Saturday evening I lounged on my bed while the younger women danced around the room preparing themselves for the descent to the village square. In one case this included a hair curler, which I thought excessive given the conditions we were living in (washing facilities comprised a hose in the courtyard in full view of the village). But they clearly found my indifference excessive, and kept asking me impatiently when I was going to start getting ready. My party outfit consisted of whatever I happened to be wearing at the time set off with a pair of diamanté earrings from Liberty's which I was given as a bridesmaid's present the day before my departure and which had been thrown into my bag at the last minute as an indulgence. The older students were less interested in dressing up and more keenly devoted to having a good time. Someone killed a rabbit one night and we drove to a deserted spot with a crate of beer and a cassette player, cooked the rabbit over a fire and danced around the flames to their beloved *nisiotika* (island songs). They were indefatigable. As always when people are removed from their regular environment for a short period of time, there was no shortage of more covert social activity, either, and it was always a surprise to see who was in the other beds in my room in the morning – if anyone.

The cave was in an outstretched jag of limestone in the valley. I was enchanted by it. First inhabited in the early neolithic period, around 5000 BC, a succession of later communities followed (though not continuously). The students said the spot was chosen for coolness, proximity of water and protection from attack, but I preferred to credit our troglodytic ancestors with some aesthetic sensibility too: few contemporary villas could match the ineffable view from the entrance to the cave.

They had arranged a string of electric lightbulbs powered by a generator which illuminated the stalactites as well as the area about three yards square from which they coaxed out their blackened treasures. The finds were carried outside, sieved, hauled up to the flat mountaintop where they were washed, and then taken to the school to be labelled, drawn, measured, pieced together and stored in shallow wooden crates. They included early neolithic clay figurines of goats' heads, jewellery and a mass of items made from goat bone. One of the pots was sculpted with an armless man and woman. In the evenings we looked at slides and Diamantios gave little talks. Inside his head he had been living with the early cave-dwellers for years. He spent all summer in a caravan on a deserted spot next to a settlement inhabited 7000 years ago, often alone, and he spoke of 'neolithic man' as a brother. It was very different from the

British tweed-skirt archaeology I had come across before, the exponents of which treat anyone who is not a professional archaeologist as a fifth-class citizen, get off on point-scoring and stalk around sites (which they refer to as 'my site') with utter contempt for the local inhabitants whom they instantly alienate.

One afternoon we drove northwest to a scraggy slope where we found paleolithic fragments, and on to the highest village on the island, Setta, surrounded by firs. Setta is a good example of the admirable orthographic contempt of Greek cartographers and signwriters alike. They will happily announce that you are about to enter Setta, which by the time you are about to exit from its wriggling streets has dropped a t and become Seta. Maps are the same – you might have Upper Seta next to Lower Setta. In the case of Tharrounia they are fairly consistent, however, in spelling it with one r. Unfortunately this is wrong (it comes from *tharros*, courage).

On the road to Lower Setta, after the beanfields and near the spot called Ammoudiotissa where there was once a lake, we stopped on a huge plateau full of apple and walnut trees, mountain tea, chestnuts and bushes laden with bitter little wild plums. Continuing in a circle, the road took us to Makrichori and Manikia and opened out into a dramatic wild gorge. I returned alone one day and climbed Dragounara Hill on the north side of the gorge. After a church surrounded by pieces of ancient marble columns and an old brown stone font, I reached a ruined wall of gigantic stones which was probably over 2500 years old. Continuing round, now looking across the gorge to the village of Gaia, stone steps led down to a cave filled with very still but very fresh water. I later learnt from an old woman that it was discovered by a goatherd who was grazing his flocks on the hill-side and noticed that one of the animals had a wet beard. It was decided that the pool was sacred, named the Holy Water of the Virgin (*To Agiasma tis Panagias*), and became a shrine. The locals drink the water. Most curious of all, there were articles of children's clothing tied to the tree above the cave and to the honeycombed rock: this, my informant told me, guaranteed health for the previous wearers. What it also did was prove the continuation of the primitive religious custom of making special offerings to God (or the gods) for specific things. (They do it in Turkey, too.)

Another local said that the cave used to be connected to an underground tunnel which served as an escape route from the castle above. The remains of this castle, which was probably Venetian, were about a 40-minute hike further up. There were ruins of other castles in the vicinity, but the more I tried to find out the more confused I became. One source said that La Cuppa was on the hill, one of the most important strongholds of the island during the Latin occupation. On 30 June 1470 it was betrayed during the siege of Chalkis and the 3000 Greeks who had fled there to safety were butchered. No one knows exactly where it was; its name probably had something to do with sitting in a cup (*coupa*) formed by the mountains and valleys. I was told of a legend involving the stolen daughter of an Eretrian king whom a band of loyal citizens came to retrieve. She was kept in a castle on Dragounara Hill, and the rescuers built a rope bridge across the gorge, but the abductors cut the rope, and the Eretrians fell to their death.

From this hill, the heart of the island, buried deep within it, the horizon was a continuous collar of mountain. On a small plain below the modern roofs of the prosperous Vrisi wobbled in the heat like a puddle of red water on a green field. The mythological giant dragons who have lent their name to the hill are ubiquitous on the island. (Most western cultures are replete with dragon images, not to mention China and Japan.) John Cuthbert Lawson, a turn-of-the-century scholar who travelled around Greece finding links between ancient religion and modern folklore and wrote a wonderful book about it, offers a succinct explanation of dragons as one type of the 'spirits' of place inhabiting the natural world. My favourite among many hundreds of dragon theories is Norman Douglas. The doyen of travel writers, he expands on the topic at great length in *Old Calabria*, one of the best travel books ever written. 'The dragon, I hold, is the personification of the life within the earth – of that life which, being unknown and uncontrollable, is *eo ipso* hostile to man.' It all started off, he says, with the identification of fountains or sources of water with things that see (the word derives from the ancient Greek *drakon*, looking), which in turn developed into a material existence looking upwards from the depths. This was the archetypal, primordial dragon, which evolved into the fire-breathing monster which gave St George so much trouble. In Greek iconography St George's particular dragon had been sitting next to a lake or spring preventing the water supply from getting through to the local village. Historically, the dragon is protean, but essentially a symbol of destructive natural forces, ... the vindictive enemy of man and his ordered ways.

As the sun was sinking dangerously fast I started the long trek back, stopping for water at Gremastos, where the villagers idling on the steps of the spring were mesmerized at the sight of a perambulating foreign woman. As usual my arrival prompted an excitable flurry of stories about British soldiers housed during the war and, also not unusually, they chewed over the embarrassing matter of Churchill's behaviour towards Greece in the ensuing Civil War. Fortunately they didn't seem to realize how obsessive and cack-handed it really was, and the subject was soon dropped. A spokesperson clasped my hand as I left and said 'Well, by God's grace we have a good relationship with our neighbours now, adding, in a fine display of Greek understatement, except perhaps the Turks, with whom we do not agree on all matters.

*

I made another solo trip, to Gimno, while my new friends toiled in the cave. After four miles along a rough track I met the Setta-Gimno road, with Mount Sterna to the left, quickly dropping away, and the vast Olympus to the right, lightly sprinkled with pines. Somewhere up there, in a dragon cave, they had found evidence of a small neolithic community, and once the archaeologists began prodding around the locals decided there must be loot, and ransacked the cave. They got it into their heads that gold statues had been found, and a deputation even turned up at the Archaeological Museum in Chalkis and demanded 'their' statues. The episode is entirely indicative of the attitude of many rural Greeks to archaeological digs. They can imagine no possible reason why grown people spend months working on the scrubland from which they scrape a living, save for financial gain. I was often told stories, as I asked my way to various obscure ancient sites, about hoards of gold coins that had been found there – all without a grain of truth in them. Diggers are constantly asked if they have found any money, and such is the local anxiety on missing out on a potential windfall that they begin arbitrarily digging themselves, hazarding guesses as to where and how they should go about it.

The area was bulging with history, even by Greek standards. The word Gimno – an unusual name of which there is only one other example in Greece – means Naked, which was curious as the plain was no more bereft of trees than most other areas. The village didn't exist before 1870, but the toponym did; the plain was used as pastureland by adjacent villages. A local historian, Theodoros Skouras, suggests that it was the base of the Gymnoi, the lightly-armed (hence 'naked') soldiers that Athens installed on Eretrian territory when it took the city-state in the fifth century BC. He goes on to suggest that the famous Eretrian horses were grazed there.

I sought out the Byzantine church of St George. It suddenly sprang into view in a small clearing in an olive grove, in the way those minuscule churches so often did, all warm and burnished oranges and browns. The inlaid decoration on the outside, probably thirteenth- or fourteenth-century, was the finest I had seen, although they had whitewashed the bottom three feet, just like they do the trees; they claim that it kills microbes. The village itself was a thriving community of about 1500 people. Several Byzantine churches had been built on the ruins of ancient temples (an edict of Theodosios II in AD 437 decreed that all pagan temples had to be replaced by Christian equivalents). I went hunting for some ancient tombs under one of them, but I couldn't see anything more than a few blocks jutting out of the earth. A man washing a donkey saddle showed me where they used to be; he said building work had concealed them.

To my enormous surprise a bus was due to pass bound for Setta, so I walked up to the northern outskirts of Gimno to wait for it. There I was accosted by a drunk who insisted on giving me a glass of coffee outside his resin shop. He seemed to dislike the idea of a foreigner roaming freely in his village, asked if I had a permit and tried to telephone the police. They were out. In the middle of his ramblings he would suddenly dive off at a tangent and ask me obscure but perfectly reasonable questions, like why are all the countries of the world of the feminine gender, and furthermore why is Poros the only Greek island of the masculine gender? These rather foxed me, and while I was groping for an answer he would swerve back to the aggressive line of argument, which inevitably led to his opinions on Margaret Thatcher, whom he held me personally responsible for appointing. This was by now a familiar and frustrating scenario from drunks and sober people alike. The rural population were suffering from the economic policies of the new right-wing government led by Mitsotakis, which bore more than a passing resemblance to Thatcherism. During my trip the Left had put about a series of posters referring to *Mitsothatcherismos*, which did little to enhance my position as the embodiment of contemporary Britain: hardly a desirable identification.

Back at Tharrounia the parties continued. I was all right as long as they stuck to the western music, and sometimes forced myself away to sleep at three, say, rather than five. But once the guitars came out and they sank into those Greek blues I was a lost woman. With their faces long since shadowy in the gloom, their strong individual personalities thickened to a single collective yearning and the harmony of their voices floated mournfully into the night. Those songs could make you fall in love with a stone. And they never stopped; each of them knew all the words, no matter what their background. It was after such an evening that I stumbled out in a haze of empty gin and ouzo bottles to catch the 6.30 am bus down to Aliveri, weakly saluted by a few hands extended from sleeping bags.

The area immediately to the north of Chalkis turned out to be rather dull. The hillsides to the right as I left town were speckled with half-built concrete skeletons. I chose not to linger at either Nea Artaki or Psachna, both throbbing satellite towns whose once-grand balconied houses of the 1890s had been strangled in a concrete jungle vibrating with the roar now endemic in Greece of motorbikes without silencers. The modern Furies. Between the two towns the bus passed through a large gypsy settlement at Kastella. The government had built a configuration of concrete boxes to house hundreds of gypsies. The universal prejudice against gypsies is particularly noticeable in Greece, perhaps because other ethnic groups aren't present in sufficiently large numbers to make racism viable. If you're going to have a target you have to be able to see it moving.

The road to Politika, which more or less followed the coast around the bay, ended at Dafni, in the southern foothills of Kandili, and was flanked by manufacturing and processing plants positioned to send their wares off speedily and easily to Athens. I made a short detour to the isolated St John the Kalivite monastery, where a genial deacon in his late twenties opened the door. He had just arrived on Evia from Mount Athos to set about reopening the monastery, which had closed in 1988. Other monks were to follow, but at present he was alone, and seemed cheerful enough about it. There was a Sharp radio cassette player in the refectory. He showed me around the *katholikon* and told me that the monastery was founded in the eleventh century as a dependency of the Russian St Panteleimon on Mount Athos. The saint himself hailed from Constantinople and died in 450, having spent most of his life in a *kaliva* (hut), whence his epithet.

Over a glass of water and *loukoumi* we spoke of our different religions, I feebly ecumenical as always, suggesting (by that time half-heartedly) that we shared the same God, he wryly insisting that in the early centuries of the Christian Church there were no Protestants, no Catholics, no Lutheran – only Orthodox. I was finding this argument increasingly difficult to counter, as well as growing thoroughly annoyed at the constant expressions of pity for my impoverished spiritual life.

An hour or two later I took this troubling conundrum to my swim at Politika beach. The village itself was pleasant enough, full of springs, and very sleepy, but the long, thin beach a mile below was distinctly unappetizing, lined with slovenly tavernas on one side and murky water on the other. I had a cup of coffee and got the freckle treatment from the contumelious yellow-and-black-scarved owner who jabbed my arm and barked, 'What's that?'

I stayed a couple of days. The room I rented was near a well-preserved Lombard/Venetian tower, now oozing pigeon shit and serving as a prop for a neighbouring taverna's television, which always seemed to be showing pictures of a heavy snow-storm. I ate there one evening and amused myself with one of the island's weekly newspapers, the *All-Evian Footstep*. The front-page story was about a butcher from Aliveri accused of stealing 41 goats.

I suddenly felt overwhelmed with loneliness, and longed for home, wherever that was. I eyed the telephone on the counter. But I resisted. Not telephoning was a rule I had made. Instead I pulled out the piece of paper in my purse on which I'd written 20 things guaranteed to make me smile. Most were personal experiences, a few were secondhand, and they were all ridiculous really, but it always worked. Number eight was that piece of film footage when the baby elephant piddled on the floor during a live Blue Peter and the keeper fell over in it. Twelve was the recollection of an endless lunch of suckling pig and Rioja in the sunshine outside the Escorial Palace; it was years ago, but when I thought of it, it seemed like yesterday.

I took further comfort in a large tub of yoghurt and went to bed with A.N. Wilson's *Tolstoy*, observing pointlessly to myself that at least I wasn't Sofia. I woke early and found myself inexorably drawn towards yet another Byzantine monastery. The road passed a small stuffed-vineleaf factory where waving white-turbaned women were standing round a table rolling up oozing green sausages. Pallets of tins were stacked outside. Half an hour further on a gentle young nun opened the door to me at the Panagia Perivleptos (Virgin Visible from All Sides) monastery; the epithet was recorded on her picture on the iconostasis. It's amazing how many different guises the Virgin pops up in. Norman Douglas says that without losing her identity or credibility she can 'subdivide with the ease of an amoeba'. The nun (one of five) showed me the domed church, which she said was founded in the eighth century. They had incorporated an impressive Byzantine marble mosaic into a new floor.

Crossing the fertile plain back to Psachna I was beginning to wonder how far from Chalkis you have to travel before the taint of the belching urban sprawl vanishes. I took a bus deep inland, high up into the mountains, until it seemed impossible that a single particle of carbon monoxide was left on the diaphanous air. I got to Steni, the largest village in the Dirfis mountains (population about 1200), found a room and went off to explore in the direction of the skiing resort of Stropones. There used to be some kind of shrine to a famous Turkish saint right on the summit, and Muslims made pilgrimages to it. If you keep walking over the ridge you eventually reach Chiliadou. The previous year I had discovered a tiny, leatherbound notebook in the British School of Archaeology in Athens containing the unpublished journals of one W. Heurtley, recording in a spidery hand that he walked from Steni to Kimi in 1924. It took 14 hours, and he was on a 'pilgrimage' to Rupert Brooke's grave in Skiros (when he got there he didn't like it; he thought the tomb was insufficiently English for one such as Brooke). Dr Sibthorp went up Dirfis from Steni in 1787 (it was commonly called Delfis then). Like all gentlemen travellers from the exotic west in that distant time he got five-star treatment wherever he went, wielding his letter from the pasha. He sounds like a sweetie, despite his relentless pursuit of botanical and mineral specimens. 'We had observed, on leaving Steni,' he wrote in his journal, 'rocks of serpentine in beds of saline marble, forming the Verd-antique of the ancients ... the higher region of the mountain was composed of beds of argilaceous slate of various colours, upon which a primary black marble lay superincumbent.' He was much younger than he sounds, and shortly after his second trip to Evia, in 1794, he died in England of consumption resulting from a cold picked up on his beloved travels. He wasn't even 38.

Greeks make day trips to Steni to enjoy the cool air, and a handful of crones were sitting around selling them bunches of thyme, mountain tea, oregano, sage, walnuts, *yigantes* ('giants', our butter beans), *chilopittes* and *trachana*. These last two are a homemade sun-dried pasta of flour and milk, *chilopittes* in thin strips and *trachana* a crumble; Greeks believe they are especially good for children, and boil them up in the winter in water and oil. The 'village-made' variety is considered superior in quality to the mass-produced version, and probably is. The thyme-servers collaborated in furnishing me with directions to the *Paleo-panagia*, a church with some of the finest sixteenth- and seventeenth-century frescos in Evia. They were assisted by the village taxi-driver, whose broken and plastered arm was not considered an insurmountable handicap to his work. As usual it was extremely hard to find, but after a couple of hours I did find it, somewhere between Kato Steni and Loutsa. It was locked, and as it was becoming dark I saw little point in mounting a key-finding operation. The outside of the original church had been entirely altered and whitewashed and so the object of the trip was confounded. I persuaded myself rather half-heartedly that it was the journey that counted.

Back in Steni a baptism had taken place, and the extended family were celebrating in a taverna off the large square, which I was able to observe from the safe haven of my balcony. The arrival of a huge synthetic cream cake did little to deter the baby's father, his brother and his cousin from their languorous, dramatic *zembekiko*, two down on one knee clapping the third. Glasses were frequently brought to the dancers, half filled, which they would down in one with their drinking arms linked together. The proud father, indefatigable on the dance floor (which was, as so often, the narrow strip of road between taverna and tables, so the dancers risked being mown down by a passing car), would throw his glass down to smash on the side of the road, among the crockery shards from plates tossed earlier. The object of the spectacle remained swaddled in her grandmother's arms at the back of the group.

*

Returning to Psachna early one morning I toiled uphill for an hour and a half, past the ubiquitous Venetian tower and on to a fertile plain where the villagers of Triada grew potatoes, cabbages, aubergines and ochra. Triada was boringly ordinary. I was looking for the house of Nikolaos Kriezotis, the Evian hero of the War of Independence. I was anticipating a fearful let-down, but a saturnine Triadan gestured in the direction of the forlorn square and, hidden behind a strip of tall trees, an imposing though roofless edifice stood between me and the mountains. From the broad yard, shaded by palms and cypresses, I looked at the front of the symmetrical house, and the mountains and band of low forested hills behind shone through the paneless windows like those little plastic Swiss chalet toys where you look through a viewfinder. It was abandoned, with bushes growing up where furniture once stood, the perimeter wall long gone and the ironwork gates, carved with the word 'Triada', forever half-open. But the grace of the architectural style, imported from western Europe in the early nineteenth century, remained impervious to decay. The neo-Classical perfection was softened by the irregular shape of the sand-coloured stones used for the walls, and from the yard a flight of steps led to a terrace lined with a row of squat pillars in front of the door. An inscription on the marble lintel read: 'Built in 1828 by Spiros D. Kriezoto, proprietor of the village of Triada', with the emblem of a sickle, an axe and an ear of corn. Clearly there had been a large family-owned estate there. But who was Spiros?

I loved the unearthly quiet; houses overgrown with weeds are potent symbols of transience. I prodded about inside, disturbing flocks of pigeons who had left a thick coat of their droppings in every room. It appeared that everything that had been made of wood was gone. That meant fire. But the decorative friezes along the tops of the upper-floor rooms were still there, splashed with faded blue and red. Half a dozen out-buildings which the locals were using for their sheep had been carefully designed in the same style as the house. The back terrace looked out towards the huge flat-topped piles of slag from the iron-ore mines in the distance.

I wandered along to the nearest shop, bought a bottle of water and tried to get the shopkeeper talking about the house. Not a chance. 'Go down to the local council building,' she said. 'They have information and books about it there.' I was delighted: I seemed to have been spending half my time piecing together pathetic scraps of secondhand and contradictory information. When I reached the office, however, it contained eight old people waiting in line to have their blood pressure taken. They looked at me as if I were the ghost of Kriezotis himself when I enquired after information. Eventually a man did start talking. His face was like walnut bark.

'Spiros was the General's grandson; he built the house here because the family owned all this land, you understand, they were estate-owners. The village didn't really exist then. The General never lived in this village, but his son Dimitris did.'

'Where are the family now?'

'There are descendants on the female side, they live in Chalkis. The estate was broken up really, you understand?' Bells began ringing.

'When was the house burnt?'

'In 1975. It was a bit of local trouble, you understand?' Only one year after the estate riots further north; it couldn't be a coincidence. Further enquiries revealed that the collection of memorabilia which used to be displayed at Triada had been removed to a private house in Chalkis. The family must have fallen out with the new generations of Triadans who, stimulated by events elsewhere on the island, couldn't tolerate even the vaguest whiff of feudalism. The house was now owned by the village council who, as ever, had plans to fix it up.

The afternoon was half-spent, and as I had no idea where I would sleep (enquiries at Psachna having drawn a blank) I was reluctant to strike off on foot for the Byzantine church I wanted to visit. I rooted out the local taxi-driver's shop, and waited an hour for him to appear over a cold Nescafé with his family. When he showed up a terrific row ensued involving a great deal of shouting. The man asserted that my church was not accessible by road, but the family disagreed. I was sure you could at least get near it on a dirt road and was beginning to grow vexed by the timewasting when it emerged that the taxi had no numberplates and so the driver was reluctant to drive through Kathenous, a largeish village en route. Further shouting disputed alternative routes. I finally demanded that we telephone another taxi to fetch me from Psachna. At this someone whooped, 'Let's all go', and into the car we piled, mother in her pinny, grandad in vest, sweating father, child with ice-cream, mewling baby and by now reluctant traveller. We proceeded along the roughest dirt tracks, stopping at each field to enquire after the health of the cabbage-tender's relations, all against a continuous soundtrack of shouting, now of a robust good humour.

We finally reached Eria, once a monastery but now just a microscopic Byzantine church with a cylindrical dome and fine ghostly frescos. It was shaded by a huge plane tree in a walnut grove, next to the Palioura river, which was reduced to a still pool. At least the spring was still trickling. The spot had long been known for its abundant supply of water, and fed the Venetian water system in Chalkis. Only a concrete shelter for the annual liturgy spoilt the scene. Probably founded at the end of the twelfth century, the monastery ceased to function around 1840, and after that the church was neglected until 1970, when it was partially restored. Inside only four slits in the dome and the tiny door allowed any light in, so I held a candle to the frescos, and Mary's huge face shone back at me from the sanctuary.

The family were absorbed in picking, peeling, shelling and eating walnuts outside the church, and pressed a fistful of fragrant clusters into my hand when I emerged. We bumped off, and after paying the modest sum demanded I was dropped on the road to the Makrimallis monastery, where I had decided to take my chance on finding shelter for the night.

The road meandered in a wonky semi-circle through lost villages, and just before Makrimallis, a scattering of houses once colonized by refugees from Asia Minor, a track darted up to the monastery. Sister Tavitha opened the door. We sat on a bench in the courtyard and she told me she and the Abbess were the only Sisters left alive. She was 70, and the ailing Abbess was 80. They had been there for 40 years. She showed me up to a room on a terrace above the rest of the monastery, over a shining pomegranate tree, pointed to a hosepipe coiled on the rosebed and assured me that I could have a proper shower outside – there was no one for miles except her and the Abbess, and they were myopic. I needed a shower badly and relished it, until I turned around and saw a man sitting on the monastery roof directly opposite banging the top branches of a walnut tree with a stick.

All the buildings were new, although there had been a monastery on the site for centuries, and at one time it was very important and controlled a number of dependencies. Tradition had kept its early years alive in the imagination of the locals and the nuns. Sister Tavitha told me that it was founded by two shepherds known for their long hair (hence *makri mallis*, long hair) who saw a light every evening on the top of the mountain opposite their huts, at the place now marked by a tall marble cross. They went up to investigate and discovered an icon to the Virgin. It had travelled (icons often do) from the monastery at Vlachia, tucked away on the Aegean coast. They took it back to the sheepfold and hung it on a makeshift iconostasis, and in the fullness of time were moved to build a monastery on the site of their huts.

It was decided that this thaumaturgic icon was painted by St Luke. (By how many do the icons in Italy alone attributed to St Luke outnumber the 70 he is officially credited with?) It sits in the church, locked in a glass case and draped with the jewellery of pilgrims. All you can see are two faces, as the rest is covered with the ghastly silver moulding beloved of Orthodoxy, a survival of the pagan custom of wrapping sacred statues with gold or silver foil as a 'thank-offering'.

The later history of Makrimallis was wretched. It was destroyed in the Turkish Occupation, then in 1941 a fire burnt down most of its forest and almost took the lives of eight monks. In January 1944 German troops arrived in search of the Evian Resistance fighters who had taken refuge there; the Greeks escaped, but the buildings were set on fire. The archimandrite saved himself by hiding under the holy table. Five days later the whole place was dynamited. The church building wasn't entirely destroyed, according to local tradition, because the Virgin, present in the form of the icon, didn't allow the dynamite sticks inside it to go off. After liberation the monks returned and rebuilt the monastery, and in 1950 a royal decree turned it over to nuns. The church, now with two large and rather odd coloured glass arches in the walls, had acquired an impressive collection of relics, all encased in jewelled caskets exposing a few square inches of brown bone. Tavitha was now the custodian of these sacred bodily remains, and she proudly reeled off the saints' names like a mantra.

The Abbess was bedridden, so Tavitha and I ate together; it was the only time that I ever sat down to meals with nuns or monks. After saying grace she asked me to say one in English. She was in the process of making *trachana*, and a tabletopful were drying in the sun, spread out under net like blobs of marshmallow. The monastery had no electricity, and no gas fridge, and Tavitha had to look after everything, including the little flock of goats, who ran away when they saw me but trotted after her like the proverbial lambs. She cut a queer figure in habit and wellington boots. I liked her. On the little balcony next to the kitchen, overlooking the gorge, we talked in the darkness.

She had grown up in Piraeus with 13 siblings. Her father owned the local bakery. She had a happy childhood, and took her vows at 22, but her brothers had never visited her because they disapproved of her vocation, and now there were only four of the family left. She said she was afraid for the world. Later she quizzed me about the other monasteries I had visited, and was keen to know what food I had been served in each and the kind of room I had slept in. I became aware of the complexities of the island's monastic culture. Tavitha was proud that Makrimallis had the oldest Abbess, perceiving this as a considerable feat and a kind of status symbol. I heard details of who had come second in the elections for abbess in one place and why, and how Sister So-and-so had been thrown out of her previous monastery before arriving on Evia, and how the word on the cloister was that Father X was really too young to be given the abbotship of such-and-such a reopened monastery.

We went to bed at 9.30 (the merest nod was given to the usual routine of services due to the indisposition of the Abbess). The guest rooms were obviously rarely used, and the paraffin lamp I tried to read by started giving out such voluminous billows of black smoke that I feared I might burn the monastery down yet again. After struggling through a couple of chapters by torchlight I fell asleep.

In the middle of the night I was woken by Tavitha's wails. I went down. The Abbess was very sick. It was not the easiest spot to handle an emergency from. A priest was telephoned, and he arrived with a doctor, who told the Abbess she would die in a matter of days if she didn't have an operation on her stomach immediately (she had been refusing to leave the monastery). So we carried her by torchlight into the doctor's car. The next few hours passed in an endless stream of incoming and outgoing telephone calls: the word seemed to have been instantly beamed around the monastic circuit as almost every abbot and abbess on the island telephoned to enquire after developments and give Tavitha, by now very wobbly, some support. The Abbess, we heard in agonizing stages (and for every successful call you make in Evia you make three that fail to connect, get cut off in the middle or in which only one party can hear the other), had been admitted to hospital in Chalkis, but there was no anaesthetist, so she was discharged, reloaded into the car and ferried to Athens, where she was undergoing surgery.

At about 8.30 am three women from Psachna who were regular visitors arrived to sit it out with Tavitha, and this was my cue to leave. She fell on my neck after kissing me goodbye, and made me promise to come back soon. I hated to go, and walked all the way to Psachna wondering what it feels like when the person you have lived with in such isolation for so long is taken away from you. After I had got back to England Sister Tavitha wrote to tell me that the Abbess had died.

The snaking main road north soon wriggled out of the tired and grubby Artaki-Psachna plains and emerged into one of the loveliest parts of the island. It headed up between two mountain ranges separated only by a series of gorges, of which it followed the deepest. For the next 12 miles or so a handful of enticing signposts pointed into a blind wall of pine trees. Just after Agios on the left, from which it was a short climb to what might have been ancient Makistos, there was an uninspiring line of three or four buildings called Neos Pagontas. But a sign indicated that the old Pagontas village was down a dirt track.

I had taken a bus from Psachna (this being no road for walking) and the driver let me off by the turning, but only after some suspicious questions as to what could possibly interest me in that spot. The walk was a silent odyssey through pine forest vibrating with its own life, punctuated by the odd pale green clearing studded with beehives and goatherds' huts. After an hour, or maybe two, I reached Pagontas, built in a curve of the hillside like most Greek mountain villages, well protected by the forest. It was composed of the usual combination of bright whites and reds and tightly packed around a modern church.

I left the village, and just as I was beginning to wonder how far I should walk along the desolate track a beekeeper drove past. He was on his way to the Aegean coast to collect some fishing nets, so I jumped in. The first leg of the journey took us through the moonscape of the Larko iron-ore mines: besides mountainsidesful of dull slag and gaping dark brown scars on the working faces, there in that lakeless island the extraction had created a huge iridescent aquamarine expanse of water with steep green and brown banks. (The company, nationalized some years ago, was still operational, but in a perilous financial state.) Soon after we emerged on to a large plateau with a luxurious counterpane of rust-coloured ferns. Pixaria, the highest peak of the northern spur of Dirfis, was on one side, and the expanse of shimmering soft country ahead left us ill-prepared for the abrupt appearance, as we rounded a corner, of the mighty Profiria. This mountain was pale grey and almost entirely naked. To the right a perfect equilateral triangle of sapphire Aegean was poised between Profiria and Mount Tanaida. There more than anywhere else I realized how much the long Dirfis chain dominated the central eastern seaboard and had preserved the coastal villages from the incursions of industrialized Chalkis, less than 20 miles from the coast as the crow flies, but the crow might think she had flown from one end of the earth to the other once she landed and looked around.

Profiria looked like a series of triangles pointing skywards, and as we approached each triangle came into focus as a mini-peak. A handful of white dots signalled the village of Agia Sofia on the opposite mountainside. As we bumped along the beekeeper was anxious to tell me about his swarms. He had 240 two-tiered wooden hives, and that year his three harvests had yielded 5000 kilos of honey. He moved them about regularly, always at night, and travelled all over Greece: in November he was taking them off to Kalamata in the Peloponnese, where it would be warmer. His honey was pure, 'without chemicals'; the factory he sold it to in Athens made four litres out of three by watering it down with sugar syrups. Greek villagers have an acute awareness of the nasty things added to foods, but only insofar as it relates to their own pure produce. So while they will always point out the difference between their own cheese or bread or wine and shop-bought equivalents, they will happily buy a tin of Spam (Zwan in Greek) or a packet of synthetic cream cake-topping. I was only too ready to accept the beekeeper's every word on the quality of his honey, but this was not enough; he reached under the seat and produced a large tin of last week's crop, prised the lid off and thrust it at me, urging me to dip my finger in. The road was very bad, equalled in quality only by the suspension of the lorry, and my first attempt, with a speck on a fingernail, provoked hoots of indignation. As he was repeatedly taking both hands off the wheel to illustrate how I should plunge my fingers in I was obliged to do as he wanted. The road had been saving up its best ridges for that moment, and the honey splurged into my lap as I licked a finger and smiled weakly.

Agia Sofia was a poor village with houses scattered up and down the mountainside. It had shrunk, and no wonder, as the land afforded precious little cultivation. Here and there they had planted a meagre clearing or a thin terrace, but most people scraped a living from goats and sheep. Just outside the village chickens were gathered on a rocky promontory where brightly coloured pieces of material flapped in the wind to ward off preying eagles. A few miles down the valley we reached the coastal settlement of Limnionas, where urban Greeks and the odd foreigner escape the heat in July and August. The beach was long and, unusually, partially of fine sand, and at the western end the cliffs formed a configuration of caves. The sea was exquisite and almost unbelievably clear; I managed a quick swim while the beekeeper was about his business. We met up at the taverna. He was a friend of the owner, whose family were the only people who remained in Limnionas through the winter. I asked him what he did in those long months, often entirely cut off. 'I play with my wife,' he replied. Two minutes later he launched into stories about a miracle-working icon in the church at Mili, the next village round the coast. Forty years ago a plague of locusts were feasting on the Psachna plain, he said, and when the situation became really desperate a priest from Agia Sofia carried the icon down to the afflicted area and the locusts took off over the Evian Gulf.

After a plate of wild *drekla* (roughly translatable as 'assorted weeds'), the beekeeper and I set off. It took a good hour and a half to reach the main road from Limnionas. We took a different route once we had crossed the ridge and emerged on the plain. Kontodespotis was hidden behind a hill. It was one of the only mountain villages in central Evia that was growing rather than shrinking, presumably due to its proximity to the industrial development of Chalkis and the Larko mines, and the fertile soil. To the traveller, Kontodespotis' greatest asset is its name, which means Short Bishop. The beekeeper recounted a rambling story about a suitably stunted senior cleric who once stopped at the spot for refreshment. A rollicking feast ensued and the swaying bishop was persuaded to dance; the spectacle made such an impression on the locals that the name stuck.

Driving almost parallel to the long freight railway which carried the iron-ore to the road, we soon reached the main north-south artery again, about 10 miles further south than my departure from it in the morning at Pagontas. I thanked the beekeeper and hitched a lift, retracing my steps as far as Pagontas and aiming hopefully for Prokopi.

Chapter Seven

I became a person among persons, rather than a unit in a thousand teams.

ROBERT BYRON *describing his arrival in Greece in* The Station

It is one of life's small ironies that the most visited spot on one of the most beautiful islands in the world is particularly hideous. Coachloads of pilgrims regularly disgorge into the grim square at Prokopi, head past the tacky shops to the large, institutional-looking church of St John the Russian and proceed to kiss the glass case displaying his shrivelled remains. A Ukrainian nobleman born in about 1690, John was taken to Prokopi (Ürgüp in Turkish) in Cappadocia as a prisoner-of-war by the Turks. After his death his body quickly became famous for its miracle-working powers, and his remains were worshipped by the Greek community, who brought them to Evia in 1924 when they were forced to move to Greece in the population exchange following the disastrous Greek campaign in Asia Minor. They carried him on their shoulders for three days. When they arrived on Evia the body was temporarily housed in a church in Chalkis, and the congregation grew rather fond of St John and his attendant icons, to the extent that they raided the truck that took him off to Prokopi the following year. Or so Osbert Lancaster would have us believe. He tells the story of his visit to Evia in *Classical Landscape with Figures*. (He only mentions Chalkis, where he says that St Paraskevi is one of the few things in Greece that Ruskin would have liked, and Prokopi, where the view at the end of the gorge reminded him of Poussin's view of Arcady.)

It is not only St John, however, who has conferred fame upon Prokopi The village is also the centre and administrative home of the vast Noel-Baker estate, the biggest on the island and so enormous that if you stand on quite a tall hill everything you see belongs to it. The forest alone covers 10,000 acres, and it incorporates mountains, several other villages, a coastal strip, a Hellenistic site, a Venetian tower, a thousand walnut trees and a reconstructed early Victorian house, amongst many other features. (Evia is unusual in the number of its large estates which were not broken up into lots and distributed to farmers after the War of Independence.) I approached with misgivings, as for 20 years the Noel-Baker estate has been the object of the most bitter and violent dispute to take place between Greeks and resident foreigners anywhere in the country since the departure of the Turks.

The story begins in 1832, when Edward Henry Noel came out to Greece at the behest of his cousin, Lady Byron (probably to look into the circumstances of Lord Byron's death at Missolonghi eight years previously). He was accompanied by a Swiss friend from his schooldays. Somehow or other they arrived on Evia after visiting Missolonghi – perhaps they were specifically looking for estates that had to be sold off hastily by evacuating Turks as Independence percolated through to Negroponte. The Prokopi estate was then called Ahmetaga (it still is, by many people) but not after the incumbent Turk as most sources state; his name was Hadji Ismail Bey. Ahmet Aga must have been a previous owner. The Bey actually owned half of the present estate; the rest, around the village of Drazi, belonged to an

Englishman called Bracebridge. Under the Aga Prokopi consisted of about 20 hovels hidden in the trees on either side of the river. The village as it is now didn't exist until the refugees arrived a hundred years later.

Both the Bey and Bracebridge sold up to the pair of fresh young westerners. After about 30 years in Ahmetaga the Swiss partner and his family felt moved to return to Switzerland, and the Noels bought them out, raising the money by selling the rich magnesite mines on the property (though they retained the surface of the mines, and still do). Edward eventually went back to London, and his son Francis took over, followed, in 1919, by his daughter Irene, mother of another Francis, the present owner. She married Philip Baker, a Quaker and prominent politician who was a junior minister in Churchill's wartime coalition and, later, Secretary of State under Attlee. He was awarded the Nobel Peace Prize in 1959.

Their son Francis, who has run the estate since his mother's death in 1956, was also a Labour MP, from 1949 to 1968; he didn't get on with Harold Wilson, and suffered rather for living in the shadow of his distinguished father. He ended his political career on a sour note and came to live permanently in his Greek home in 1968. He also became a Conservative. There was a groundswell of feeling, locally, that the original foreign purchasers of the estate had bought it for a song, exploiting the weakness of an emergent nation. This idea found fertile soil among a people still keen to establish and assert their national identity, and was nurtured further by a certain degree of personal ill-feeling towards the present owner of the estate, not least because of what was perceived as support for the Colonels, leaders of the right-wing military junta who seized power in the 1967 coup. (Though antipathy towards the family was nothing new. In the 1850s Mr Noel wrote of a vicious attack on his property, and in 1859 the British Minister to Greece quotes the nomarch of Evia thus: 'You are credulous, to think the government will do anything for Mr Noel. What they want is not to keep but to get rid of strangers.') In addition, the local economy had been transformed by the development of the mines, and consequently the villagers (or some of them) had the confidence to rebel against what they perceived as an oppressive feudal hangover.

The movement against the Noel-Bakers, orchestrated by the Communists, escalated out of all proportion, culminating in 1974 in attacks on property, including arson and the desecration of a Noel grave, huge demonstrations in the village square with banners hung across the street saying 'We'll get you out, Englishman', intimidation of any Greeks who dared support the family, a refusal on the part of the villagers to work any of the Noel-Baker land, and, eventually, sequestration of most of the forest by the government. The court cases have dragged on literally for years. In the early days of the Socialist government in power in Greece for almost all of the eighties the British Foreign Office, through their embassy in Athens, got very near to concluding a deal with the Greek government whereby the Noel-Bakers were to keep a small portion of their land and be relieved of all or part of a huge tax bill. The family withdrew at the last minute and Pasok let it be known that they could therefore forget any kind of deal. As a result, in 1990 the Noel-Bakers still had to apply for permission to use the timber from their own forest – permission which was usually refused – and still had no real idea when, if ever, they would regain legally-recognized ownership of at least part of their vast estate. Successive land reforms had expropriated nearly all their arable land, and in 1988 locals were still lying down in front of combine-harvesters attempting to work the cornfields.

It was a traumatic period for the community, and a devastating one for the family. They had, after all, been kingpins in the area for 140 years, and had contributed a great deal to the well-being of the inhabitants, mainly under the auspices of their

North Euboean Foundation, which was registered as a charity in 1961. Its work included the provision of doctors and agricultural advisors and the construction of a health centre which was opened by the Greek King and Queen in 1962. It even sent a group of poor local children to England on a visit. These actions, of course, might well have militated against the Noel-Bakers in the end: several Athenian journalists I spoke to expounded the theory that Greeks hate charity, and that once they were in a position to do anything about it their pride couldn't accept patronage.

Francis Noel-Baker, in 1990, was working on an impressive project to turn 1500 hectares of his mountain, forest and seashore into a private nature park, properly protected and maintained. The plan was to introduce flora and fauna, beginning with wild pig and deer. The whole concept was based on the assumption that the government would buy the other two-thirds of the forest, thus partially financing the park and providing ample land where locals could shoot and cut wood so that they would leave the nature park alone. It seemed highly unlikely, however, firstly that the Greek government would ever actually pay the family anything remotely approaching the true value of the forest, or secondly that people would be happy to hunt and cut wood legally when there was a perfectly decent illegal forest to do it in next door. There were already letters in the local press claiming that the idea of a nature park 'is a new form of oppression, just under another name'. The complainants used the word 'feudarchs' to describe the Noel-Bakers and asked in high rhetoric if the park planners loved the forest more than the villagers of Prokopi and Drazi, who had watered it with their own sweat and blood. 'We do not want', they wrote, to be nannied by foreign protectors, and one day, when we have got the proprietor out, we will be capable of looking after the forest on our own.'

A complicated sequence of connections resulted in an invitation to stay on the estate as a guest of the resident potters, who ran courses in an outbuilding. The big house, where at least half of the gentlemen travellers in my carpetbag had stayed before me, was an elegant blue-shuttered creation in early Victorian style. It was almost entirely rebuilt after the war, as the occupying Italians managed to burn it down, or rather blow it up, one drunken evening when they put too much wood on an upstairs fire which roared out of control and met a pile of explosives.

One day I walked up to Drazi (now called Dafnoussa, though you'd never know it), where I first saw the mines and the destruction they have caused to an otherwise idyllic landscape. Hideous scars in the hillsides and great piles of slag obliterated chunks of the view. The overriding characteristic of the countryside remained, however, thick, lush pine forest – the very hallmark of the north (in the south they even have to buy their own resin from the mainland). Most north Evian pines are Aleppo, whence the pungent resin is collected. A professional feasibility study on the nature park project concluded that the area was rare for southern Greece in that 'many parts have not been subject to human intervention and so constitute a natural laboratory ... It is a wholly integrated natural ecosystem.' Drazi was full of huts with walls made of tightly woven branches. Just beyond it the top of the Beza tower poked out over some tall pines on a small hillock. It was once a square, three-storeyed building, built by Franks in the mid-thirteenth century (or so Buchon thought). Beyond it the road proceeded up the mountain towards the village of Troupi – and I was still well within the boundaries of the estate.

The next day I went to have a look at the gigantic plane tree on the other side of the river, long a well-loved feature in the northeast of the island. It was one of the largest and oldest trees in Greece, over 15 feet in girth at the base of the trunk and at least 2000 years old – about the same age as the famous one on Kos which Hippocrates sat under. But the now obsolete Paraskevorema mine had ruined it, and it was barely recognizable as the same tree against which black-hatted men lounged in sepia Noel-Baker photographs. The mines had deposited a viscous sludge all around it, and the roots were dead or dying. It would break Buchon's heart.

Almost all of Prokopi lies west of the main road. If you strike off east, as I did one sun-flooded morning, a smaller road plunges through dense pine slopes and meets the coast at Pili, a sprinkling of houses behind a wide bay. There was a large lump of rock around the corner, rising out of the sea, and a woman chivvying some goats along told me it was called Stone Ship.

'Once, many years ago, the village was celebrating St John's festival at that little church there. While they were dancing a goatherd boy from another village ran among them to say a boat full of pirates was coming to get them. They fell down, they were so afraid. Do you know what happened? The saint turned the ship into stone!'

She finished the story with a flourish and wished me well, muttering about the munificence of God. I had a job to understand her as she spoke with a peculiarly strong accent, and during the course of the day, as I snaked my way along the precipitous coast road southwards, I noticed that everyone did. They were isolated behind the mountains, and before the road opened the nearest shop from one village had been a seven-hour walk away. At Sarakiniko, where I ended up, all the residents still had the same surname. A hundred goats' cheeses were hanging from the rafters of the largest house there, and below them a toothless woman in her forties was dispensing frothy warm milk to her six barefoot chocolate-brown children. The little bay, accessible only on foot on hidden paths, was a base for Saracen pirates, hence the name of the village. The pirates must have thought they had found paradise, it was so beautiful there, with pale grey towering mountains behind, endless expanses of thick green pine forest and a delicate coastline curling gracefully into bays and coves disturbed only by luminous waters reflecting a strong blue sky.

On the long journey back my feet hurt and my face prickled with sunburn. A young man on a motorbike stopped after a couple of hours, as the sun was setting, and told me to jump on. His helmet was strapped onto the back – a common sight, as if the law only stipulated possession of a helmet whilst in motion without specifying its relationship to the rider's head.

I slept deeply in my cool white room and woke with the sun in my eyes. On my way to buy provisions a fisherman I had met at Pili hailed me from the window of his van and asked if I wanted a lift through the Derveni gorge. I decided it was the day for it, so I bought a kilo of oranges and got in. The man had lost a hand dynamiting fish out of the Aegean. The mysterious gorge, cut by the Kireas river, played an important role in the history of the island during the period of Lombard and Venetian rule. It was famous for its impassibility, and it remains the gateway to the wooded north. The key to a free passage, centuries back, was control of the fort less than five miles south of the Prokopi plain. This fort controlled two iron gates several yards apart across the floor of the gorge, and marked the border between the baronies of Chalkis and Orei.

The ruins weren't visible from the road, and they were fiendishly difficult to locate. One of the problems was that the fort didn't have a name as far as most of the locals were concerned. Its name used to be Klisoura, a word sometimes used for the whole sequence of dramatic gorges and a common Greek toponym. I knew vaguely where to start looking, and parted company with the fisherman opposite the tiny St George's church, whence I headed up a dirt track and after a few hundred yards came upon a charcoal-maker sitting outside his knot of tin-roofed huts. The first attempt at eliciting information was a failure.

'There is no Klisoura mountain. There's only a Klisoura spring, and that's on the other side of this one' (points vaguely south-west).

'What about the fort?'

'You can't go there' (begins digging).

'Why not?'

'You just can't' (digging increases in intensity).

When was I going to learn? You can't expect to tease out any information until your interlocutor has got the measure of you. Accordingly I sat down on a rock nearby and waited. It was an extraordinary spot, with gorges shooting off south and east, rocky escarpments, thickly wooded bottle-green slopes full of promise, a shining blue sky and silence.

After five minutes he began shouting the usual questions: where was I from, why was I alone, why did I want to see the fort, how come I could speak Greek. I answered them all, and sure enough he soon ambled over with a polystyrene flask of water, offered it to me, and sat down. He would have taken me to the fort himself, but unfortunately he had a job in Prokopi to attend to. It was really worth climbing up, and as long as I had plenty of time I would be fine, although there was no path at all, so it was rather a battle through the forest. He embarked with great enthusiasm on a story about an old woman called Menko who lived in a cave in a gorge thereabouts and betrayed the way up to the castle to the Turks, adding as proof that local children still use the word 'Menko' for anyone who cheats.

I bit my tongue waiting for the crucial piece of information.

Eventually he pointed to the nearest mountain, between the Kireas gorge and the next one westwards, directing me up a bare rocky slope. (I never successfully reconciled the position of the fort with Buchon's account of his journey.) I started up the mountain. K.A. Gounaropoulos, doyen of Evian historians, recounts the myth that it belonged to Aktis, illegitimate offspring of the sun god Helios, and so was charmingly named Bastard Mountain. There are endless myths and folk stories woven around the Evian mountains – as there are in all mountainous places, as where they dominate the landscape they tend to dominate the imagination too. The pale grey honeycombed rock was easy, if vertiginous, but the forest was troublesome. On my travels I often ended up doing exactly the opposite thing to that which I had planned, simply because an opportunity arose, and consequently I was often wearing exactly the opposite type of clothing to that which I should have been wearing. This day was a case in point: a sleeveless, thin cotton frock is not the most sensible attire for hacking through dense, prickly undergrowth. From the look of the pine trunks even the resin collectors had given up a few years previously. (Hardly surprising, as resin-collecting is gruelling work even in accessible forests.) Above the tree line I eventually found some unedifying ruined walls. Buchon thought the fort was much too large to be Venetian, as other sources claim. He thinks it was built by Franks, by which he meant Lombards, in the first half of the thirteenth century. The perimeter walls, he said, dropped right down to the bottom of the Derveni gorge and closed the road at the place called Iron Gate. Klisoura went through the usual cycle of occupancy by Lombards, Likarios and Greeks, Lombards again and then Venetians. The Turks destroyed most of it.

The panorama from the top was overwhelming. I lay on a bed of needles near the edge of the forest where the strong sunlight filtered through branches like eyelashes, and I reflected on the blood that had quite literally seeped into that earth throughout the wars and battles strewn through Evian history. During the Civil War which followed the Second World War the bodies found on Klisoura were subsequently laid out in the warehouse of another estate, further north. An old woman told me once that she found her two dead sons in there.

I usually stowed my carpetbag halfway up the mountain when I was climbing to save carrying it, and then spent hours relocating it on the way down. In this instance it was particularly vexing as it meant more scratches and pokes in the eye as I searched. At least I didn't get caught in a wolf trap like Buchon's companion and host Mr Noel.

The only interesting thing I ever read about Mantoudi, the next village if you continue along the road from Prokopi, was that in 1895 the inhabitants decided to exhume and burn one of their number who was believed to have turned into a vampire and killed various people off. They dug her up again because if you become a vampire you don't rot when you die but are reanimated. It might have been a hundred years ago, but a woman in Stira had talked to me with prolix conviction about vampires only two months previously. In contemporary folklore the incorruptibility of the dead is the most dreaded condition, as it was for the ancient Greeks. Buchon had a vampire experience not far from Mantoudi which he recounts not in his book but in the pages of the *Revue de Paris*. The Greeks always took him for a doctor when they saw his western clothes, and he was forever dishing out quinine or cream of tartar and prescribing chicken soup. On this occasion he was consulted over an exhumed body that had failed to decay after 10 years underground – clearly a sign of vampirization. He shut the worried villagers up with a story about the dead man needing a longer sleep than most and suggested a further 10 years underground.

A newspaper cutting was pinned on a noticeboard in the square in Mantoudi showing a man in black tie surrounded by a swarm of glamorous young women in silly clothes: it was (said the caption) Mr Mantoudi, who the previous week had reached the pinnacle of his profession by being crowned Mr Greece. I wandered around and was amused by the Disco Yuppy just outside the village, because it would be difficult to find an area of Europe more bereft of young upwardly-mobile professionals than there. The local economy had disintegrated, because Mantoudi lies at the heart of what was once magnesite country.

The story of the Fimisko mines is, to a certain extent, the story of modern Mantoudi, and even the story of northern Evia. It is a tragic story of incompetence, mismanagement, corruption, quick riches and sudden poverty, and the whole truth of it will probably never emerge. During my visit it even included murder in its grim catalogue. The rich seams of magnesite within the neck of the island have long been an important mineral resource in Greece. They took off as an industrial concern after the promulgation of the 1861 Mining Law. In 1897 the British Petrified Company Ltd began working on mines on the west coast belonging to the Galataki monastery, and in photographs of Limni taken in the first decade of the century you can already see the scar on the hillside where the white stone was brought by rail to the coast. At that time the firm was turning out 50–60 thousand tons of raw or calcined magnesite annually. A Greek company had been established for some years already, and specialized in fire-bricks which could withstand high temperatures. Both companies sent magnesite ore in large quantities (both crude and calcined) over to the US and Europe, where it was mainly used for lining furnaces. It also facilitated the extraction of resin during wood-pulp production and was a component in the manufacture of carbonic acid and cement. The mines were the hub around which the community revolved, like the textile mills in Lancashire once were. Small children worked all day carrying stone or chipping off defective pieces. Years later, the mines around Mantoudi and Prokopi were bought up by a Kirios Skalistiris. The operation was divided up into a group of smaller companies, each dealing with a separate area of the business, from excavating to brick-making to distribution: presumably the idea was to establish separate profit centres. At some point there was trouble over alleged financial irregularity, and the owner was accused of funnelling vast profits off to Switzerland.

Whatever it was that happened, an important fact to remember is that the mines had brought considerable employment to the area, and over a period of years there was a dramatic improvement in the standard of living of the northern islanders. They almost all had proper houses, or at least cottages, rather than huts. The mines were nationalized over 10 years ago under the name Fimisko, although everyone still calls them Skalistiris. The enterprise was profitable once. But at some point it started leaking, and then haemorrhaging money. It received injections of foreign cash, but something, somewhere, went horribly wrong. There is a very real consciousness now, and has been for years, that a great number of workers were employed at Skalistiris to sit around, sleep and read newspapers. You meet them, and they tell you that's what they did. (Not everyone, of course, had an easy time: there are men in Mantoudi with serious health problems as a result of working in the galleries.) So to a certain extent people could see it coming. But that didn't make it any easier when it came. During the course of my trip, amid yet more stories of EC grants being salted away and an employee responsible for spending them despatching his three sons to an expensive school in France, the government announced that enough really was enough. It turned out that Fimisko had actually been buying magnesite from Turkey for years and just processing it, because it was cheaper that way.

If workers get paid for doing nothing it's the fault of the employer, not the workers: to think otherwise would be a gross misunderstanding of human nature. Whether the private employer or the subsequent state employer bears the heaviest responsibility for the catastrophic mismanagement of the mines is a complex issue beyond the scope of this book. The situation became so highly politicized that you could barely believe what anyone said, least of all the protagonists or the newspapers. The Right used the situation as a stick to beat the concept of nationalization out of people's heads, and claimed that all was sweetness and light while the company was in private hands. What there can be no doubt about is that the huge number of redundancies in and after 1990 have ripped the community apart. There was an appallingly stark illustration of this during my visit when two men who had recently been made redundant from the mines spent an evening in a *kafeneio* in Kourkouli. Discussion on the subject grew heated, according to newspaper stories and eyewitness accounts; the two men were from opposing political parties, as so often in Greek disputes (it is ironic that a population with a heightened political awareness is consistently served by leaders with a heightened political incompetence). Shortly after leaving the *kafeneio* one man stabbed the other to death in the street.

A very even-handed article appeared in the local press written by a respected village priest, discussing the role of the Church in the matter of the mines. He was convinced that both private management and state were to blame for the plight of the community, and he also attacked the union members, who were, he said, never independent, but served a party line rather than the united good of the workers. Having laid into both employees and employers he ended up with an emphatic plea that if 'I' became 'we' and if party and personal interests were left behind, a solution could be found. This was faith indeed.

In order to protest about the mass redundancies and about the lack of provision for a sliding scale of redundancy payment according to years of service, the workers organized a programme of industrial action over the summer. They marched through Chalkis and picketed the town hall, strung up banners in the squares and organized meetings. Then they staged a five-day blockade of the only artery from Chalkis to the north. They cut down plane trees and laid the trunks across the road just outside Prokopi, and sat there on a rota, with a bonfire going. Several people with an eye for the main chance set up drinks stalls. The doughty wives and a few female employees sat around knitting. A curious thing was that on at least four occasions when I spoke with the miners and their families I was told that the women were doing what the British miners' wives had done during the great coal strike of 1984. The supportive role of the wives was the one aspect of the whole British dispute that had left a lasting impression on the villagers, either because of some quirk of media coverage or, more likely, because it appealed to the sacred concept of the indivisible family unit.

The blockade caused chaos, and everyone had to come and go via the Arkitsa-Aidipsos ferry. I crossed the picket-line on foot one day: I thought perhaps they wouldn't mind a foreigner doing it. They looked at me suspiciously and I smiled feebly, clutching my NUJ card in my pocket. Naturally enough, this being Greece, some people made it their business to beat the system. The commonest method was to produce a doctor's note saying you had to have an urgent operation in Chalkis. I saw one man pull this scam, and as they dragged a trunk aside to let his car through he was recognized as a Mitsotakis supporter. A great shout went up, but all they could do was hurl abuse as he sped off.

I have often wondered about this Greek compulsion to beat the system. While we all get a certain amount of pleasure from minor tax dodges, the Greek sees it as a matter of personal honour and pride to get the better of anything and everything. Perhaps it was ground into the national character during four centuries of Turkish occupation. After all, then it was one's patriotic duty to outwit the ruling class. Now it's not only the authorities that inspire the maximum range of wiles and ruses. The Irish-American author Kevin Andrews, in his sadly long-out-of-print book *Athens*, says, 'Outwitting is not only a national compulsion but a national relaxation too,' and goes on to tell the story of a parquet-floorer who bought up a job-lot of used coffins, saved them up and laid them with the result that two blocks of flats had a plague of worms.

So it was in Mantoudi that I felt the tragedy of the mining community most intensely, even though the workers came from all over the north. It was a crucible of discontent. I reflected on the irony of the mines' history. In 1902 a diplomatic and consular report was submitted to the British parliament from their legation in Athens, written by one Percy Bennett, the commercial attaché, who had assiduously toured around every mine he could find. He cited the Evian magnesite industry as among the most important, and wrote encouragingly, 'Labour is very cheap in Greece, and the peasant population intelligent, well-disposed to foreigners, and quite free from the Socialist tendencies of the age.' What a long way they had come.

The blue Fimisko buses shuttling people to and from their jobs had been a common sight all over the area for years. The funny thing was that now virtually everyone was laid off the empty buses still plied up and down. I never worked this out. I did wonder if they had forgotten to sack the drivers.

At Kirinthos I solved the mystery of Skiloyanni. People often mentioned this enigmatic and obviously reasonably large village, but I couldn't find it on any of my maps. Although each map was woefully inadequate, I generally found that if I used them all in conjunction a reasonably accurate mean emerged – but not a single one mentioned Skiloyanni. The answer, of course, was simple. It was Kirinthos. They changed its name to give it an ancient flavour in another desperate attempt at cultural recovery.

Rather a cack-handed attempt too, because old Kirinthos was not there at all but down on the coast. And everyone still called it Skiloyanni anyway.

Just outside the village I left the main road that was the guiding principle of my movement northwards and set off for the coast. I was vaguely thinking I might stay down there for a night or two. Events were to turn out rather differently.

After two or three miles I found Kria Vrisi (Cold Spring), a collection of a dozen houses surrounded by glossy, high-cropped cornfields behind a long, sandy beach. Greek refugees from Turkey were settled in the village, but it became malarial and was abandoned in the thirties. In recent years summer homes have sprouted, but at the time of my visit only two families were year-round residents. I picked my way down to the beach, where the Greeks had been careless with their rubbish. It wedged itself among the remains of an Italian artillery line in the dunes. Like many other peoples they keep their houses like new pins but have no sense of individual care for common property like the sand and sea. At one end of the beach a saltwater river washed under a rickety wooden foot-bridge, and at the other the freshwater Voudoros (the confluence of the Kireas and Nileas) flowed along the foot of a sheer-cliffed hill. From halfway up the hill I could see some of the large estate belonging to the former leader of New Democracy and long-time minister Evangelos Averof, an Epirot who played a key role in the first Karamanlis government in 1974. The estate was run by his sister, and there were stories of trouble and local opposition. The remains of the ancient city-state of Kirinthos were on the top of the hill, now overgrown and barely visible, but once important enough to rate a mention by Homer. He refers to it in the Catalogue of Ships as *ephalos*, which means 'on the sea' – perhaps not his most imaginative moment. It was founded, they say, by the mythological Cothus.

I swam in the deserted bay, but not for long: it was named

Peleki (Axe) when a number of locals were slaughtered on the beach by axe-wielding pirates, and it was easy to imagine the scene. But there were no boats on the melting horizon, just the shadowy outline of Skiathos and Skopelos. Buchon liked it there, and predicted a renaissance for Kirinthos, '... if ever there are enough people on this fertile island to exploit so much excellent land.' Well, Kirinthos was reborn, but in name only, and not on top of the hill for its beautiful and practical position, as Buchon thought. It was reinvented in the fond hope, beloved of Greek bureaucrats, that the past glories of the name alone would, by some kind of unexplained transference, absorb themselves into its modern namesake.

I found a room to rent in a holiday house, and spent the evening in the taverna behind the beach. Late into the night the farmers started telling tales of objects they had found while poking around in the ancient graves, and when there were only three of us left one man disappeared, returning 10 minutes later with a plastic bag. He unknotted it and carefully spread the contents on the table, revealing, to my amazement, two *lekythoi* (oil flasks for funerary use), in good condition and almost certainly early fourth-century. I had seen one from Eretria just like it in the Louvre.

There was nothing aesthetically startling about Kria Vrisi; the square was scruffy, and blighted by one or two hideous concrete holiday homes. And the beach was unspectacular. But I liked it, and fell in with its rhythm. I started using it as a base for expeditions. The first was to Agia Anna, elided to Ayianna, a large prosperous village to the north with a horrid beach community below called Angali. Besides the usual types of local farming, the Ayiannians used to produce natural dyes from almonds and unripe walnut rind, and the women were famous for their cultivation of a red dye from the roots of a plant (*Rocella tinctoria*). It was indelible, and in great demand domestically and abroad until it was superseded by chemical dyes.

Ayianna often crops up in the context of Evian folk customs and rural traditions. This is not entirely because its folk heritage is richer than elsewhere. The village produced the most assiduous folklorist and chronicler that Evia has ever seen. Dimitris Setta, who died in 1989, painstakingly recorded every aspect of rural life in northern Evia but especially in Ayianna; he wrote whole books on such topics as north Evian curses, for example, and riddles, and mills. You have to admire the stamina of a man who can catalogue 679 riddles.

Nonetheless Ayianna did have a particularly impressive traditional costume – or rather, it gave its name to the costume worn, with topical variations, in about 50 villages in central Evia. Some old women still wear it. The most idiosyncratic feature is the *singouni*, a sleeveless, collarless, thigh-length jacket or waistcoat worn on top of a vast quantity of other layers with an apron and belt on top. The *singouni* was first worn on the girl's wedding day, and even the poorest had 12 in her dowry. The garment has given its name to the whole costume: you still hear people say 'she's *singouna*', which means she wears traditional dress, or the opposite, 'she's *foustana*', which means she wears a regular dress. (The Greeks call this latter 'European style', which shows which part of the world they identify their heritage with.) Shoes were only worn on special occasions. The extraordinary aspect of the system was its complexity. Different styles of garment and different embroidery designs and colours were used for each stage in the woman's life. The period of marriage was the most sophisticated, requiring subtle alterations and a range of garments and accoutrements, each to be worn only at its time. Nothing was left to the imagination or to the personality or wishes of the individual – even hairstyle was dictated – and thus were the women safely ritualized. (There was a traditional male costume called the *foustanella*, a stiff white kilt worn with pompommed shoes, a short waistcoat and a loose shirt. But it was less elaborate than the female version, did not indicate at a glance if the man was single or married, and was abandoned much earlier.) There is, of course, an argument that the system facilitates individuality through non-material modes of expression. But it seems unnatural and pointless to allow individuality to manifest itself in some areas and not others.

Observed purely as a linguistic construct the costume system was impressive. Each design had a name, and so did each local variation of the thick cotton blouse: Setta recorded 37. Many were on display at the tiny folk museum at Ayianna (which the administrators, with the true zeal of the amateur, had signposted at the most peculiar spots all over the north, as if it were an international conference centre). It also housed a collection of old agricultural implements and goat bells. I learnt that there are 18 Evian words for nannie-goat, a further 14 for billy, and yet more for kid.

I spent the afternoon in the village on St Anna's day (the saint's day festival, called a *paniyiri*, is the most important date in the local calendar). The crooked streets were buzzing in preparation for the second round of festivities (celebrations begin on the eve of the saint's day) and people were emerging from yesterday's fog, all spruced up, to start again. In fighting spirit I sat down in the square for an ouzo (a foreign woman drinking alone in the sticks is a cultural anomaly of the highest order). Soon, however, the word got round that a foreigner had come to their *paniyiri*, and little glasses of ouzo started arriving with alarming regularity. When I tried to pay my bill at the end I was told that it had all been taken care of. It wasn't the first time that I had experienced this while travelling in Evia, and it was not to be the last. It never, never ceased to amaze me.

There was an abundance of local festivals, and I spent a happy week sitting outside the taverna in Kria Vrisi and visiting various local *paniyiria* with Alexandros, the farmer who owned the taverna, usually on the back of his moped. He knew a great deal about local history, which was how we got talking in the first place, and he had an easy, spontaneous manner, a quick wit and a charming smile, all of which appealed to me. On the terrace of his place there were usually half a dozen men who divided their time between the taverna and their work (but more was allotted to the former). I was ploughing through a book written in *katharevousa* (the artificially created, formal Greek) – always an unhappy experience – on the Turkish Occupation of Evia. As my dictionary was in Chalkis I used the group as a human replacement for it, and a word might lead to half an hour of discussion as each person offered his own explanation, and quarrelled with the others. It was possibly the slowest method by which anyone ever contrived to read a book, but it was enjoyable, especially when words were acted out.

There were several St Paraskevis in the area, so on the eve of the festival we headed down to Farakla, a small village in the cornfields where she had a church. We didn't arrive until midnight, by which time two eight-piece bouzouki and flute bands were vigorously outblasting each other only a few hundred yards apart. Alexandros stood around talking to people, and a great fuss was made of leading me to 'another foreigner'. My spirits fell. They used to love introducing me to anyone who was western. Firstly they assumed we were all the same and so would automatically enjoy being with our own kind, and secondly they liked to watch us interacting, like animals in a zoo. In my experience the whole performance was usually a disaster, and I would find myself wriggling out of conversations with people I would normally take some trouble to avoid. On this occasion nothing could have been further from the truth; as they took me to a wonderful Englishwoman called Tina who had married a Greek. We struck up an immediate friendship, at which point all the interest went out of the thing for the watchful facilitators of the meeting.

In the olden days each *paniyiri* had its own idiosyncrasies, but the breakdown of rural society has largely led to their disappearance in Evia, as in most of Greece. But other annual customs have survived. In several of the villages north of Ayianna they still enact the ritual of the *piperia* (pepper plant), or *perperouna*, on the first of May. A young girl or boy dresses up as a tree and a singing procession accompanies him or her from house to house. The object is to ask the tree to ask the saint to intercede with God and beg him to send rain. It must have its origins in the pagan raindance – one of many traits that linger of a religion that believed the natural world was responsive to human acts. This particular custom was known all over northern Greece, and previously among other peoples too, like the Vlachs. (John Cuthbert Lawson thinks the name didn't begin its life as 'pepper-plant' but as *perperia*, which evolved from the ancient word *periporia*, meaning 'walk'.)

The next morning we went up to another St Paraskevi, on a hill above Kria Vrisi overlooking the plain. Several families had slept out all night next to the church and a thousand-year-old oak tree (they often do so at *paniyiria*, as their pagan ancestors did when they slept in the sanctuary of a god whose healing touch they sought). When we arrived at 11 the liturgy was over and they were spread out on blankets getting stuck in to the quantities of retsina they had brought in large plastic Sprite bottles. Huge copper cauldrons were bubbling with *revithia* and *manestra* (a chickpea and pasta mixture) provided by the church, and the bouzoukis had already started up. Alexandros and I settled with a large family group from Skiloyanni, and one old man began talking about a Sarakatsani boy he had known 60 years before. I was fascinated by this elusive, aloof transhumant tribe with beguilingly mysterious origins. They fanned out all over the Balkans and are most closely associated with the Pindus and Rodopi mountains in the northern mainland; in the fifties there were about 80,000 of them. For centuries they spent half the year in their mountain pastures, which they went up to on St George's Day (23 April) and the other half in their lowland village, bringing the flocks down on St Dimitrios' Day (26 October). Their rootlessness was balanced by an elaborate ritualization of almost every aspect of their lives, from costume to moral code. The classic text on the subject in English is *Honour, Family and Patronage* by the social anthropologist John Campbell, published in 1964 and providing a fine analysis of a fascinating para-culture. (The following sentence from it, too, describing the Sarakatsani world order, had indelibly stamped itself on my memory: 'Women and goats are conceptually opposed to men and sheep.')

Evia was the only island used by Sarakatsani, except Poros, which was the furthest south they ever got (and perhaps Aegina too); I suppose you wouldn't expect a transhumant people dependent on flocks to use islands. In Evia they were, until this century, only found in the chunk of the island from the Chalkis-Kimi axis northwards about as far as Limni and Ayianna, and the cluster of villages around Skiloyanni constituted the most heavily settled Sarakatsani region on the island. The great Sarakatsani chronicler Angeliki Chadzimichali discovered many still living there as recently as the German Occupation, mainly settled and assimilated into the villages, but not exclusively by any means: some still spent the summer in the mountains and wintered either over on the mainland or in the grazing areas around villages such as Artaki, Psachna, Skiloyanni and Mantoudi. By that time they had spread as far south as Marmari. There were 50 Sarakatsani families living on Mount Kandili then too, and a middle-aged man in Limni told me that he could remember seeing them up there as a child, working as resin-gatherers encased in layers of elaborate costume. Chadzimichali has photographs taken only a few decades ago of Sarakatsani women in traditional costume sitting outside their wigwam-shaped branch-woven huts near the very spot where we were picnicking. Many of them had quite un-Greek looks, and were fair; perhaps that explains the blond heads you see now. It's a more charitable explanation than the locals leeringly offer.

The Sarakatsani were known by various names by the indigenous population, usually based on where they were perceived to have come from, and in Evia they were generally called Roum, Romii or Roumeliotes, after the Roumeli region in northern Greece. People often spoke of them to me misleadingly as Vlachs. They are settled now, mainly as farmers, with their own permanent pastureland. Their story is one of almost total assimilation.

I didn't have the opportunity to talk to the man further as his grandson, wearing a t-shirt saying 'Greeks do it better', arrived on a motorbike to take him down to the village. I never saw him again.

By this time I was milking goats and peeling potatoes with Alexandros and eating with his family. I felt at home with him: we even went shopping together. The rhythm had taken over, and I didn't mind when I fell off the back of his moped into a pile of donkey shit. We used to go to a hill on the other side of Skiloyanni where he shot birds when he was a teenager. It was up beyond the oldest church in the area, St Luke's, a barrel-vaulted building surrounded by evergreen oaks. Up behind it, in an olive grove, were the remains of a Byzantine settlement. Alexandros knew every hidden inch of the ground.

The last thing I had expected of my trip was to undertake lifelong responsibility for the spiritual welfare of an Evian child. We were all sitting round a table engaged in idle conversation in Kria Vrisi one day when Nikos the plumber from Skiloyanni asked me if I would be his baby daughter's *koumbara*. It would be difficult to overestimate the strength of the bond this role represents. As a *koumbaros* (if you are a man) or *koumbara* you baptize the child and undertake responsibility for its spiritual life; it is like being a godparent, but in practice much more meaningful. The *koumbara* and all her or his family quite simply join the child's family, and vice versa. The perceived importance of the relationship is illustrated by the traditional rule that the child is not allowed to marry its *koumbara*'s relations. (The other kind of *koumbara* is the one who marries a couple, regarded as a less crucial position than that of bringing a child out of the wilderness into the family of God.) Baptism is one of the most important *mistiria*, or seven sacraments, of the Orthodox Church.

Which was the problem. As far as Orthodox doctrine is concerned, a Christian of another Church cannot perform the role, as Orthodoxy is the one true Church and the child must be led into it by one of the faithful. I tentatively mentioned this to Nikos (who knew I was a Protestant): as I suspected he would, he dismissed my misgivings, confident that Christianity was the important thing, that we had the same God, and that it was the spirit in which baptism was undertaken that mattered. This was a touching faith, blissfully unaware of the entrenched complexities of ecclesiastical reality – if they could argue bitterly for literally centuries over one little word (the *filioque*) which the Romans wanted to insert in the creed, they were certainly going to take a dim view of an Anglican baptizing a child. Everyone urged me simply to go ahead, but I felt obliged to confront the priest with my heretical status. Because of old family connections we were inconveniently using a priest from a distant village. I caught him after a session casting out demons, and my non-confrontational approach seemed to work, much to my surprise. I had the suspicion that he was on my side. He said that it was absolutely not correct, but that he would allow me to participate in the service 'as far as I can'. In the event he let me do virtually everything. When I told my Athenian friends later they raised their collective eyebrow, and I got the vague impression that they didn't like it very much, but I was thrilled, as it felt like true rapprochement in its small way.

Kevin Andrews, travelling in Greece during the Civil War, became a *koumbaros* and wrote about it in *The Flight of Ikaros.* He was one of the first writers to deal with the reality of modern Greece, as opposed to its ancient past. I often had cause to envy Andrews and his peers their 40-year advantage, as if the true traveller had been disenfranchised in the age of mass travel, where there is, in Greece at least, a German camper van at the end of every secret path. But my *koumbara* experience was a gratifying one, as it showed, in its own way, that the western traveller can still experience some kind of meaningful journey in the much-altered country. It's in books like Andrews' that you understand most clearly that real travel is something that goes on inside your head. At one time it looked as though all modern travel books had to have a whacky hook to make them different – *Abseiling up the Amazon Blindfold: My Story* (although a remarkable Victorian called Annie Hore published *To Lake Tanganyika in a Bath Chair* in 1886) – just because the world isn't as mysterious as it was for the travellers of the thirties. The transformation of the journey into the book and the imagination brought to bear upon the material is what counts, and perhaps the best writers of all could dispense with the journey and write their travel books without leaving the study.

Alexandros was to be the child's other *koumbaros,* and he and I went to Athens for the day to fulfil our preliminary duties in buying the baptismal clothes. This was a really gruelling experience. You go into a baby shop where you buy the whole lot: frock and maybe coat, shoes, socks, cap, fancy underclothes, a bottle for the oil, soap, a sheet for the child to lie in when it emerges from the font, a satin pillow spiked with little pins which the guests wear, three candles for the edge of the font and a huge flounced *lambada* candle. After that you buy a gold cross and chain. The depressing aspect was that the vast majority of items offered were hideous, over-elaborate, frilly, synthetic, repulsive confections which were vastly overpriced and which seemed paradigmatic of the rampant, undiscriminating consumerism that is itself consuming Greece. I was perfectly happy to spend the money, but I wanted to see my goddaughter in something aesthetically pleasing, not a grotesque parody, and in particular I wanted something she could wear again, as her family was poor.

This was far more difficult than it sounds. Again and again I asked to see special winter dresses and a classic felt hat rather than a bonnet (the bonnets I was shown were indescribably appalling). Again and again I was told that I should dress my baby in ugly crap because that was the way things were done. Alexandros supported me, but in that rather passive way that men do when you take them shopping, and after half an hour he wanted to take the next thing offered and go for a cup of coffee. But I refused to succumb. In the end I found a beautiful midnight blue velvet dress trimmed with cream cotton lace. There was one final row about the socks. The salesperson tried to force me to buy frilly white ones.

'But cream-coloured cotton would go better,' I protested.

'No. For a baptism you must have frilly white nylon.'

'But there can't possibly be a rule about what kind of socks you must have.'

'You don't know, because you're foreign.'

This was a typical example of the attitude of a certain kind of Greek. Foreigners are another species. Thus one Greek person addressing a foreigner feels that he or she can speak with the authority of the entire Greek nation. The notion of identification with a group, so essential in the traditional social structure, still means that when foreigners are involved, 'the group' expands to become all Greeks. I won the day over the socks, found a cream felt hat with a small brim and a midnight blue velvet ribbon, and sank weakly into a chair as she wrapped it all up in two huge boxes. My final memory of the shop was seeing her put the baptismal soap into the box. It was a bright pink naked baby.

People like baptisms. We carried the boxes on the journey home and were constantly hailed by comments and questions about when the event was to take place and whether it was a boy or a girl. The woman next to me on the bus wanted to know all the details, and congratulated me on becoming a *koumbara*: it was 'a beautiful thing to do', she said.

The appointed day arrived, and we processed to the little church at Kria Vrisi, I holding the child, who was 13 months old and still had no name – they get called 'Baby' until they are baptized. The doors were left open to the glare of the Aegean and sunlight slanted into the little nave. First Alexandros and I renounced the works of the devil on behalf of the child, facing the priest and holding Baby. This included spitting on the floor three times and blowing into the air. Alexandros said the ancient *apetaxamen* responses, and we recited the creed together, reading from a book held up by the priest. Suddenly all those years of learning to read ancient Greek aloud were given a purpose; I never thought they would be. The priest asked us what name we were to give the child. Although it is the *koumbaros*' right to choose the name, we were constrained to agree to Stella, as they wanted her to be named after her grandmother – they almost always do. Presumably it symbolizes the regeneration of the natural world. It would be rare too not to be baptized with a saint's name: it represents the unity of the whole church, heavenly and earthly. The name is supposed to be a secret until pronounced by the *koumbaros*. There have been cases of a name being agreed in conjunction with the parents in advance, and then a *koumbaros* shouting out something totally different. The temptation to pipe up 'Clytemnestra' was overwhelming.

The priest held an icon to our faces for us to kiss, and then his hand, and we moved to a copper font shaped like a huge wine goblet in the centre of the church. The baby at this point was wearing ordinary clothes, and they were taken off while her grandmother poured two buckets of water into the font. Someone held the *lambada* up, the priest intoned and poured olive oil into the water, crossed it, took the baby and crossed her with oil – whereupon she started screaming, very loudly. The priest poured oil into my cupped hands and I spilled it over Stella's head as he tipped the rest on her body, and we rubbed her all over. Then he plunged her into the water three times, invoking one member of the Trinity for each immersion. (The time-honoured sacrament of threefold total immersion is of fundamental importance, symbolizing burial and resurrection with Christ. When people asked me how we went about the business of baptism in the west they made it clear that they thought the concept of a little cross on the brow was feeble in the extreme, but only what was to be expected of such a half-baked religion and its Laodicean followers.) Stella became quite hysterical. She looked as though she thought she was being murdered.

I was handed the baptismal sheet, and little Stella was laid on it for the Chrismation, the Orthodox equivalent of confirmation. (This means that the child is sealed with the gift of the Holy Spirit, and thereby becomes a full member of the Church, ready to receive the first Communion the following Sunday.) Various parts of the blue-faced Stella's body, including eyes, nostrils, hands and feet, were anointed with a cross by a little stick dipped in oil. Alexandros and I then marched round the font with her, led by the incense-swinging priest.

At last she was returned to her mother, who dressed her in the new clothes. The priest washed his own hands and then ours over the font with the pink infant-shaped soap, and the final part of the service involved a session in front of the iconostasis where Alexandros and I kissed the icon and the priest's hand again and he announced our names as *koumbaros* and *koumbara*. He hung the cross around the child's neck and her mother curtsied before us and kissed our hands, acknowledging our role in her daughter's life. I found this faintly embarrassing. Before we signed the register and the baptismal certificate everyone rushed up to shake our hands and greet us with the traditional wish for a long life.

We adjourned to Nikos and Maria's tiny cottage, where five people slept in the only bedroom and the toilet was outside and flushless. The evening passed in a celebratory haze of wine, music and dancing. Perhaps the oddest experience of my new role was that I was now attached forever not just to the child and her parents but to every member of the extended family. In such small communities most people seem to be related to most others, and so from then on whenever I wandered around in Kria Vrisi or Skiloyanni, and sometimes further afield, I was hailed as *koumbara* by almost everyone, including, frequently, people I had never seen before. It took a bit of getting used to.

The time came to move on, not least because I was sinking into a comfortably indolent existence which threatened to immobilize me. Early one morning I told them I'd be back soon, and put my carpetbag over my shoulder.

Chapter Eight

To the north are several good ports, and there the inhabitants live more secure than to the south.

BERNARD RANDOLPH *writing about Evia in*
The Present State of the Islands in the Archipelago, 1687

I called in to the post office at Strofilia to send a telegram to my friend Sabine Gardener, who was on Samos. We had planned to meet up on Evia, and I wrote that she could send a telegram back to Istiea in four days. She never did, which I later discovered was because my telegram had taken five days to reach her, and was carried for the last 10 miles of its journey on the back of a donkey.

I continued my trek northwards. Beyond Ayianna the road surface was excellent, for once. But I soon branched off, up a deserted road sweeping through land ravaged by the great fires of 1977. Everyone in north Evia is deeply conscious of the aesthetic loss the island regularly suffers from fire. A complimentary remark about the beauty of the landscape, even if it is not in a fire zone, will undoubtedly provoke the remark, '*mas ta ekapsan*', 'they've burnt our trees'. The local economy has been badly affected too, as resin and wood constitute an essential source of income for many mountain villages –

although that hasn't prevented large tracts of forest being deliberately destroyed. Dimitris Setta wrote in the seventies, 'The destruction of the Evian forests is indescribable,' and went on to criticize the 'technology of progress' as 'foolish and chaotic', largely blaming the mines, which, he said, have had a disastrous environmental impact on the island for well over a century. People generally think of ecological destruction such as deforestation as a crime of our own age, but in the 1850s the British Minister to Greece, the Right Honourable Sir Thomas Wyse, travelled in Evia and wrote a scathing attack on the wanton felling of pine trees in the north. It's a wonder there are any left.

An irresistible dirt track took me along to the hamlet of Strafi, tottering precariously on the mountainside and consisting of a handful of scruffy old houses and a large church. A kindfaced shepherd appeared and pointed a blunt and shrunken-nailed finger at two stones on the outside wall of the church, painted with red crosses. To the right of each cross was a kind of red asterisk in a circle. He insisted that this was hugely significant, and very old, but unfortunately we were unable to establish what the significance was. It was enough for him that it was endowed with a special meaning, as that confirmed the continuing sanctity of the church, which had existed in an unbroken line for so many generations, a cornerstone of the once-inviolate social structure. For that old man the structure hadn't been so badly skewed by its collision with the modern world that it had collapsed – but it might not have long to go. I was groping towards an understanding of what the traditional social system entailed. It subsumed the individual, because it provided everything, in terms of values and moral code. It was no wonder, therefore, that it was difficult to grasp, as a proliferation of individual choices was an essential component of my own culture – or my generation's interpretation of it.

Back on the road uphill a van passed, and it stopped for me, as they always did. The driver, who looked extraordinarily like the Dalai Lama, had been hunting birds on the coast, but was glum about his catch, blaming the drought. I didn't recognize the name of the bird in Greek, and when I asked him to describe it he plunged his hand into a canvas bag and threw two dead quails in my lap. We reached Kerasia (Cherry Tree), a mountain village, and I continued beyond it in search of the Evian petrified forest. It turned out to be something of a non-event, as extensive cultivation and removal of the petrified wood had all but obliterated the evidence, but eventually I found some granite-hard chunks of wood on a cornfield. Sections were entirely nacreous.

I turned back and walked for an hour or two along a dirt road to Amelantes, trying to follow the course of the river Nileas (the ancient Greek version transliterates as Nileus). It was named, they say, after Poseidon's son, the offspring of a brutal alliance with the mortal Tiro. He had a twin brother called Pileus who was cut into pieces and boiled. Nileus had 12 sons, and Heracles killed all of them except Nestor. In the shop at Amelantes, over fresh walnuts and honey, an animated debate took place on the ancient tradition surrounding the Nileas and the other great river of northern Evia, the Kireas. Sheep who drank from the Nileas apparently turned black, and from the Kireas white. (The identification of rivers with black or white is a familiar theme in Greek topographical mythology.) A further variation was that dough kneaded with Kireas water produced white bread, and with Nileas water, black, and another – more fantastic still – that pregnant women who drank the river water correspondingly gave birth to black or white children.

The village had shrunk to a fraction of its previous size, although an Athenian family had recently installed themselves. The decision to abandon the metropolis for a rustic backwater was the cause of some derision on the part of the two younger men in the shop. They enthusiastically showed me the ruined mosque built for a television series shot in the village a few years previously, and could still remember the names of the Athenian girls they had met when the team were on location. The older people said they felt shame that their village was failing to maintain its size and thus was losing its identity.

I was eventually accompanied to the last house through a swarm of glistening silver guinea-fowl, and put on the track for the Arapis gorge. The dirt road ran along a sheer, wide gorge, heartstoppingly close to the edge. An old man who grew up in Strafi told me later that he could remember a loaded mule plunging down when the track was only a narrow path. After some distance and one (intentional) descent to the bottom, an even rougher track ended in a clearing on the edge looking straight towards the narrow, sheer, sandy-rocked Arapis gorge. It had caves in the vertical rockfaces like holes in a Swiss cheese. In the minds of the villagers it was richly embroidered with stories. The most famous, repeated by everyone on the north coast, was that of Boulovinena. On the run from the Turks in the middle of winter, a young woman from Ayianna took refuge in a cave near the top of Arapis. It was connected to a higher cave by a hole in the roof wide enough to climb through. Boulovinena had a cat, and the pursuing Turks followed its paw tracks in the snow, and found the lower cave. They lit a fire with bales of straw to smoke her out, but she had already flung herself to her death on the rocks below from the top cave.

In less than an hour I was back on the main road. Unsure of accommodation prospects immediately to the north, as it was getting dark I made for the coast at Angali and rented a room with a couple who kept urging me to stay until the weekend so that I could meet their son, who was doing his military service near Athens. When I left the next morning the man said, 'Pity you can't stay to meet him. You've got such good child-bearing thighs.'

Once again I continued north – it was beginning to come

naturally. The hills between road and sea were striped with narrow terraces of young pines, and the deep red soil gave them a queer appearance. By mid-morning I was walking on a ledge between a precipitous cliff-face and a huge gorge. The two stubby Lefkonisia (White Islands) loomed ahead in a vast sea, and then, around a bend, Vasilikon Bay appeared, where the Persian fleet anchored before the great Artemisium sea battle of the Persian War in 480 BC, hence the name (Royal), used to describe the ships (the Persians were led by King Xerxes). The road descended rapidly in a series of excruciating hairpins and then bisected the largeish village of Vasilika. An enquiry at the *kafeneio* as to the likelihood of a bus was swiftly dealt with in the negative, but the owner's cousin was about to leave for Ellinika and told me to hop in. I knew there would be trouble as soon as I saw the fake-fur seat covers.

We turned down a dirt track before the village to its beach, Mavrika, which my new friend thought might interest me. Actually it did, but not for the reason he had in mind. The Greek fleet anchored in Ellinikon Bay while the Persians were around the corner. After three days of fighting the Greeks were forced to withdraw. Their colleagues posted at nearby Thermopylae also fared disastrously, and the result was that Xerxes won control of the whole of central Greece.

Before I had absorbed the scene he of the furry car seats had all his clothes off and was splashing around noisily in the calm sea, beckoning me in. Despite my profound irritation I thought it probably wasn't wise to strike off back to the road through 20 minutes of forest affording plenty of privacy should he pursue me. So I got my book out and sat with my back to the sea and to him. Fairly categoric body-language, you might think, but far too subtle a signal to cut any ice with my chum. Within five minutes he was sitting an inch away from me, naked, dripping and grinning. Muttering something offensively anatomical I stalked off down the track, ignoring his shouts. Now he was angry it was imperative not to disappear into the forest. There were six sheep on the pastureland ahead, so there had to be a shepherd; I found him sitting under a tree, sufficiently aged for me to feel confident that soliciting his help would not mean doubling the problem, and after taking the story in he signalled me behind his hut with his crook. I heard my assailant inquiring after my whereabouts (presumably by then with his clothes back on), of which the inscrutable shepherd claimed no knowledge, and shortly after the car passed. The old man whistled to let me know the coast was clear, and we sat talking to allow plenty of time for Lothario to lose interest and disappear. The shepherd pointed out a wooded hillock called Kastradaki between the road and the beach and said he would show me ancient remains concealed upon it. Shortly after we set off I realized the sheep were to come too, and they all did, in a long line, conspicuously uninterested in the items of archaeological worth.

Agriovotano, the next place I came to after Ellinika, was the northernmost village on the island. The name means Wild Herb. I stood on the top of the seahorse's head, looking down towards the modern Cape Artemisio, which was almost certainly the ancient Cape Artemisio too, where the famous naval battle took place. Herodotus tells the story that Themistocles, leading the Greeks, held a meeting on the beach after their defeat. The locals, quite naturally, were driving their sheep along the shore, as I had seen them do hundreds of times during the summer. Themistocles gave instructions to his men to kill as many sheep as possible to prevent the Persians. Herodotus sniffily concludes that it was the Evians' own fault because they had ignored an oblique oracle warning them to keep the animals away from the island. In 1928 the famous bronze statue of Poseidon, dating from the late fifth century BC, was dragged out of the sea there. Ardent local historians have petitioned for its removal from the National Museum in Athens and installation in an as yet non-existent museum on the north Evian coast – a kind of domestic Elgin Marbles scenario.

I hitched on to Gouves, and climbed up to the house of the poet Yeorgios Drosinis, whom my Athenian literary friends (they prefer to be called intellectuals) dismiss as 'very minor'. He was born in 1859, and cut his literary teeth on the satirical paper *Rabagas*, along with his exact contemporary Kostis Palamas, an intellectual powerhouse and one of the finest modern Greek poets. The same can't be said of Drosinis, who went in for rather limited, trite lyric poetry, though sometimes it manages to be quite elegant. The two rather nauseatingly address poems to each other as 'fellow travellers'. Drosinis wrote quite a bit of prose too, and was reasonably successful; he certainly had staying power – he was still churning it out at the time of the Second World War.

Visiting his house was more fun than reading one of his poems. A grey crumbling turreted affair with the traditional external staircase, it has kept only a little of its roof, and it presided over the village like an abandoned but dignified relic of its past, an architectural pariah next to the neat modern red-roofed boxes below. It looked like it would be a pile of rubble in a few years as far as anyone cared, but the crone next door, spitting watermelon pips into Drosinis' front garden, told me that the municipal council had been round to check it out, and they were going to fix it up in honour of their one and only famous son. I thought it was highly unlikely that they would.

My attitude towards Drosinis was transformed when I read his columns in the pages of the weekly magazine *Estia* from 1882. They are lively accounts of life in Gouves during a four-month period when he was collecting folksongs, and exude the author's personality, unappealing as it appears at times to have been. They make compulsive reading as, far from conveying the rural idyll, he displays, at least at first, utter contempt for his peasant neighbours, writing them off as 'semi-barbarians', ridiculing their naive questions and seeking solace in his only 'civilized' or 'cultured' neighbour, who was Swiss. With the customary injustice of posterity we have no record of what the villagers thought of the man in the tower. As the months go by he mellows, however, and his pronounced Romantic streak is activated by the natural beauty of the area (resulting in some awful purple passages). He even succumbs to the charms of the locals.

The village, set in three deepish valleys, was composed of 150 people, he wrote, spread between 20 families, with 500 goats and sheep, 100 hens, 50 oxen, 30 pigs, 25 horses and donkeys, 15 dogs and 10 cats. Not one of the peasants owned their own land, and they paid a third of their harvest, chiefly wheat and corn, to the landowners. Few could read, and he says that a person from Xirochori (now Istiea) up the road was their idea of humanity which had reached the acme of sophistication.

I stopped for a few days at Pefki, a typical small Greek resort. There was nothing particularly aesthetic about it, but the people were friendly, the sea was good even if the beach was crummy, and there were plenty of bars and tavernas. I walked to the end of the jetty where some Egyptians sewing up tiny holes in huge red nets called to me from under a green tarpaulin. They were hoary old salts from Cairo, smiley with flashes of gold, working as hired hands on a large Greek fishing boat moored nearby. One asked me in pidgin Greek if I would go for a walk with him later. When I declined, the other, with the true instinct of a sailor, put his hand in his pocket and offered money.

It didn't take long to explore Pefki. The village of Artemisio was just along the coast (confusingly the site neither of Cape Artemisio nor of the temple of Artemis Proseoa, but it must have acquired its name from the latter). Wandering through the lanes down to the scruffy beach I was hailed by people working in their orchards, and they gave me handfuls of green suede almonds and hard little pears. They all spoke in the pronounced 'semi-northern' dialect, swallowing certain final vowels, and it lent the language a curious staccato rhythm.

Nobody had any idea where the temple was. I found the spot where it probably had been, just outside Pefki, and the Pefkians had built a cemetery on top of it. A fuss was made over it a couple of years ago, someone told me, and *I Melina* - Melina Mercouri, the former Minister of Culture for Pasok but better known in the west for her role as the blonde prostitute with the heart of gold in *Never on Sunday*, a film directed by her husband Jules Dassin - came in person to plant a sign on the road nearby saying 'Archaeological Site'. This was rather a pointless gesture as absolutely nothing could be seen of the temple, but it seemed to make everyone feel better. The word in Pefki, however, was that there was still a pressure group to move the cemetery elsewhere, but it was being fiercely resisted. Drosinis got terribly excited in the pages of *Estia* when he discovered the temple. As far as I could make out he reached the same conclusion as me, as he says it is at a place called Agios Yeorgios (as my cemetery church was named) near the Swiss man's estate. This man, revealed as one Herr Bild, had a marble slab in his house with an inscription listing 35 citizens who contributed to the restoration of the temple of Artemis.

The fact that the temple is not particularly near what is now called Cape Artemisio is a problem, and there is always a chance that the whole edifice was somewhere else and has fallen into the sea. Jacques Cousteau appeared some years ago with a team of divers and looked for it. On the other hand the temple might not have been on the actual cape. People used to think that it was at Kastri, a little village near Gouves, on a small but sheer hill in the middle of the beach. Drosinis struggled up there, but had so much trouble with the thick undergrowth and sharp incline that he gave up, so I thought the least I could do was learn from his experience and not attempt it.

Back at Pefki a man had installed himself outside the house where I was renting a room selling Batman t-shirts with the yellow-on-black logo, only it said Patman underneath by mistake. A subconscious case of bathos, perhaps, on the part of a Greek t-shirt printer.

Istiea, situated right on the seahorse's eye, is the largest town in the north, and was an important settlement during the earliest periods of Evian civilization. Its geographical isolation from the centre of the island (the journey through the long narrow gorges is arduous even now) has lent its history a different hue, yet its strategic position overseeing a vital and exposed sea-passage prevented it from becoming a backwater. Its geography meant that it was always vulnerable – and it always will be, a fact recognized in 1938 when a defence zone was set up from Istiea to Ayianna. It was a territory to be coveted, and it was fertile. Very little is known of the origins of the settlement, but the mythological version is that Ellopas, son of Ion, the first Ionian Greek, founded the kingdom of Ellopia in the north of Evia, and its capital was Histiaea, as the ancient name is usually transliterated. (Modern Greek has lost the h-sound.) Homer says that Histiaea sent a contingent to the Trojan War, and Herodotus, much later, that the Persians did a spot of sightseeing there after the Greek withdrawal from Artemisio. The problem with the ancient history of the region is that Histiaea is frequently jumbled up with neighbouring Orei, and the exact relationship between the two is unclear. Orei was probably a satellite of Histiaea, and when Pericles destroyed the latter as punishment for its rebellion against Athens in 446 BC he expelled the Histiaeans and settled 2000 Athenians in nearby Orei. After the Peloponnesian War this Athenian settlement was probably broken up by Spartans, and the exiled Histiaeans were recalled to their former home. The city-state owned a considerable stretch of territory, and controlled the small settlements of Dion and Athenai Diades to the west for at least some of their history, and likewise Kirinthos and its fertile plain to the east. Histiaea probably joined the Euboean League at about the middle of the fourth century.

This was the beginning of the Macedonian period, and Histiaea was particularly important to the newcomers as they used it as a base for crossing to Thessaly. A battle for the city-state took place in 303 and the Macedonians took it, and most of the island with it. A century on, in about 200, the Roman fleet captured it. Philip II of Macedonia was only too aware that Rome and its allies were on the lookout for territory, and he tried to fortify the island; he succeeded in winning Histiaea back – but not for long.

The contemporary town is the capital of an eparchy, the smallest of the three on the island both in land (318 square miles) and in people (less than 24,000). Both eparchy and town have shrunk in population terms over the past few decades, not least because there has been virtually no industrial development, with the result that people have migrated towards Chalkis or the mainland in search of work. Farming remains the chief employment, and whilst it sends a good deal of produce to other parts of Greece, the eparchy has the lowest overall official income on the island – although the hidden economy is not to be underestimated, and there are certainly some rich farmers on the plain.

I left my carpetbag at a kiosk and had a look around.

Although the architectural hotchpotch of the town itself included concrete constructions bearing the unmistakeable stamp of the sixties and seventies, it had not entirely lost its character, as old buildings lurked, particularly in the web of backstreets. They were either elegant, nineteenth-century town-houses or tiny asymmetrical stone cottages with uneven brown-tiled roofs, generally very low slung but sometimes two-storey with rickety outdoor wooden staircases, painted in a variety of earthy colours. The one hotel in the town only had a handful of rooms and was full (I couldn't imagine with whom), and there was no other accommodation available. Things obviously hadn't changed much in 149 years, as Buchon couldn't find anywhere to stay in Istiea either and was on the point of sleeping rough when he was taken in by a kindly stranger. Once again I found myself walking in his footsteps. I slept on a marble floor in the studio of a local artist called Maria Doriza-Delki. The studio was a huge room filled with half-finished paintings. I dreamt in watercolour. Buchon went to a *paniyiri* and dreamt of the perfectibility of human nature.

Just off the acacia-lined Square of the Heroes I came across the HQ of the Hunting Association of Istiea. I was amazed to find the chairman working at a desk-top computer. Three assistants were processing hundreds of blue licence books for people who wanted to hunt the particularly rich local country legally. The chairman was suspiciously anxious to impress upon me that absolutely no professional hunting went on whatsoever, and that absolutely the only creature hunted was the turtle dove. The hunters give them away to friends, he said, who eat them. The story would have seemed unlikely even if I had not met two men down the coast who sold the birds on a regular and professional basis. The office doubled up as an animal museum. Besides casefuls of local specimens they had procured some from abroad, including an African mongoose with a cobra curled around its belly.

Istiea is situated on a huge plain which extends beyond it down to the sea. The area is extraordinarily fertile: Homer calls it '*polystaphylos*', land of many vines, though now the vines are lost in the mass of other cultivation. I swam near Kanatadika, a handful of crumbling old houses with low roofs separated from the water by a narrow strip of fine sand, and, behind them, a scattering of modern holiday homes. Someone had lovingly restored a fine old building among them with portholes and graceful arched windows. It used to be a salting plant for fish, and before that it may have been the pottery works for making the *kanata*, or pitchers, that gave the village its name. Around to the east a small lake had been converted into a fish farm by the local council. Before the fishermen took to dynamiting the channel, seals from the mainland opposite used to come to Kanatadika to have their babies.

One day I called upon the mayor of Istiea, whose town hall was a kind of prefab. He was a wily Pasok man with a boisterous sense of humour, and sat behind a huge desk while his bejeaned and sockless sidekicks barged in and out: there was little evidence of any real work going on, but plenty of shouting and handshaking. I had read, in Chalkis library, that a small collection of ancient finds were kept in the basement of the town hall, but when I put this idea forward there were hoots of laughter. 'They are at Orei,' shouted the mayor. 'They stole them from us. But we're going to get them back because we'll build a museum.' Much later I met an archaeologist from Leeds who had published a paper on a fifth-century BC statue bearing an epigram in the local dialect: he saw it in a shed belonging to Istiea town council, covered by half the Mayor's supply of firewood.

The last trip I made before leaving Istiea was to the village of Nea Sinasos a couple of miles northeast, where plain slopes into mountain. It was bland, modern and stultified. There was a small display of folk costumes in the school brought by refugees from the largely Orthodox Christian town of Sinasos in Cappadocia. I walked back feeling depressed.

I knew I was lonely because I listened to The Farming World on the World Service. I decided to skip off for a weekend of conviviality at Kria Vrisi. It felt like going home. I hitched down on the spur of the moment and got a lift in a vast fuel tanker whose driver insisted on taking me all the way to the village, much to everyone's amusement when I descended in the square.

If you look at a map you can see that Evia was once part of the mainland: the peninsula at the northwestern tip fits into the bay opposite like a piece in a jigsaw. I decided to go straight there rather than continue creeping along the north coast, and then to double back on myself. After a sweaty bus journey I boarded a boat under a huge overhanging eucalyptus tree and chugged across the bay to Yialtra from Loutra Aidipsou (also called Aidipsos, although strictly speaking the latter is the inland village). The spindle of land linking them was dominated by stumpy dark green mountains. The boat moored opposite a straggle of buildings and the smell of oregano grilling wafted through the air. The little resort, officially called Loutra Yialtron (Yialtra Baths) but usually lumped together with the head village of Yialtra on the hill, owes its existence to hot mineral springs which foam over the beach, a manifestation of prehistoric volcanic activity. Knots of old people were crouched in the streams on the red, mineralized rock or at the water's edge, tipping plastic cartonfuls of it over themselves. Later I swam off the beach and was washed over by foamy currents as warm as bath water.

I found a room to rent with warped green shutters, overlooking the sea; there was a television in the courtyard where all the grannies gathered for the soaps in the evening. After unpacking I walked to the main village thinking of Benjamin Powell, who came all the way from Seneca Falls, New Jersey, to Yialtra in 1899. In his unpublished papers, lodged at the American School of Classical Archaeology in Athens, he writes that he arrived in a boat, as I had, continuing, 'A new road is being made from the little port up to the village.' Above this line someone had written in pencil: '1950: still not finished.' I was longing to sneak back into the School and add my piece, but although they had failed to finish the road in half a century, 91 years had been long enough, and it rolled triumphantly on to Yialtra.

Powell's typescript, embroidered with his scribblings, is an inelegant delight which tells the reader far more about 1899 than about the ruins he pursued so ardently. The ingenuous nature of the author, too, enhances the text. Powell solemnly reports a story recounted to him by Mr Noel about a large stone with a strange hole in it. The well-known Evian dragon had attempted to cross to the mainland to kill a rival dragon. Tired from his failed exertions he sat down on the stone to rest, farted and blew a hole in it.

A crowd of people buzzed around the butcher's in the village, waiting their turn to buy wine out of a barrel; this must mean (I thought) that the wine was good, and so, a victim of the universally irresistible temptation to join a queue, I emptied my water bottle and got in line for a kilo. Yialtra is one of the wine-growing regions of Greece permitted by legislation to use its name on bottles of resinated wine – though as most of it never gets as far as a labelled bottle the privilege is largely honorary. The island as a whole has been granted the same right, and it is commonly accepted that the retsinas of central Greece and Evia are superior to all the others. The butcher's wine was scandalously cheap, and it tasted like scrumpy cider; the first few mouthfuls made me wince. But if they could drink it, so could I.

For the next three days I explored. The peninsula was almost all mountain. The main feature of the landscape in the eastern half was fire damage: three-quarters of the crops had been destroyed two months previously, and flocks had subsequently been banned to allow the new shoots time to grow. The only road – a good one – ran along the south coast, past a hill called Kastelli where there were remains of an ancient settlement which may have been Dion, a community referred to in the *Iliad*.

Idling along the deserted road, mentally turning over episodes from my past, as I often did during the months alone, I suddenly found myself in front of a surreal encampment that appeared to have no connection whatsoever with anything around it. It was a barbed wire fortress covering perhaps a hundred acres within which slender gaps between tall trees afforded glimpses of multi-storeyed concrete blocks and floodlights. I discovered that it was no more accessible down at the coast, as the section of beach attached to it was sealed off. The only human life to issue from the heavy gates while I observed them was a squadron of local cleaners, about to be bussed to their villages. It was Club Med Gregolimano. I don't know how the management picked that spot: it would be difficult to find a Greek island with less of a Club Med style than Evia.

By this time I was out of fire country, and the slopes were covered in thick pine forest. After a hot hour I reached Agios Yeorgios, a hugely long line of holiday flats and houses. There was something depressing about it: perhaps it was the rough edges of Greek families on holiday, shouting, aggressively hustling their way up the aisles in the tiny shops and conspicuously consuming at high speed. Real life began to reassert itself only a short distance inland, and a man gathering prickly shrub branches to make brushes stopped for a toothless chat.

The early nineteenth-century German traveller J.L.S. Bartholdy, generally rather sniffy, loved this area, and expounded in his book on its pleasant aspect, in particular the orderliness of the cultivation, the neatness of the houses and the methodical industriousness of the population. He made such a deal of this orderliness that it began to irritate me that the only German traveller in my band of paper companions conformed to every cultural stereotype in the book, damn him.

Up at the top of the mountain, at the modern Lichada, I saw the small, half-cultivated plain at the tip of the seahorse's snout which petered out into soggy inlets. The mainland loomed to the north and south, and what looked like the open sea stretched away to the horizon in the west; in fact it was heading for Lamia. After lunch under a mulberry tree I began walking down to the coast, and to my surprise was overtaken by a bus bound for Yialtra. It seemed a wasted opportunity not to get on it, seeing it was there. It kept stopping for the driver and conductor to pick bagfuls of almonds and pears.

One morning at half-light I joined a knot of pinched-faced workers on their way to the Aidipsos hotels and caught the first ferry over the bay. After a mouthful of coffee I took some dry sesame bread with me on a bus along the north coast. We passed through the inland Aidipsos – a village with more heart than its coastal counterpart – then hit a strip of gentle holiday-making from Agios to Neos Pirgos. The latter was founded by refugees, hence the New in the name. A million and a half Greek refugees came to the motherland in the brutal population exchange following the Greek military defeat in Asia Minor in 1922. Just before Nisiotissa, a tiny island dominated by a ruined Venetian tower, cars were disappearing to the ferry service to Glifa in Phthiotida. It was the quickest route from Evia to northern Greece. In Neos Pirgos the old fishermen still speak of a submerged mole, and the whole area was called Molos until the refugees renamed it: a rising sea level has meant that much of what was Evia is under water, and the whole of the North Evian Gulf is characterized by intensive seismicity and crustal movements. At Orei I got off the bus.

At a café table at the water's edge I had a bizarre encounter with a black South African waiting for a fisherman to arrive to ferry him over to the small island on the horizon where he lived. He was employed as a handyman by a travel company, and once the tourists left he and his wife spent the winters alone on the island. They had left their children behind with relations in Africa; he missed them, but he hoped that one day he would have saved up enough money to go home.

It was a strange story. Argironisos was a long and thin island shaped like a camel with two humps and covering 60 acres. According to mythology, or at least the local version of it, when Zeus tried to destroy the earth with a flood, Prometheus' son Deucalion and his wife Pyrrha escaped the inundation in the manner of Noah, and built the ark that saved them on Argironisos – hence its ancient name Deucalion, as it appears on a sixteenth-century British admiralty chart. A fisherman later told me that monks used to live there, and in 1882 they built the chapel that still stands, dedicated to SS Kosmas and Damianos, a pair of doctors who ministered to the poor and refused to take any money for their services. (They were victims of Diocletian's persecutions, but death didn't stop them: they healed Justinian, for example, over 200 years later.) The name Argironisos is supposed to come from the saintly doctors' epithet *anargiri* (without money), although a fisherman told me it came from the silvery colour of all the snakes. During the early part of this century a handful of families eked out a living there from olive trees and corn, eventually to leave for a more user-friendly home where at least there was enough water to go around. Enter a Greek who had somehow ended up in Mozambique, where he made a modest fortune out of beans and married a Greek-South African girl whose heart's desire was her own private Greek island. They bought Argironisos, which they used for holidays until a few years ago, when they decided they should do something with it. Reluctant to sell up, they walked into a hotel management company in Athens and asked the owners if they would like to run the island as a tourist destination.

Fortunately for Argironisos the next phase of its history was not one of nightclubs, souvenir shops and coach parties. The agents decided that its chief selling-point was that the punter could have the entire island for his or her own party, and so it is hired out by the fortnight complete with cook, housekeeper, 38-foot yacht and skipper, sailing dinghy, pedalo, windsurfer, snorkelling equipment and waterskis. While I was travelling on the north Evian coast opposite Argironisos I noticed how frequently people spoke of it, and always with great fondness, especially the older ones, who used to go over in fishing boats as children to swim. Like many landscapes of childhood it had come to symbolize a lost paradise. But they all mentioned an article about it in the newspaper *Kathimerini* which had reproduced an ad from the *New York Times* quoting the cost of a trip. The luxurious holidays sound horribly expensive when converted into soft drachmas, and the object of the piece was to point a finger at those who had and were prepared to pay that kind of money.

Orei was one of those Greek coastal villages that almost manages to be pleasant but doesn't quite make it. It was built on a grid of overwide and dusty dirt streets with self-conscious pavements and a mite too much concrete. It did have a splendid muscle-rippling marble bull on display, however, whose beauty had survived the loss of most of his extremities. It was a fourth-century BC grave monument fished up from the sea in 1965, the product of a flourishing ancient community at Orei on a hill on the eastern outskirts of the village. The acropolis there was one of two, according to Livy, which is why the name of the town is plural in Greek. The Venetians put a fortress on the hill, and in about 1415 they used Turkish slaves to build a rampart around it. Now there was a peculiar church shaped like half a cylinder below it, largely constructed of coloured glass and resembling a Victorian railway station.

The archaeological finds of Orei were kept in a tiny room in the middle of a row of shops, and considerable energy had gone into the task of ensuring that no one ever saw them. The long-windowed room was entirely curtained and there was no indication of what might be inside. The door was ajar, so I knocked and pushed it open. I glimpsed a couple of marble capitals and then a manic individual eating a peach leapt forward and hustled me outside, fretting lest I had caught sight of any Oreian relic. Once we were standing in the street he announced, clearly rattled by the near disaster, that a person could only view the dozen or so bits of stone under his protection with written permission from the Archaeological Service in Chalkis. His occupation, beyond eating peaches and shooing off the one visitor per five years who expressed any interest, remained a mystery. After I had bandied Diamantios' name around he relented to the point of allowing telephonic permission: the Service had to call him with instructions to allow me in. The prospect of such a complex manoeuvre involving the Greek telephone system defeated me. I was pleased to discover later that the room had been burgled the previous year and 20 pieces of marble stolen. Considering that it was directly underneath the Orei police station this was either quite a coup on the part of the thieves or a staggering piece of incompetence on the part of the officers on duty.

Buchon landed at Orei in his boat on the eve of his fiftieth birthday. He slept in the open, and was enchanted by the beauty of the bay when it unfolded before him at dawn. He could see Mounts Parnassus and Olympus on the horizon. A Turk called Mehemet Bey was still a landowner at Orei; he was the grandson of a former pasha of Negroponte, and used to own huge amounts of land. During the Lombard-Venetian years the port of Orei (known then as Oreos) was the chief town of the northern third of the island, dished out to the Veronese Pegoraro dei Pegorari in 1205 (although the Crusaders' Partition Treaty had specifically assigned it to Venice). The territory included some of the Sporades. It remained more Lombard than Venetian for many years. An argument over the feudal rights of the barony of Orei led to a war when the incumbent Carintana, a dalle Carceri who married William de Villehardouin, died in 1255. According to Buchon the town was attacked in 1263 by the Genoese Benoit Zaccaria, supported by troops of the Byzantine Emperor Michael VIII Paleologos. Other sources state that it was taken by the Greek fleet during the siege of Castel Rosso and Karistos in 1276. During the fourteenth century Venice was keen to acquire it from the Lombard fief-holder, and others had designs on it too: in 1351 a Genoese fleet of 62 ships laid siege to it for two months, but failed to get in. It was on an excellent trade route, and the small Jewish community maintained a lively business. It was always important to the Latins.

The plan for my day trip was to strike off into the mountains. I turned up to Taxiarchis, where the asphalt ended, and from there walked southeast through sumptuous fig orchards and clumps of pear trees. Thousands of figs were drying on black netting on the ground; those still on the tree tasted like pouches of honey. There were quince trees with fruits like furry green apples, and the odd pomegranate, interspersed with smoking mounds of charcoal made from solid igloos of branches covered with hay and soil. The whiff pursued me through the fig trees. Shortly I reached the chestnut-wooded Kastaniotissa, a mountain village with a white concrete square the size of a football pitch and a history blighted by the gruesome Leeves affair.

The Rev. and Mrs Leeves, retired British Bible Society missionaries, had settled on the Kastaniotissa estate in the mid-nineteenth century. They owned the whole village, and several other villages too. Philanthropic by disposition, they befriended a local priest's son and offered him their patronage. Before it could be put into effect he murdered them in their beds, apparently out of terrified desperation when a robbery was bungled. The incident took place soon after a vicious attack on the Noel estate, and the Greek government panicked, fearing that the western powers would get difficult. But once the guilty party was himself killed the affair seems to have faded from public consciousness.

I climbed to Yaltsades, where everyone was asleep, decided to take the low road and hitched a lift with a passing gravel lorry. The hill behind us was black from a fire two weeks before, except for the first pale grey streaks of erosion. 'You'd better take a good look at that forest where you're going,' said the truck driver bleakly. 'It might not be there next year.' There is a shocking lack of preventative measures against fire in Greece. Prime ministers appear on television holding forth about how serious the matter is, but the few fire breaks that have been cleared in the forest are generally not maintained, so within a year they are overgrown and not fire breaks at all. The Forestry Service claims a lack of money, just as everyone else does. Of course there is little anyone can do to prevent arson, which seems to be perpetrated by woodcutters, who can sell half-burnt trees, and by people who wish to build on the land but are forbidden by laws protecting the forest. These laws apply even to privately owned land, so it is conceivable that someone might burn down their own forest.

From Voutas I climbed to the ridge between the Telethrio and Xiro ranges. It plunged down to a deep valley, and the simmering pine forests were mottled with planes, oaks and chestnuts. The luxuriant covering softened the appearance of the mountains, and I thought how extraordinarily different it was from the savage nudity of the south less than a hundred miles away. Later, off to the east, the tiny village of Kokkinomilia hung like a fragile decoration on a huge Christmas tree. Suddenly asphalt appeared on the road, and an hour later a car passed, and the driver took me the last seven miles down to the wide coast road. The mountains ended abruptly and a flat olive-thick plain extended to the sea, scarred by the dried-up course of the river. I had a series of lifts along the glorious Rovies-Ilia route. The road rose high above Monastery Bay, until it was near the clifftops, and ahead I could see only jagged rocks jutting into the air and the sun setting behind them.

The trip – a 55-mile circular tour – ended in a boat from Loutra Aidipsou, and I decided that I couldn't postpone a proper sojourn in the spa town any longer. I wasn't fully aware of why I'd been postponing it, except I didn't like the look of it very much.

Two days later I liked it even less. It was packed with elderly Greeks seeking comfort in the thermal springs; they bathed once a day and spent most of the rest of the time eating. Everywhere I went men in vests and women in towelling robes were chomping their way through cheese pies, *loukoumades* (sweet, deep fried dough balls), ice-cream and *souvlakia*. Avenues of eucalyptus trees (introduced in Greece early in the century to drain swampy land, though Norman Douglas claims that they actually foster malaria) did little to mitigate the overbearing claustrophobia. Loutra Aidipsou is the largest spa town in Greece, and the springs themselves – over 60 of them – bubble up in the most unlikely places (rising from over 7000 feet), turning the surface of the rocks red with alkaline deposits. In one place the rock formation was shaped like a jacuzzi, and I sat in it surrounded by swirling warm water with a faint sulphurous smell.

The spa was very popular in ancient times: at one stage it was known as the Baths of Heracles, as the story goes that he used to go there to recuperate when he was injured. The Romans were particularly keen on it, and General Sulla went for his gout in the first century BC. It was a fertile cultural centre too, and people used to engage in literature and philosophy discussions after 'taking the waters'. (How times change.) Under Byzantium it declined, and there was even religious opposition to the use of the waters. The Lombards and Venetians called it Lipso or Lepso, and had to rebuild it completely after a Turkish raid in 1415: Lichada across the bay suffered the same fate, and they fortified both in a last-ditch attempt to save themselves. When the Turks were duly installed they weren't particularly interested in the spa, the fortunes of which again waned until the Kingdom of Greece was formed. At that time the waters were claimed to have healing properties for just about every medical condition anyone had ever heard of, and by the 1890s Murray's *Handbook* was even saying they were good for gunshot wounds. Now they seem to attract only those trying to fend off impending death, the indigenous equivalent of what Lawrence Durrell wrote of the Dome Hotel in Kyrenia, Cyprus, in *Bitter Lemons*: 'It was as if every forgotten Victorian *pension* between Folkestone and Scarborough had sent a representative to attend a world conference on longevity.'

One woman I passed was listening to a church service on a radio perched on the bonnet of a car. She used her crutches to stand up at the appropriate moments. It struck me as a tragic image of dogged desperation – but perhaps it was really one of hope.

Among a hundred or so cheap boarding houses there were a handful of old hotels, redolent of past grandeur, all flaky pastel paint, chandeliers and heavy gilt-framed portraits. If you wanted to spend an illicit romantic weekend on Evia, the Heraklion would be your venue, although you would be obliged to spend all your time in the bedroom, as once you descended the sweeping marble staircases it would be difficult to avoid the tawdry souvenir shops and confectioners' palaces.

The *Panayias* (Feast of the Virgin), commemorating the day she 'fell asleep', is celebrated all over Greece, and on Evia at least the fifteenth of August is the equivalent of a bank holiday. (The bodily assumption of Mary constitutes a very important part of Orthodox theology. Typically, however, immediately after the Pope declared it to be part of Roman Catholic dogma in 1950, a reactionary Orthodox fringe group announced that they didn't believe it after all.) Three villages near Kimi are famous on the island for their *Panayias* festivals, and as the day approached I decided to break off my journey and return to the centre of the east coast.

Many of the churches around Kimi used to mark the occasion: there were charming dog-eared photographs in the folk museum of crowds of people staring beadily at the camera around steaming cauldrons. Only Ano Potamia, Kalimeriani and Oxilithos still keep up the tradition, but they do so in grand competitive style. When I had indicated in Ano Potamia earlier in the summer that I might return for the *Panayias* I was informed by more than one person that it was imperative I was at their festival rather than either of the others 'because we don't have bones in our stew'. That year the fifteenth fell on a Wednesday, and this, with Friday, is traditionally a meatless day, so the bishop doesn't allow the *paniyiri* to take place. The villagers select instead either the next day or the following Saturday. Only Oxilithos scheduled the event for the Thursday, the day that suited my programme, so the decision was made for me. Nikos, my friend the Village Chairman at Ano Potamia, put on a brave face at this blatant slighting of his invitation, mentioning again several times the boneless advantages he offered in a tone of voice suggesting that I might regret it.

I rented a room in the village the night before and turned up at 9.00 am on the day at the Byzantine church of the Dormition of the Virgin. More than 130 *kazania* (copper cauldrons) were already bubbling with *stifado* (beef and onion stew) over logs in special stone compartments. A throng of about 50 sweaty cooks wearing white hats and aprons were assiduously stirring with huge wooden ladles a yard long; they had been at it since 6.00 am. If you consider that each *kazani*, two feet in diameter and over a foot deep, was half full, it was a staggering amount of food. Even though some people brought pots in which to take food home, the fact that all the stew disappeared was something akin to the miracle of the loaves and fishes in reverse.

Behind the church concrete tables and benches stretched up the hill, and families began to settle themselves around them. After numerous false starts when each table I sat at was claimed by the aggressive representative of a family who had 'booked' it, I was herded towards the table reserved for *xeni*, the ubiquitous word translated as foreigner but more accurately meaning 'not one of us': a powerful concept in Greece. I had made friends with an 86-year-old man with a scarred face who was blatantly ostracized by his fellow villagers (I wondered why) and we joined up with an eclectic bunch of Greek spare parts at the outcast table.

After the liturgy a raggle-taggle group of embroidered-robed boys in flip-flops processed in a large circle from the church carrying the icon and banners, and the Bishop read from the gospels on a podium near the cauldrons, requesting no smoking while he did so. People completely ignored him. When the time came for the food to be dispensed there was a cacophonous scrum as doughty villagers shoved forward with their dishes. (Shouting and squabbling are almost part of the tradition at *paniyiria.*) After an hour the cauldrons were carried around and plates were produced for the uninitiated (like me) who hadn't brought their own. Hatted individuals dispensed wine from plastic tanks, and boxes were circulated for financial donations. The *stifado* was unimaginably delicious, bones and all: I simply can't imagine how mass catering on such a grand scale can produce such good food.

Barba Thanasis, my 86-year-old friend, produced a series of empty bottles to be filled with wine. He was miffed because the *stifado* was finished, and in revenge began picking bunches of grapes from the trellises above the tables, for which he was vigorously upbraided. Everyone was disagreeable, and there was practically no exchanging of greetings between tables. At four in the afternoon they all drifted off – no one had danced, despite the loud-speakered music. Oxilithos is a prosperous village, and obviously its residents no longer feel the need to engage in the community spirit of the *paniyiri.* In the old days their life was hard, and people were determined to enjoy themselves if they had the opportunity to spend the whole day without working; festivals would continue until midnight at least, and in some villages they went on for three days. Now people have other concerns, leisure is cheap, the role of the community is accorded no value and the *paniyiri* is simply less important. The clash of the traditional and coherent with the urban and fragmented is an old story – social anthropologists have been writing about its effects in the Mediterranean for years. But in regions relatively unpursued by modernity, like much of Evia, the phenomenon is still working its painful course. It takes a long time. Juliet du Boulay published a brilliant study of a north Evian community almost 20 years ago, called *Portrait of a Greek Mountain Village.* She wrote that the villagers were materially far better off than they used to be, but if poverty can be judged by the discrepancy between what people have and what they want, they are poorer than they have ever been.

Barba Thanasis invited me back to his home. It was a single room in an old cottage, without water or electricity, and he cooked his food in a dented iron kettle on a tripod in a fireplace. Besides a narrow bed, a rickety wooden table, a chair and a stool, the room was full of piles of what appeared to be junk but presumably were his life's possessions. We drank wine and I asked about the yellowed framed photo on the wall of a young woman. He began to cry, and told me it was his wife, whom the Germans had killed in the courtyard outside. It depressed me profoundly to leave as he asked me over and over to stay longer, and tried to elicit a promise that I would come back the next day. He never even asked my name.

On the bus back up north I was joined by a German man in bermuda shorts. He was about 50, an ex-headmaster and now Director of Education of some vast tract of Germany, and he was holidaying alone. He was a classicist, spoke English in that sing-song way Germans do, and clutched at the straps of his bag as he reeled off his itinerary. He exuded a kind of desperation, and sure enough when we both alighted at Aidipsos he continued to trail behind me even after we had said our polite goodbyes.

'I would very much like to come to the monastery with you.'

'I'm sorry, they won't let you in with shorts on. Anyway, you said you were checked into a hotel on the coast.'

'I would very much like for us to spend the evening together.'

'I'm afraid that's not possible. I hope you enjoy the rest of your holiday. Goodbye.'

'I like you very much.'

And so on. I had to threaten him with the police to shake him off.

I wanted to see the mountains, and St George's monastery

hidden within them, and to make sure I found the best views I took the long route. From almost 3000 feet the sea and cliffs looked as if they were made of the same substance but painted a different colour. After a proliferation of red-berried arbutus the landscape grew stonier, and by the time I reached Polilofo there was little cultivable land. I could see it, too, in the gaunt state of the half-ruined village, whose inhabitants looked worn out with years of struggle with the earth. But they did have water, as a fecundity of plane and walnut trees around the village testified.

Several miles further on, red and white monastic buildings appeared, nestling near the top of a gorge. I was soon installed in a guest room overlooking the cramped courtyard, and idled away the afternoon talking to Sister Magdalini as she darned a huge pile of thick black stockings. In the evening there was a fierce storm, and the swirls of thick mist that hung on the mountaintop descended to absorb almost all the valley. The nuns celebrated the last service of the day up in a cell they had half-converted into a makeshift chapel, and a 16-year-old novice came running down to fetch me. It was a tiny room with a bed in one corner and a huge crucifix on a wall, illuminated by a single candle. Indistinct black shapes crouched on the floor. The thin pane of glass rattled, and the lashing rains competed with the Sisters' incantations.

Olives for breakfast again. By now I was an old hand at monastic fare, which was good, and always plentiful. There was never any meat, but occasionally fish, and a variety of lentils, chickpeas, home-made *chilopitta* noodles and other soupy concoctions, and sometimes boiled greens. I was usually given a tomato salad, and always fruit. The yoghurt bore little relation to what Marks & Spencer fondly label 'Greek-style yoghurt': it was sharp and solid with a strong tang of goat and a pungent fragrance. Homemade cheese and rock-hard bread made daily appearances, and if I left a piece of the latter it might reappear at each meal for a week until I ate it.

I fossicked around in the barrel-vaulted catacombs. They were probably originally used as storerooms, and still were: 10 porcelain toilet bowls stood in a line, awaiting installation in the unattractive accommodation block under construction. The nuns had only been there five years. The previous lot left after a long and acrimonious fight with the bishop, who had tried to make them sell some of their coastal land, allegedly to pay for the Chalkis bishopric. Things reached such a pitch that he forbade priests to liturgize at the monastery. It all became too much and the nuns took themselves off to a monastery on Spetses; a few renegades returned later, and the rest were replaced.

In 1959 a theology student discovered a handwritten document dated 1727 amongst a pile of papers near the monastic ovens. It was a description by the Abbot Ananias of the persecution of the monks by Turkish troops under the leadership of 'Ahmet Pasha Bezir'. They were accused of being '*yiatakia ton klefton*' – providing sanctuary for the klephts (the first word is from the Turkish *yatak*, a mattress or couch). The klephts were a kind of socially-integrated bandit operating in northern Greece, most conspicuously in the eighteenth and nineteenth centuries. It's not surprising that there were klephts on Evia, as they were all over the place in northern and central Greece, although they aren't normally associated with the islands – like Evia itself.

The next morning the three-month anniversary of the death of a Sister was marked by a memorial service. We ate the bowl of *kolliva* (a 'remembrance food' mixture of boiled wheat, raisins, almonds and walnuts) in the upstairs room after the service. An urgent discussion took place about the monastic walnut grove, as some trees had to be cut down, and by chance three merchants interested in walnut wood (a ferociously expensive commodity) had presented themselves the previous day. The nuns interact with the outside world far more than I had imagined, often struggling to grapple with its sordid complexities. A particularly abrasive collision ensued in the late eighties when the Socialist government introduced measures to appropriate monastic land. Important figures within the Church colluded in applying pressure on the monks and nuns, and a defence campaign circulated information among the monasteries. The situation remains unresolved.

Chapter Nine

There is perhaps no country of the same extent where nature is so varied as in the island of Euboea.

EDWARD DODWELL, A Classical and Topographical Tour Through Greece, 1819

Negrepont est une des plus belles Iles de L'Archipel: elle est abondante en toutes choses.

PAUL LUCAS, Voyage du Sieur Paul Lucas, 1714

From the road sweeping down towards Limni an apparently aleatory configuration of red roofs suddenly appears, reaching round the bay. I got off the bus, and the village felt like home after my months on the road, simply because I was familiar with it from my previous visits to the island. I was going to stay with the old friends two valleys along who had originally brought me to Evia, and it is difficult to imagine an experience anticipated with greater pleasure than being with your own people after the extended company of strangers.

The road to their valley had been ruined by a line of vast concrete blocks dumped on the shore. People told me they were for a *marina*. A ferry service used to operate between Limni and the mainland, and ever since it stopped there have been rumours about it starting up again. Limni probably sees more independent tourists than any other spot on the island (though admittedly this is still not many), and so far seems to have avoided the perils of the tour group brigades. A ferry, perhaps, would be the beginning of the end.

For the next few days I did very little – just swimming and reading, really, and of course sitting up late talking outside the little cottage hidden in the pine trees. For some reason the coast south of Limni is the only place on the Evian Gulf where the sea is as pellucid as the Aegean – and naturally the west coast has the huge advantage of sunsets over the water. On the other side the sun disappears into igneous mountains. Just at that time one day, as the colour was draining out of the sea, I met my friend Bruce Clark on the beach. He had just arrived from Moscow, and tried to give me a dog.

Zeus and Hera were married in Limni – or Elimnion, as it was called then. The ancient settlement was almost certainly destroyed in the earthquakes of 426 BC. It reappeared about 700 years later and prospered until the late ninth century, when it was probably sacked by African pirates. It was rebuilt inland, and destroyed again by Turkish troops before Chalkis fell in 1470. The coastal site was reoccupied in the sixteenth or seventeenth century, was colonized by Greeks from other islands, then in 1790 50 Limnian families left for Skiathos; they probably couldn't stand the Evian Turks any longer. Bartholdy's boat put in to Limni in 1804 after a storm. He describes it as a miserable little village, and criticizes the poor state of cultivation in the fields nearby, which he claimed was entirely due to the fact that the population was Greek not Albanian, Greeks being less capable of hard work. He quite liked the look of the women, who were sitting outside their houses engaged in sewing and other tasks, except that they were rough and dirty. I don't suppose they were wholly taken with him, either.

During the War of Independence the Turks attacked Limni again, but the inhabitants managed to sail off to Skopelos and Skiathos before they did so. They came back after about eight years, and by 1831 the population had risen to around 1000. It was soon a flourishing town, largely because it developed its sea trade, and by the middle of the nineteenth century the Limnians were known throughout the Aegean for their seamanship, and sent boats as far away as the Black Sea. In the 1880s in particular the newly created wealth manifested itself in a surge of construction, as the grand neo-Classical houses of modern Limni testify. It became one of the most important seafaring towns in the country with, at its peak, 150 wooden sailing ships. The advent of steamships was a disaster, of course, as it was for Galaxidi and the other major Greek ports, and although some of the tall sailboats struggled on till 1950, it was over, in reality, before then. The last of the great Limnian sea captains died in 1990.

I was surprised to discover a children's ballet company in Limni – not something normally associated with the Greek sticks. They performed *Orpheus in the Underworld* at the annual Limni Festival. You wouldn't see that kind of thing in the south.

One of the most important annual events in Limni was the Virgin's birthday on 8 September – the first of the 12 great feasts of the Orthodox calendar (which begins on the first of that month). It quite simply took up the whole weekend, and revolved – or it was supposed to – around an icon in the church.

The first event was a service at five in the afternoon on Friday. I sat on a bench outside the church for most of it and watched the men, awkward in their suits, escape for cigarette breaks. Two people next to me on the bench started a conversation about personal miracles they had experienced, largely in the form of visions. One saw the Virgin regularly in her dreams, and the other had seen a saint when he was a child; he was 70, but the vision was still with him.

At the end of the service the icon was rather self-consciously carried out of the church on a kind of sedan chair and borne up to the old threshing floor, preceded by gold-robed boys and followed by several hundred Limnians. After some readings the priest launched into his sermon. His theme was that the Virgin was a joy to the world, but were we a joy to each other? He suddenly quoted Sartre's 'Hell is other people'; it was unclear what the Limnians made of this existential turn. They began to shuffle from one foot to the other.

Immediately after the sermon the auction took place, whereby the priest flogged off the right to carry the icon up the hill. Everyone perked up a good deal. The idea is that the Virgin goes to spend the night with her mother, who has a church up there, as a kind of birthday treat, and because she is so excited she wants to get there quickly, so the icon becomes light and easy to carry. (It doesn't always oblige. One year a sea-captain's widow – generally the people with the cash in Limni – won the auction but tottered around under the weight of the icon until they were constrained to relieve her of it.) The priest opened the auction with a church bid of 20,000 drachmas. After a slow start it rose in chunks of five to ten thousand. Once it reached six figures the crowd on the threshing floor was taut with tension, and a murmur rippled through it with each new bid. It came to a halt at 165,000 (not a record, as one year someone paid 300,000), offered by a cosmopolitan-looking young couple who went up to undertake their task in a great fluster.

The business of auctioning off a sacred task is, of course, a curious concept, a fact which has not gone unnoticed by some of the more perceptive residents of Limni. Some refuse to have anything to do with the festival. 'I want to carry the icon,' one 23-year-old told me. 'So why shouldn't I, just because I haven't got enough money?'

Meanwhile the procession was assembling. After the short journey up to St Anna's (Mary's mother's church) the priest led a *Paraklisi* (Petition to the Mother of God). It had scarcely begun when I was spontaneously invited to dinner by a couple renowned for their parties, so, with the instinct, I hope, of the true traveller, I forswore the cultural experience for the sybaritic one. Very late in the evening I passed through the village on my way home and was surprised to see they were already hard at it, with loud music and exuberant festivities at every taverna, despite the fact that celebrations aren't supposed to begin until the birthday itself. At first I thought that like Christmas at home it was becoming increasingly difficult to dig up a grain of meaning in the celebration, but it was not so simple, and the comparison was not a good one. The meaning was as true for them as it had ever been; it was the availability of cash to celebrate it that had changed, and all the other 'true' things they now had to think about.

They made an impressively early start on Saturday nonetheless, and struggled back up to St Anna's to process slowly through the stifling church and kiss the icon, clutching their bunches of basil. Over the loudspeakers the priest interrupted his chanting three times to tell them to keep quiet. (This is such a regular feature of religious festivals that I think people would feel something was missing if they didn't get told off.) At 11 he conducted a little service outside to bless the row of bubbling cauldrons full of meat and *manestra*, dipping bunches of basil into holy water and sprinkling it on the crowd before various dignitaries came forward to kiss his hand. Meanwhile the front ranks of the crowd queuing for food were jostling for position with increasing vigour. Of all the scrums I have seen at *paniyiria*, and I have seen a few, this was beyond doubt the most spectacular, requiring three policemen to maintain order in the crucial moments leading up to the removal of the rope between the people and the food. They actually stampeded up the stretch of grass to the cauldrons as if it were a 100-metre sprint ground.

People sat around eating in the sunny glade and small boys patronized the stalls, celebrating the Virgin's birthday with the purchase of a plastic machine-gun. People drifted away, but at four in the afternoon they were back to return the icon to the lower church. The procession stopped at various points, and people whose houses were on its route lit candles outside. When they arrived the icon was held aloft for everyone to pass under and thus be blessed. Another *esperinos* service and another sermon followed, but I slunk off for a siesta.

In the evening the celebrations reached a crescendo. The owners of the packed tavernas exploited the occasion by offering bottled wine only (far higher profits); calling for another bottle, I felt, was never quite the same as calling for another kilo. Individuals or groups paid, in turn, for the privilege of dancing to the live music, so you couldn't just get up and dance when you felt like it. (I could, because a foreigner, assumed to be ignorant of all procedures in all circumstances, was exempt, but that was hardly the point.) Nothing dampened the collective enthusiasm, however, and when we left, at three, it was as if the evening had just begun.

The next day the village was infused with the familiar Sunday air of recovery, mitigated only by the preparations of the travelling bazaar which had arrived for its annual week in Limni. The stallholders claimed their usual positions on the front and in high good humour began setting out their displays. I wandered rather aimlessly in the backstreets and came across a tiny marble-strewn church in the corner of a car park. It was part of a huge early Christian basilica built on the site of Roman baths in about the fifth or sixth century. It had a brand new roof, but the floor was bare uneven rock, except for a small portion of dirty mosaic. An old woman came over to check me out. She told me that nobody wanted to live in the houses nearby because the square was inhabited by spirits, and that people living next to the steps above the church used to be woken regularly at night by the clip-clopping of St George's horse making its way down to the square. That was why the site next door was derelict, she said, which I knew wasn't true, as it was an old school which nobody knew what to do with, but it didn't lessen the validity of the story; once a place is invested with that kind of significance the fertile Greek imagination won't forget it.

Besides an odd block of modern art near the bank inscribed with a cryptic quotation from the work of the famous Communist poet Yannis Ritsos, they had put a bust of Angelis Govios with a handlebar moustache opposite the post office. He was a local freedom fighter who led the Evian forces in the infancy of the Greek revolution, when Limnians were the first on the island to fight. Govios was killed in the spring of 1822 near Politika and much lamented under his soubriquet 'the Evian eagle'. By that time there were two main revolutionary forces on Evia, one in the north with its sights set on the fortress at Chalkis and one in the east, led by Nikolaos Kriezotis, aiming at Castel Rosso. Activities dropped off in 1824, and it was at that time that many Evians went to fight on the mainland.

I washed my face in an eighteenth-century spring with a row of original rectangular washbasins. At one end of the front the slender terraced houses, each slightly different, backed on to narrow lanes of uneven whitewashed steps flanked with crooked buildings with wooden external staircases. At the north end of the seafront, beyond the last house, a candle was still burning in St Christodoulos' cave shrine. After locating the key to the heavy iron gate I climbed the few steps to the tiny, once whitewashed and now smoke-blackened cave; he must have been very short. He was born in or near Nicaea in Bithynia, Asia Minor, in the eleventh century, and began his monastic career there at a young age. After travelling to Rome and Palestine he was made abbot of a monastery near Miletus, but the Turks were persecuting Christians in Asia Minor at the time, and he had to flee, eventually settling on Kos. He didn't much care for it there (too worldly) and in 1088, as soon as he was granted a Bull by the Emperor Alexis Commenus, he took the monks from Kos to found a monastery on the then lonely Patmos (where the apostle John saw the Apocalypse). Most of the monks didn't like it and went home, but Christodoulos pressed on and built the now famous monastery of St John the Divine.

Some time later he decided he wanted to dedicate his remaining years more fully to God (an alternative version is that he squabbled with the other monks) so he came to Evia, where he lived an ascetic life in the cave until his death in 1093 or 1111, according to which source you follow. Tradition has it that as soon as he died his corpse began working miracles, but not for long in Evia, as monks from Patmos soon pitched up to take his remains back, as the saint had requested in a 'secret will'. They are preserved in his chapel in the monastery on Patmos. The Limnians are proud of Christodoulos and see him as one of their own; at the beginning of this century a Merchants' Guild built a church for him in a pine grove on a cliff above the cave. The curious thing is that if you ask them when Christodoulos lived or where he was from, they don't have a clue, but the 'theft', as they put it, of the body has bitten deep into local consciousness, so much so that if the saint or the church come up in conversation it will undoubtedly provoke the explanation '*mas to eklepsan!*' – they stole him from us.

When I took the key back the women of the neighbourhood were crowded round a leathery old man with two donkeys. He walked them two hours each day from his village, loaded down with produce to sell to the Limnians. They bullied him dreadfully, and I saw two of them pinching bunches of parsley when he wasn't looking.

*

We used to go to an isolated but very popular taverna a couple of miles along the dirt road south of Limni, and one night I went out fishing with the owner and his wife in their boat, called *Poseidon*. The nets had been laid several hours earlier, out at a depth of about 120 feet, and we chugged around traumatizing the fish by beating the water with a plunger. I sat back while David winched the nets in, twisted with 30 pounds of red mullet and a few vicious-looking scorpion fish. He also had handfuls of coral plant in the nets, a mass of friable orange lungs. Koula said that if you dry and crumble it you get the very best cure for a nosebleed: two snorts and the bleeding stops. The sea was inky glass. On one side the lights of Limni glittered enticingly, and on the other the black-ridged back of Kandili dropped down to a half-submerged snout. Back at the noisy, fluorescent taverna the fish were packed into a fridge, and new arrivals enquiring after the evening's catch were rewarded with some of the tender baby squid a bigger fish had brought into the nets.

Beyond the taverna the coast road deteriorated, and after several miles it ended at the Galataki monastery, on or near the site of the ancient settlement of Aeges (though Pausanias confidently places Aeges in the Peloponnese, and at least one modern archaeologist claims that Aeges was only Mount Kandili and not a settlement at all). Homer tells how Poseidon had a golden palace under the sea at Aeges, and he picked up his chariot there in order to go over and help the Greeks in the Trojan War. He was in Samothrace when he saw that they were in trouble, and came to Aeges by taking four giant strides across the sea.

Galataki, tucked in at the foot of Kandili, is the oldest working monastery in Evia. I went to stay with the nuns for a week, sleeping in a little room directly opposite the polygonal-domed *katholikon*, and chants drifted in through the open window against the constant tinkle of a lion's mouth fountain. I loved the nuns, and sat endlessly in the courtyard (filled with the usual clouds of bougainvillaea and coral, as well as acacia and a cypress) talking to them as they crouched sieving corn or sorting walnuts. They told stories about the saints they were named after as if they knew the women personally; I suppose they did, inside their heads. Some evenings we sat in the weaving room and I watched them through the strings of an enormous loom and saw the Minoan pattern in the carpet creep upwards, inhaling the acrid smoke from the wood burning in the huge iron which a Sister pushed over priestly robes. As I often asked them questions it was only fair, of course, that I should answer theirs, which were frequently ingenuous to a degree that made me smile. 'What's it like in an aeroplane? Are there beds?' Sister Evgenia asked me one day. Before I could reply Sister Sinklitiki piped up, 'No, of course not. I've heard that it's like the bus that goes from Limni to Mantoudi.' They often saw me sitting around reading or writing, and soon began to treat me as a kind of encyclopedia, calling me over to ask arcane questions such as what was the population of Iraq (who had just invaded Kuwait), and I always felt compelled to make up an answer rather than disappoint them. Half the time the questions shocked me with my own ignorance, as children's often do: how could I not know what the religion of the Kurds was?

I could even swim every day, as Galataki presided over the string of Glifa beaches, which by September had already been abandoned by summer campers. All the land belonged to the monastery; it used to extend as far as Mantoudi, but at the beginning of the century the state bought most of it, and there have been bitter disputes virtually ever since.

On 14 September we celebrated the discovery and erection of the true cross in AD 327 by St Helen, Constantine the Great's mother, another of the 12 great feasts of the Orthodox calendar. The service carried straight on from morning prayers and the whole thing ran from 4.15 to 8.30 am. Towards the end the priest carried a wreath of basil and carnations studded with three candles round the church, preceded by the Abbess, walking backwards and swinging incense. It was placed on a table in the middle of the nave, the priest walked round it three times and then everyone went up to kiss the wreath and the priest's hand and was given a small bunch of basil. The five loaves of *antidoro* were brought in and blessed. Shortly after the *epiklisis* (invocation of the Holy Spirit upon the sacraments), the priest offered the eucharist, bread and wine taken together from a long-handled teaspoon.

It did feel rather like running a marathon, and it was difficult to know whether the sense of elation apparent in the courtyard afterwards emanated from spiritual elevation or relief that it was over. We adjourned to an upper room where we ate marzipan peaches and *loukoumi* and drank coffee. Five middle-aged women from Chalkis were on retreat, and inevitably I ended up spending a lot of time with them, not least because we ate together. They bossed me around dreadfully, and told me off for not eating enough preserved walnuts and for wearing espadrilles in church. I enjoyed it; it made me feel like a child, absolved from responsibility in an adult world. Some of their loudly expressed opinions, however, were less appealing, and I soon realized I was holed up with a bunch of right-wing reactionaries. They got terrifically worked up about the mines, absolutely certain that everything had been all right until they were nationalized. They perceived the world in black and white, as if they suffered from a genetic disorder which rendered them incapable of seeing that it was all grey really. In addition, one woman irritated me beyond belief by constantly urging me to become a Christian.

'But I am a Christian. I'm just not Orthodox.'

'Oh yes, I'm sorry,' she would say, but the next day the same exchange would take place. The commonly-observed strong identification between being Christian and being Greek dates from the Turkish Occupation, when the Greeks were the Christians and the Turks the enemy. (The Turks actually turned the Church into the administrative infrastructure of the Greek community. Church was State, in a very real sense, albeit within a hostile super-state.) In addition, Greeks think of themselves as Christians rather than Orthodox because they perceive no difference between the two: Christianity and Orthodoxy are indivisible. Thus there is a distasteful tendency to treat Christianity (let alone Orthodoxy) as a Greek preserve. I have actually been asked, in Greece, are you a Christian or a foreigner?

The presence of the women irritated me. I felt more alienated from them, with whom I shared a worldly, urban existence, than from the nuns. I have found on my travels that the absence of any point of cultural contact creates a vacuum which is filled by a simple recognition of humanity – the romance of the total stranger – whereas the semi-familiar triggers associations and the tendency to categorize. I remembered feeling closer to Amazon tribespeople living naked in huts with whom I couldn't exchange a word than to the Portuguese-speaking boatman from Manaus with whom I hitched a lift upriver to them and got by with in Spanish.

Sister Sinklitiki used to take me up to the library, where we sat on the flagged floor surrounded by books and documents, piecing together the monastery's long history. As it was founded on the site of Poseidon's temple it was dedicated to St Nicholas (the sea-god was usually transformed into the sea-saint). It was plagued by pirates, and later by Turks, and was eventually abandoned. The story goes that in the middle of the sixteenth century the captain and owner of a merchant ship from Constantinople got caught in a storm in the Gulf, and was saved only by his imprecations to St Nicholas. His ship was washed ashore below the monastery and he climbed up, found the ruined buildings and undertook their restoration as a thanks offering. Being from Galata (a quarter of Constantinople) he was called Galatakes, hence the name. Or is it? There is another, less plausible story that it comes from *galaktagogeion*, which means a milkery: the monastery once owned a flock of sheep so huge that they had to construct a system of underground channels and cisterns to bring their milk from the sheepfolds.

In about 1547 another sailor had a similarly providential experience and paid for the walls of the church to be painted with frescos. Two centuries later Galataki was partially burnt by pirates again, though the Turks then appear to have been quite keen on it, and went to some trouble to keep it in order; the library had several imperious firmans (orders from the Sultan), one on goatskin, referring to monastic territory. In 1896 a rich seam of magnesite was discovered on land belonging to Galataki and exploited by the British Petrified mining company.

In 1946 it was converted into a nunnery by ecclesiastical decree. I saw the dusty and yellowed bones of the monks in the roof of the St John the Baptist chapel adjoining the main church, reached by an impossibly tiny secret passageway. Both chapel and church were covered in frescos. One of the most extraordinary was the Last Judgement, in which people were climbing up a ladder to heaven, with angels flying above trying to help them up and little brown beasts below trying to drag them down into dragons' jaws. Two men were being pulled off by their beards. It was a fearfully riveting picture. It must have been an effective tool for terrifying people into submission when sacred paintings constituted the main, if not the only, plank of religious education. (Or of any education, come to that.) In the nave most of the frescos had been systematically destroyed with a small, sharp tool which had left marks like a snowfall. Even the eyes of the great Christ Pantokrator in the dome had been dug out. The row of images on the iconostasis was interrupted by a maverick far more recent than the others, painted under western influence, all sickly sentiment and realism. I felt suddenly irritated at being told what to feel by Latin art.

They used to say the *apodipno* in the narthex. At the beginning of the service the only light shone from a tiny oil lamp back in the nave, so it was very dark, and one night I sat on an elderly Sister's lap by mistake. During the service they lit a candle in a niche, in front of an icon to the Virgin, and it cast its flickering light over the entire biblical cosmogony while the arches cast long shadows, and black shapes crouched on the chequered floor. If God was anywhere, He was there, I knew that.

On one side of the courtyard a peeling pink-plastered tower overlooked the sea. The monks built it in the thirteenth century to protect themselves against pirates, as far as I could find out, and it was an architectural feat as it appeared to rise straight out of a huge block of rock. I went up it, through a succession of tiny-windowed guest rooms. There were photographs and paintings of bishops and saints everywhere, and right up at the top Lord Byron had wheedled his way in. Typical.

Next to the tower one day Kirios Yannis, the monastic handyman, was preparing the wine barrels for the impending grape harvest. He was about four feet tall and looked like a troll. (Most of the nuns I had come across were a similar height. This was a great mystery.) He began by washing out the sludge at the bottom, the residue of last year's wine. Then he boiled up the *stifaria*, a mixture of pinecones, bayleaves, oregano and a multitude of other herbs, and swilled the barrels well with it. The monastery stank like a winery, which must have been rather a surprise to the group of German tourists who arrived.

I went off on several expeditions on foot. Whenever I

announced that I was about to depart the nuns would come swarming round, gabbling about routes, heaping provisions upon me, arguing about whether I had enough clothes with me and generalizing wildly to each other about foreigners' habits. (Their feelings on foreigners were going through a particularly sensitive phase, as the previous month a German woman had stayed with them who was training for the priesthood. The shock of the concept of women priests had nearly killed them.)

After about an hour and a half on foot inland one day I reached Pefkeli, a mountain clearing and the site of one of Galataki's dependency chapels. I went up after two days of rain and the pines shone an iridescent green; even before I got to the top I could see both seas, which was always a thrill. With each turn of the hairpinning track the sunlight slanted on another slice of the landscape.

One morning I prepared the nuns for a long absence and wrote down the Abbess' directions to Troupi. It was a long and silent walk with mountain vistas on every side, although the mines soon loomed, until they seemed to blot out most of everything else. The Kakavos site alone stretched forever, and its flat brown ridges and mighty slopes made it look like the Rockies. After a fire-shorn valley I was in Fimisko territory proper, entirely surrounded by artificial lakes and mountains of grey-brown slag tufted with whatever brave scrub managed to live there; Paul Theroux would have called it kitty litter.

The church in front of me, owned by the monastery, was a nondescript modern affair – or so everyone thought until recently. The mining company applied to bulldoze it when they realized there was a seam of magnesite underneath. On a hunch, the Abbess launched emergency investigations, the Archaeological Service was alerted, and experts confirmed that under the whitewash and plaster there was a twelfth-century Byzantine church. The archaeologists sprang into action, and even organized a police guard until the company backed off.

When I went in slants of sunlight beaming through a small window captured the motes of dust in the air like particles suspended in a shining tube, and the image hit me in the stomach, because it took my mind straight to my own church in Regent's Park, where I had observed the same phenomenon many times on silent Sunday mornings. I would have given anything, at that moment, to be there.

As I approached the heart of the mine I became aware of an insistent humming – from the overhead cables, I supposed – punctuated only by the occasional bird squawk. It suited the desolate scene of sudden departure: pens lying on half-written pads on desks under corrugated iron shelters, half-drunk plastic cups of coffee, fuel pumps still dripping petrol, a rubber glove with the fingers turned inside out. Massed ranks of huge lorries stood in rows next to enormous fuel tanks, empty, hugging the barren railway line spanning the valley which for years brought the white stuff to the depot. Where it ended, iron hoppers, hulky as Leviathan, tangled with pipes and more railway line connected with a concrete hangar. A handful of rogue pine trees and oleander bushes dared to survive. A pyramid of brightly painted tin drums stood out against the dull slag spotted with magnesite, and pieces of machinery everywhere were poised in mid-action.

It was as if a spaceship had carried all the workers away in a moment. The maniacal humming grew louder, and I felt as if I should put my hands up in surrender as I walked towards the office block. But then I heard a man whistling, and the tension snapped. He was one of the skeleton security staff still employed, and he pointed the way to my destination. The track passed Papastratis, another state-owned mine which had just been closed, where men were eddying around belligerently. I pressed on to Troupi (or, more usually, Troup, the semi-northern dialect form), at first just a red church roof high up in the pines against the background of Kandili's tallest peak. About three

... out of Galataki I hit the narrow, broken concrete road leading through the village.

Troupi showed all the signs of mass emigration. It had avoided most of the 'modernizations' that have been grafted on to most Greek villages over the past 40 years. The houses were all one-storey and most of them consisted of one long room only roughly divided up (second storeys and proper room divisions were comparatively recent developments). Stone ovens, whitewashed inside and out, were still in operation in one or two yards, and hens swarmed around a proliferation of rickety outbuildings. There seemed to be no one about. Suddenly a man with a creased face appeared and immediately hailed me. Once he had got over the shock of meeting an itinerant foreigner he would brook no refusal to his hospitality, and we sat outside his crooked house, overlooking a patch of reeds, a valley, and then the soaring mountain. His wife brought us coffee, water, goats' cheese and bread.

'You should have seen our village 30 years ago,' he started. 'It was the best in the area. Many people, and beautiful. Now the mines have ruined it. Nobody wants to live here any more; there are only about 15 families left. My two sons live in Piraeus. I used to have 500 goats, you know, but I sold most of them when I went to work down the mine. Ha! Now that's gone too. But I'm not leaving here. I'll stick it out, with a few goats.'

I saw for myself the ruins of houses. Without a fire going in the winter the simple, unprotected buildings soon crumble. The tragedy is that the closure of the mines will probably mean the end of Troupi.

On the way back I passed through the mine again and was apprehended by Chrisanthi, a telephonist, leaning out of a window. When she found out how far I'd come she suggested I take the company bus with her as far as Limni. She was about to go on strike. 'Now we're saying it's all 2500 of us or nobody; we won't agree to a few hundred staying. There's never been any decent investment here – look at the machinery. The government have left us high and dry. The union is OK but it has no power.'

'People say it's corrupt.'

'Look, if you had honey on your fingers you'd lick it, wouldn't you?'

'Well –'

'Everyone's corrupt here, they all eat money, don't you know that?'

'People say that Skalistiris might come back.'

'If it's not him it'll be someone else with a different name but the same attitude. We're the only ones who will suffer. Where do you suppose we'll find work? There isn't any here. North Evia is finished. I'll probably have to leave my village and go to Athens – it's the last thing I want. But what can we do?'

She stared at me, then laughed and took my arm as we went to punch her card. The bus took us down through arid villages and a plain filled with acres and acres of ripened corn. Just before the main road I remembered a small whitewashed church entirely hidden in those cornfields; Alexandros took me there once. It looked ordinary, but there was a configuration of Byzantine tiles on the outside wall of the sanctuary, and the ground was strewn with pieces of marble. Round the corner they were digging a pit for the foundations of a corn-processing plant, and if you picked away at the subterranean layers you could see there was a wealth of ancient and Byzantine objects embedded in the earth. I looked it up afterwards, and found that the church was built out of the debris of a monastery on the same site. At the time I thought that next year the concrete plant would be up and the fertile soil would be hidden for another century or two. This time I thought how typical it was of the island not to reveal itself; you have to seek everything out, and it holds all its secrets. Maybe that was what I liked about it.

*

It was impossible not to be aware that the grape harvest was approaching. Glistening fat bunches beckoned from every trellis, barrels began appearing in the autumn sunshine after their year of darkness, and in the backstreets of Limni huge iron cauldrons boiled away with *stifaria*. Some people filled their barrels with seawater, leaving them to infuse on the beach for a day before cleaning them. Everyone was talking about when they were going to press their grapes, and the topic seemed to dominate every conversation.

Early one morning in my friends' valley we set to with secateurs and huge black leather bags. When the vines were bare the whole team (11 of us) sat in a circle under a trellis of vines removing leaves and bad grapes. It was like picking sardines out of a fishing net. At two o'clock a long table was laid and a huge meal appeared, together with several demijohns of last year's vintage. Over lunch (punctuated with frequent toasts of '*kali krasia*' – happy wining) the oldest picker, 80-year-old Stavros, who was nearly blind, regaled us with stories of harvests of his youth. The landlord used to offer all the workers a meal at midday, brought in baskets by the women and eaten sitting at the edge of the vines. Waving his crook abstractedly in the air, Stavros slowly worked his way round to the familiar lament for the passing of the old order, let out a deep sigh like a bicycle tyre being deflated and concluded, 'Life was better then; things were done correctly.' It was like a litany: love didn't exist any more, sex was too free, the divorce rate was scandalous. He claimed that in his youth courtship involved serenades under a balcony. One of the main causes of 'all the trouble', he said, was that villagers had taken to marrying strangers, people from elsewhere (the older ones present grunted in agreement). When I asked what sort of places these strangers came from he cited

Rovies, a village you could walk to in an hour. Until a few decades ago virtually everyone took a spouse from within the village, and older people still resent it when young ones 'marry out', perceiving it as evidence of the collapse of a world that was good, self-sufficient and introspective. The man looking outside the village for his wife has become the symbol of the man looking outside the village for his values and goals.

In those days, every aspect of rural life was welded to iron-rigid customs. I was sad when it came to the first pressing that one of my favourites had disappeared. When I had come from Athens for a weekend to work at this same harvest eight years previously Stavros had announced, just as we were about to press, that the first person in must be a *parthena*. This word has acquired a similar ambiguity to our 'maiden': it can be used to mean an unmarried girl, but strictly speaking it means a virgin. As out of the 12 of us I was the only unmarried woman I was quickly co-opted in without further etymological debate. The symbolism of purity is clear, and Stavros had also checked that I didn't have my period, as this would have disqualified me: the age-old concept of menstruation as unclean. Women with their period used to be barred from various rural tasks, and at one time villagers even used to say that they shouldn't enter a church (later in the summer an old woman asked me if I was 'clean' before allowing me to look beyond the threshold of a sanctuary). It links in to a wider concept of fundamental female impurity of nature; a weakness and fatal tendency to sensuality which handily distinguishes women from men. The latter's nature is *de facto* superior in quality, and although there is a proper place for a woman in the system her role is based on this premise.

(My own culture certainly had difficulty with it all, too. The logic behind the regulation in force in the UK until recently that you could advertize toilet paper on television but not tampons is breathtaking in its patriarchal absurdity. Even an intelligent western travel writer refers to 'embarrassingly ... feminine physiology'. I ask you.)

The cleaned grapes were tied in hessian sacks and slung in the stone press, and the juice, once extracted, ran through wooden sluices into the trough below. (Most islanders don't use sacks but tread the grapes directly. They also generally toss the pressed skins and stalks into the juice and let it all ferment together for a short period; the juice is then filtered out through an implement resembling a toilet brush. The juice that doesn't ferment with the skins, or does so only for a short time, becomes white wine, while the more extensive mingling of juice and skins produces red.)

I felt grapes burst under my feet and the sticky juice ooze through my toes, squinting into the sun with the sound of hornets in my ears. When the juice had stopped flowing the pulverized fruit was removed from the sacks and pressed again in a wooden screw-action contraption which coaxed out a little more. (There is some commercial wine production on the island, and hydraulic presses are used. But very little.) The wooden sides of this second press were let down and Stavros took out the by now dry, cake-like substance made of skins, pips and stalks. Most people distil it to make raki or, in northern Greece, *tsipouro*, a delicious firewater with powerful after-effects.

As the sun went down we washed and hosed the empty bags, baskets and sacks and covered the press. The sugar level was measured with a special gauge; they add sugar or honey if necessary. The next day we burnt a sulphur tablet in the prepared barrels as a final cleansing agent and filled them with juice, adding a soluble cleansing tablet to each. Later in the week we crumbled in gluey handfuls of resin.

Many farmers supplement their own crop with *mousto* (unfermented grape juice) from other vineyards. (Very approximately 75 per cent of Evian wine is made from the *savatiano* grape, but other varieties are grown too, and they are frequently mixed.) This year the harvest had been poor throughout the north, and so *mousto* was in short supply (and expensive). Although the drought was partially responsible for the diminished harvest, the main cause, I was earnestly told by three people, was hedgehogs. Apparently they stand on their hind legs and knock the grapes off the low vines, then roll over, spear them all and make off. Each time I heard this story I was convinced that it had been contrived solely to make a fool of the foreigner, but a joke of such sophisticated orchestration – the three sources were entirely separate – seemed inconceivable. (Much later I read exactly the same account of hedgehog behaviour in the Byzantine *Physiologos*, a popular work describing various creatures and drawing Christian morals from their behaviour, possibly written by Peter, Bishop of Alexandria, who died in 311.)

When I walked past the stone storeroom over the next week or two I heard the delicious fizz of fermentation. In a month, Stavros informed me, he would pour in a layer of paraffin oil to seal the liquid, and then plug the barrel with resin. Over on the east coast the harvest took place several days later, as exposure to the Aegean means a slightly damper, colder climate. There portable presses were shared around. They looked like huge wooden buckets with a layer of slats across the top. At Kria Vrisi they took the grapes up to the village cooperative press for the second pressing, and stuck to the old tradition of quaffing last year's wine while the production of the new vintage was in progress . . .

Shortly after the grape harvest I was invited to a baptism several villages away. As the father was from a wealthy local family the party afterwards was an elaborate affair at a taverna in the mountains involving endless plates of food, rather bad wine and loud music. The *koumbara* was wearing a navy suit and a clustered pearl ring the size of a bunch of grapes, and immediately after the church service she abandoned the suit for a skin-tight, strapless leopardskin number. She had emigrated to Canada, and her knowledge of and access to such a 'sophisticated' and modern culture lent her great prestige in the eyes of the villagers. (I often came across emigrés returning home to the island for a holiday. Once I hitched a lift with a villager who had settled in Florida; he had brought his enormous phallic car over for the summer. They become symbols of the never-ending, superabundant world of materialism outside the village, unknown, unfettered and always desirable.) The collective dress code at the party was reminiscent of a circus, and many guests favoured shiny satins, net and gold shirts. The cake was a three-tiered, synthetic cream confection, and there, in that land of plenty, they had decorated it with tinned pineapple rings. The whole event was being videorecorded, so a bright white light kept going on and off, making everyone feel self-conscious, and hot. To make matters worse Baby's father had tried to pick me up at least three times over the past month. But the formality was slowly displaced by the wine, they began dancing, forgot about their clothes, their money and their tinned pineapple rings, their faces came alive, they lost themselves, and everything was all right.

The road up to the monastery of St David *Yeronta* was quiet and gravelly, surrounded by dense pine forest broken up with the odd stubbly wheatfield. The three villages *en route* consisted of about seven families apiece. The trouble with the said road was that all eight miles of it were at a steep angle. The exertion did little to enhance my appearance, and the monk who opened the door was, unsurprisingly, very circumspect, and left me sitting in the courtyard for two hours with a piece of *loukoumi*. This at least gave me the opportunity to explore.

The monastery was situated on a kind of balcony overlooking vast tracts of forest on the slopes of Kavalaris, the western spur of the Xiro range. St David had found the mountain conducive to asceticism. Despite being known as St David in Evia, he wasn't an islander by birth: he came from a village in Lokrida. He was born at the tail end of the fifteenth century, and by the age of three already had miraculous tendencies; his epithet, *Yeronta* (old man), refers to the wisdom he displayed even as a child. He became Abbot of Varnakova monastery, near Nafpaktos, in 1520, and then left to live as a hermit near Parnassos. He was eventually obliged to leave there too because of trouble with local Turks, and he ended up on Evia. He lived in a cave on the mountain, and decided to found a monastery below it. Once it was established David continued to go off on his trips, teaching and healing, and he finished his life's work in the Peloponnese, whence he returned to die in his monastery. His sacred remains were kept in a small box, though I didn't see them, as at the time of my visit they were being hawked around his native Lokrida.

The monastery was burnt by the Turks in 1824, and the abbot, a revolutionary leader, was murdered. By 1990 the blooming courtyard had been spoilt by a modern belltower which looked as though it ought to be scaled down and stuck on a wedding cake. The tiny candlelit crypt to the two Anargiri saints, decorated in the seventeenth century, had survived intact. I had never seen a church so completely covered with frescos. It made me realize just how important images were to the Orthodox concept of worship, and why the challenge mounted against them in about 726 had led to strife as intense as civil war for well over a hundred years. In broad terms the Iconolatry faction were in favour of images, and the Iconoclasm faction dead against on the grounds that they distracted the worshipper and smacked of idolatry. It wasn't about art, of course, but about the human nature of Christ, the danger of creating idol-substitutes, and a range of metaphysical issues that were relentlessly chewed over (and fought for) until the Empress Theodora gave icons the all-clear in 843.

I was eventually shown a tiny room with two beds about three inches apart. I had the name of a monk whom I specifically wanted to talk to, but when I enquired I was told he was absent, and I was left alone. There were about 10 pilgrims in residence, and after evening prayers they disappeared into the refectory; eventually a cook-priest appeared with a mound of *revithia* and *manestra* for me, and I ate it in darkness in the courtyard while everyone else chattered away over their meal inside. Whenever anyone left the refectory, light spilled out into the courtyard. I was a freeloader, after all, I rationalized. And I was a single woman, representing threat, danger and dark forces. Christian compassion? It has its cultural barriers. I went to bed with Jane Austen. Shortly my room-mate arrived, the elderly and half-lame Maria from Paleochori. She stood in her nightdress for 10 minutes staring at the bare lightbulb mouthing her prayers.

I have slept on many rectangular constructions that I would hesitate to call a bed, but the one I lay on that night was perhaps the worst ever. It was like sleeping in a wheelbarrow. I was woken by Maria squawking, and as the room came into focus I realized that she was telling me off. Because I had closed the shutters, she said, she had slept until 7.30, and now had to face the 'shame' of arriving late at the liturgy.

After the service I met Vasilis the plumber, who was about to go up to St David's spring with a monk to discuss the construction of a new pipe (St David had tapped the ground with his staff, and water miraculously sprang forth). I asked him if I could go along too, as I was anxious to leave – once again everyone else was seated around the refectory table in animated conversation while I fidgeted awkwardly in the courtyard. As we were about to set off a monk took Vasilis aside and said the Abbot had decreed that it was not appropriate for a girl, a monk and a plumber to be seen on the mountainside together, and I wasn't allowed to go. As the accompanying monk was at least 75 I rather admired this feat of ecclesiastical imagination.

I left, stumbling over my thanks, and set off downhill, branching off cross-country to the village rejoicing in the name of Retsinolakkos (not Retsina Lake, but Resin Pit). From here it was only a short distance to the coast, where the cypress-lined promontory of Kochili and Sipiada, dotted with houses, separated Limni Bay from the long stretch of coast up to Ilia. There was a cave there called Agia Kiriaki where, Maria had told me, a dragon with a goat's head lived. He swam over to the mainland every summer to see his girlfriend and once, in the olden days, he had helped some distressed sailors get home by pushing their boat. Oh yes, she said, spirits could be good as well as bad. Every village, it seemed, had its resident spirit or ghost. At Kerasia up in the mountain they had told me about some kind of anthropomorphic spirit which was terrorizing three villages in the vicinity. If it wasn't the spirits it was this person or that person who was a witch.

I walked along the beach to Rovies. The village was anciently called Orovies, but the remains of that first settlement may be under water now – people have reported sightings of ruined houses out at a depth of 60 feet. Ancient historians noted that the 'infallible' oracle of Selinountios Apollo was at Orovies. In late Roman times the residents probably moved inland to Paleochori to get away from the pirates. I met a woman sitting on a barrel knitting, leaning against an old tower. She told me that her great-grandfather had bought the tower from a Turk, and I realized it must be the one built by the Frankish Prince of Achaea, William de Villehardouin, some time after 1255.

The modern village was affluent, with wide streets and a crop of new concrete buildings at various stages of construction. There was a paper manufacturing plant near the old road which had presumably paid for some of them. It had a spacious feel. The outskirts were dominated by one of the largest olive estates in Greece, owned by the Papadopoulos family. Half of it was given to the people of Rovies as a gesture of anti-capitalist defiance, but they didn't bother to maintain it, or so the story goes.

Maria had asked me to visit her at Paleochori, and so a week or two later I did. Walking through the village was like stepping into the past, except for a couple of impeccable new red-tile roofs, which looked embarrassingly out of place. The present I took was tossed under a chair without being unwrapped. I suppose the Greek custom of disregarding the gift of a guest is preferable to the forced effusions of the English equivalent, but it always irritated me. The house, which had belonged to Maria's great-grandfather, was a two-roomed stone cottage, without running water and with a toilet at the end of the garden. In the kitchen the two huge wooden grain stores were still in place, and next to them the roof had collapsed after a heavy snowfall. A pair of old wooden loom pedals hung on a rusty nail next to the door.

Maria flapped around preparing coffee. The floor was almost entirely covered with bags and boxes. A huge old black-and-white television dominated the room: it had been given to her a couple of years previously. 'It doesn't work very well,' she said. 'So I don't turn it on because I'm afraid it will catch fire.'

She lived on a pension of 10,000 drachmas a month, and as there were no shops in the village and she could barely walk she relied on friends and neighbours. This natural social system seemed to work, in that she survived, but only just, and it must be hard being partially lame and fetching all your own water. My friend Joy in Primrose Hill in London is disabled to a similar degree, family-less, and surviving in a one-room council flat on a pitiful pension. She is surrounded by an unwieldy lumbering infrastructure of social workers, health visitors, home helps, specialist charities, meals-on-wheels and day centres, but the quality of her life is not superior to that of Maria. How far this is merely a comment on urban British life compared to rural Greek (in that the former needs considerable bolstering even to match, in quality, the self-supporting state of the latter), or how far it is a poor reflection on the inability of the more sophisticated system to be anything more than a soulless provider of the bare minimum rather than a life-enhancer, is difficult to assess. Being old and sick and alone puts you rather beyond the pale in any culture.

I went back to Kria Vrisi four times during the last weeks of summer. I was beginning to get used to a rhythm of life dictated by the land. In late August they cut the beans, and contract balers came in to parcel up the dry stalks and pods, which were sold for fodder. At the beginning of September the walnuts were picked. In the middle of the same month, the grapes, and at the end the corn was harvested. Then the stubble was burnt, and the women picked through the blackened fields for fallen cobs. In November they were going to sow the wheat, and so it went on. Once it became cooler, in late September, the sheep were kept lower down, and the days were punctuated by the bells of a large flock and the whistles of the shepherd taking them down to the river. The corn harvest transformed the landscape and opened up whole new vistas. The contract harvesters moved in again, and dusty lorries heaped with dark yellow corn pellets lumbered in and out of the fields. The village thinned out, until only the two families permanently resident were left. We lit fires in the taverna, and I learnt to make *mizithra* (you boil goats' milk, add citric acid, water and salt, and strain it. It sets and keeps all winter.) Sometimes the extended family would gather, and there would be as many as 40 of us round one long table, gorging on plate after plate of food, and dancing. They knew how to enjoy themselves better than any people I have ever met.

For two days in late August we had experienced torrential rain, thunderstorms and gale-force winds, cutting off mains water and the telephone. It was nice to feel holed-up, and curious to be cold and wet in an utterly transformed bleak and grey midsummer landscape. A donkey was struck by lightning and killed, which everyone found hilarious. The beach disappeared entirely under layers of wood, leaves and other debris, including three drowned sheep, and the tall corn was beaten down. Roads were blocked by alluvia from the mountains all over the north of the island. The mood altered radically when we learnt that at nearby Vasilika seven people had been drowned in a house built on an old riverbed. Ghoulish photographs of swollen naked corpses appeared in the press, with screaming headlines accusing the local police of not rescuing the bodies because they didn't want to get their uniforms dirty.

A series of strikes throughout the nationalized industries paralysed the country in September. Anyone can live without electricity, but not if your water is brought up by an electric pump. Fortunately the old hand-pump in the square still worked, so we spent days ferrying buckets around. Everyone got bad-tempered.

The golden days of early October, however, conspired to make me miserable about leaving. The sea was an exquisite mass of clear greens, a gauzy haze hung over the mountains, and the air seemed to breathe a sigh of relief over us after the heat of summer.

Chapter Ten

... over tranquil seas you will come to your own country, and your house, or anywhere else where you would like to go. Nor does it matter if the place is even more remote than Euboea, which is said to be at the world's end by those of our sailors who saw it, that time they took the auburn-haired Rhadamanthus to visit Tityus, the son of Earth.

The Odyssey, Book 7

The goatherd, I learnt over a crackling telephone line, had been obliged to change the date of his daughter's wedding for the third time. (This struck me as a remarkably cavalier attitude towards an event involving 250 guests.) The summer was over, and I had a freelance job in London to rush off to and a plane ticket home; I shouted my apologies down the receiver. A few seconds of confusion followed and I heard his daughter Vangelitsa's voice. 'Come, Sara, can't you change your ticket? We're expecting you.' I said I'd call her back, and sat under an olive tree. I had been carrying their invitation around in my head all summer, ever since the day it was spontaneously delivered in the middle of the Stira mountains. I couldn't bear to miss it now. The vision of London lurched before my eyes, and my resolution quivered.

At the telephone exchange I wormed my way out of the job and then caught a bus to Athens. I loved that journey through the gorges. As I watched the familiar villages appear and disappear I thought of the number of times I had made my way along the same road on weekend visits to my friends. I had travelled in first gear all the way, sitting on sacks of onions in the back of a clapped-out gypsy truck; in a rattling Pony in the middle of the night pouring retsina from a wicker demijohn; on a mountain bike (down only, thank God); in a lorry carrying 40 tons of cement from the factory at Aliveri; on numerous buses, and even in a BMW convertible with the roof down. The dying days of summer were the best, as the plane trees were just beginning to turn orange. They were the most poignant, too.

In Athens I wasted time with airline officials and idled five days away with old friends, then the morning before the wedding I took a boat over to Nea Stira and travelled by taxi up to the old village. The air was warm and pellucid, and it felt good to be back.

The house (as opposed to their hut near the flocks where I had first met them) was at the top of the village, and it had a view over half the Evian Gulf. Vangelitsa and her mother came running out to the courtyard to embrace me, covered in flour, which I soon was too, and introduced me to the other daughter, Dafni, and an Aunt Tassia. They were making the special, highly-decorated wedding bread in the old kitchen underneath the house – the only remains of the ancestral home, which they pulled down and built on as soon as they could afford it; goatherds do all right these days. Vangelitsa glowed through the flour.

The bread, huge circular loaves with intricate dough mosaic-work on top, including acrostics of congratulatory messages to the bride and groom, was soon finished, and we moved to the modern kitchen upstairs. All the items downstairs were old and well-used – the roughly hewn olivewood bowl and dagger handle worn smooth in the middle – and each had a kind of individuality, part of the bond between the users and their environment. Upstairs the anonymous plastic utensils and redundant white goods operated – blatantly – as reproachful symbols of the ever-advancing alienation that is the result of a culture clash. The family gravitated downstairs and felt guilty about it.

Visitors came and went, and the family tackled the apparently self-renewing list of preparations. We had lunch. During the course of the afternoon Dinos, the bride's father, sloped in from the goats, obviously in a state of confusion, and began playing backgammon with Uncle Sophocles.

The groom was to come and live with the family, and the nuptial bedroom had been prepared. He was a goatherd too, with 400 animals which he looked after with his father and brother. It had been decided that he would bring 200 of them to his marriage, joining them up with the 300 owned by Dinos. I tried to imagine him herding them all 11 miles south. The dowry was expertly displayed in their bedroom-to-be: handmade sheets, pillowcases, blankets, tablecloths, mats, cushions and rugs, intricately embroidered and edged. The bridegroom had sent a similar dowry over (because he was coming to live in the home of his new in-laws), and there must have been 100 items on display, all starched and folded so that only a strip of each was visible, like rolls of material in a draper's. It was completed by a magnificent collection of woven *tagaria* pinned on the wall. Visitors were required to stuff a banknote in between the rolls to safeguard the good fortune of the marriage, and Vangelitsa and Dimitris could have paid for their entire honeymoon with the money sticking out between the brightly coloured wads of material.

Xenophobia is not a uniquely Greek characteristic – far from it. In Japan you come across far more highly developed notions of national genetic superiority, not to mention the attitude of many British tourists. But you do often hear, in Greece, the general theory that foreigners are out to get us. Even the Socialist party have made a deal of exploiting this paranoid nationalism in the crudest possible way, instilling a belief that foreign investment or intervention in any form has been and still is responsible for many of Greece's problems. Uncle Sophocles, a Swiftian master of denunciation, was keen to express his unsolicited view on foreign policy towards Greece, and seized the moment. We heard on the radio that the government had announced a reduction (by two months) in the length of military service. I remarked quite casually that this was a good thing. This provoked a masterful speech, a model of how to build on a particular and construct a massive general in one flowing movement. It went something like this.

'It's not a good thing. We have a powerful enemy right on our doorstep ready to pounce, and we must be prepared. Do not forget that we were enslaved by the Turks for 400 years.' (Extensive details of Turkish oppression end Phase One.)

'Of course, foreign countries exacerbate the situation because they support the Turks – buying their goods and so on. They do so for their own ends, because Turkey is important strategically, and because they need the goods. The US, Britain, Germany and France in particular do us a great deal of harm by the cordial relations they enjoy with Turkey.'

Phase Two continued with a lengthy extrapolation of the many instances throughout history when Greece had been poorly treated by foreign nations. Lloyd George in particular got it in the neck. I braced myself for Churchill, whom it seemed certain was being saved up for the grand finale, but Sophocles had already worked himself into Phase Three and was reaching a crescendo.

'All of this exploitation and manipulation is particularly repellent when we consider that the light of civilization dawned here in Greece! The light of civilization!' (Considerable expansion.)

'When we were building the Parthenon you were still living in caves! Caves!' This last was accompanied by a jab of the finger towards me, indicating that now we were very much talking in personal terms. Having thus made his ultimate point (proving the superiority of Greek civilization), Sophocles ran out of steam rather. The speech appeared to have gone over the heads of the rest of the family, who were locked in debate over how many meatballs would be required the next day, and I was stymied as to what to say to Sophocles in the pregnant silence that ensued: it was a speech as incapable of tackling as ever there was. Fortunately the Greek language came to my rescue with a word we could well do with in English: *malista*, which broadly speaking in this context means 'Well that's all fine and understood and the topic is more or less closed or at least I don't want to say anything else about it so let's move on to the next thing.'

Over a supper of egg-and-lemon soup we toasted the bride-to-be with the words, '*kali stepsi*' (happy crowning), and ate amid constant interruptions by swarms of aunts, great-aunts, second cousins and other members of the complex extended family structure that characterizes every Greek village. Shortly before midnight it was decreed that we should all go to bed and get a good night's sleep in preparation for the rigours of the next day. I was delighted to escape from Sophocles' demented rantings to the girlish chatter of Vangelitsa and Dafni, with whom I was sharing a room. It felt deliciously young and innocent to be lying there in the dark, idly speculating on the concept of marriage and the oddities of men. Dafni was 22, and married for two years, and she exploited her superior position mercilessly, firing advice and instruction at her elder sister, who refused to be bullied, and conversations frequently ended in explosions of laughter, which were in turn followed by a volley of rebuke from mother in the room opposite. I was in a tricky position, as way back in June when I first met the family I was so tired of people trying to pair me off that I made up the story that I was engaged if anyone asked. This rebounded on me now as I found myself involved in an ever-increasing complexity of lies about the arrangements for my non-existent wedding. By the end I semi-believed that I was indeed to get married soon, and even had the person in mind (he'd die of shock if he knew), and surprised myself by being mildly disappointed that it wasn't true.

The big day dawned. Or rather, everyone got up before it had the chance to do so. Although the wedding was not until four in the afternoon, at five-thirty in the morning they were all running about. The bride's parents had actually slept on the floor, without a mattress, as they had given up their bed to an aunt and uncle, and the sanctity of the made-up bridal bed was not to be defiled.

There was a good deal of work to be done, as they were having a *meze* lunch (light buffet) for relations and neighbours before we set off for the church. The previous day I had barely been allowed to do anything, given the traditional honoured position of the guest in the home. But as the activity intensified in the morning and the pressure increased, so did my tasks (which I had been urging them to allot me). At first I was permitted to engage only in the most basic work, such as washing up, peeling potatoes and moving furniture, as being a foreigner I was sure to muff anything more complicated. (I was in fact removed from tomato-cutting duty as I was not cutting them into the correct shapes.) As time wore on, however, it became clear that the extensive *meze* were well behind schedule, so there was nothing for it but to delegate more important jobs to me. Thus I made 500 *keftedakia* (baby meat-balls), though each stage of the process was carefully monitored, and six aunts blustered past regularly to check that I was using the right sized hole in the grater to grate the garlic.

When it was almost finished we had to sit down to one last family meal. Once more I was faintly irritated at the toast raised to all unmarried girls on these occasions, *Sta dika sou*, which means let's hope you get married soon too, with the subtext God help you if you don't because then you'll really be a reject and an utter failure and we'll all feel dreadfully sorry for you and your parents will die in shame.

It was quite straightforward. In rural Greece marriage is a social necessity for both partners, and you are simply perverse if you don't want to do it.

A hairdresser arrived, and Vangelitsa disappeared into the bedroom, while the rest of us took it in turns to get ready. The water was cut off (still rationed) in the middle of the proceedings, which caused a furore, and we had to carry up reserves stored in the kitchen underneath and call on Dunkirk-spirited neighbours to appropriate their spare bucketfuls. While Vangelitsa was having her hair curled a cassette player was set up and her mother and aunts danced around her, singing and whistling (the mother was an ace whistler, you could hear her about two miles away). The goatherd himself, who had escaped to tend the flock for most of the morning, now sat around looking bemused. He was eventually coaxed into a suit. It was like a child dressing a docile dog: the victim accepts the treatment without complaint but the incongruity of the result is comical, and you feel sorry for the dog. A tie, however, was evidently beyond the pale, and he wore his collar open.

Guests began arriving at about two. The women went into the bedroom, where Vangelitsa was still seated in front of the mirror, and threw handfuls of rice on the bed. I was co-opted in to carry round trays of *parfait amour*. The *parfait amour* phenomenon is one of the great mysteries of Greek life. For no apparent reason they imbibe it, alone among liqueurs, in huge quantities – or sometimes they tip it down the sink in huge quantities, like now, when the form was that each person took a microscopic sip from his or her glass and replaced it immediately on the tray, whereupon the remainder was thrown out. This struck me as the most monumental if not criminal waste, and I would have stationed myself by the sink and drained all the barely-touched glasses myself were it not for the fact that *parfait amour* is utterly repulsive, and also that it would have been embarrassing to get drunk before the church service.

Other guests evidently had no such scruples, and proceeded to sink jugs of retsina at an alarming rate. Vangelitsa eventually emerged, resplendent in her white frock, hired from Chalkis, and sat on a chair in the middle of the room. She remained stock still for an hour, eyes glued to the floor, while people danced in a circle around her, led by her mother and aunts, singing special bridal songs, and guests threw banknotes in her lap. She held her hands straight out in front of her as if she were waiting for her nails to dry, and she looked terrified.

Someone shouted that the car had arrived, there was a terrific scuffle, and Vangelitsa and her parents processed out of the house and shot off to the church, with all of us in pursuit, honking furiously. In the main square everyone thronged outside the church, and once the bridal party, by now including three little bridesmaids, was arranged inside, we swarmed in. There were about 250 guests, on the whole dressed fairly casually, including a few with shirts open to the waist and gold medallions languishing on hirsute chests. Most Greek services are fluid affairs (not least because there are no pews), and this was no exception, as people came in and went out, chatted amongst themselves and greeted long lost relations. The priest did request quiet at several key moments, but everyone carried on as if he wasn't there. After the Office of Betrothal, when rings were exchanged, the *koumbara*, responsible for swapping the bridal crowns symbolizing grace from the Holy Spirit, held them in place while the party walked solemnly round in a circle, led by the priest. This was our cue to throw rice, which had been mixed with flower petals at the house and was now offered round for each guest to take a handful. Some people had brought their own supply, however, and approached the task with considerable enthusiasm, hurling pounds of the stuff, which lodged in the priest's beard and behind his glasses so that he couldn't read his chants. It all got rather out of hand.

As we filed out we were all given little net bags full of sugared almonds and greeted the bridal party. Then we piled back into the cars and drove the 11 miles to Mesochoria, where the reception was to take place in the bridegroom's grandfather's taverna. All 250 of us squashed behind long tables in the courtyard and began quaffing retsina from plastic Coke bottles. Goats' cheese and other appetizers soon appeared, followed by a huge chunk of spitted goat each, roast potatoes and then bunches of grapes. The band consisted of two bouzouki players, a lute player and three singers; the bridal party led the dancing, and soon the floor was full. They were indefatigable dancers. The band played their last number at 7.45 am. The cake was produced in the middle of the festivities, along with the special bread. There was also a little present-giving ceremony, when the bride's family offered gifts to their opposite numbers. (The gifts are in recognition of the new relationship between them – a highly important one in the context of the village social structure.) The dancing didn't stop for this, however: the ceremony was incorporated into it, as the bride and her mother threw the gifts over the shoulder of the recipients as they danced round (fortunately they were things like goat-hair blankets, which was just as well, as you couldn't fling a cut-glass vase over someone's shoulder, but perhaps they had that in mind when they chose the gifts).

One of the most amazing things about the whole wedding was the tenebrous group of yellow-and-black-scarved old women, and a handful of old men, who sat for hours looking through the fence on the road high above the taverna. Every time I looked up they were there, crouching in the gloom watching the pretty bride dance in the bright lights.

I have a vague recollection of Uncle Sophocles bearing down on me, eyes blazing, fulminating about the behaviour of the British government in the Cyprus débâcle. The goatherd continued to look like a fish out of water, but this was amply made up for by his wife, who whistled demoniacally all night. The wine kept coming, and spirits began stirring. Whenever one of the young men asked me up to dance, after 10 minutes one of the squadron of aunts would sally forth into the middle of the dance floor, grab me by the arm and suggest that I might like to join their group.

The collective staying power was impressive. When the sun rose things began to look a teeny bit seedy, despite the watery morning view of the pale Aegean. The last guest finally staggered off at about eight, and I was left with the bride's parents and a man I'd never seen before. We chatted to the groom's family, who lived above the taverna, and for a long time I wondered why we weren't going home: enough, surely, was enough. The family didn't possess a car, only mules, and these had been deemed inappropriate wedding transport. It emerged that Dafni's husband was supposed to be giving us a lift home. He was nowhere in sight, and I didn't like to enquire. Half an hour later Dafni appeared and asked me if I could drive. Her husband was dead drunk in the back of his car, and no one in the family could drive. Refusing would probably have meant that we had to stay up until all the alcohol had passed out of his system, which would certainly have been days not hours (possibly weeks), so we set off: Dinos, the unknown man and I in the front, mother, an aunt, Dafni and her husband in the back. There was no traffic, but the road was, I realized, a succession of hairpins balancing above a cliff face, and in addition we had to keep stopping to let the owner of the car be sick. Once he didn't give us the opportunity to stop, and was sick anyway.

When we got home we had to have a little more music and a little more dancing and several kilos more wine. The unknown man lay on the couch in the kitchen. I can't remember what time we went to bed, but I do remember getting up a few hours later and realizing that I had to catch a boat shortly. The Greek insistence on hospitality can kill you at these times. As I sat at the table wanting only black coffee and aspirin and feeling as though I might have died, a jug of retsina mixed with Coca-Cola and a plate of cold goat was set before me.

I made the boat, and sat feeling ill. There were only about 20 passengers, and they were all hungover wedding guests – it was like a transportation ship to a penal colony. I was going home. I felt curiously dispassionate about my imminent departure. Nothing seemed to have ended, and nothing would end. It was exactly as Laurens van der Post said: 'Where the body stops travelling, the spirit takes over the trek.'

Select Bibliography

There is an abundance of material on Evia (though only in Greek) in the hefty tomes of the Society of Evian Studies, published annually under the title *Archive of Evian Research (Archeio Euboikon Meleton).*

Kevin Andrews, *The Flight of Ikaros*, London, 1959

S.C. Bakhuizen, 'Chalcis-in-Euboea, Iron and Chalcidians Abroad', *Chalcidian Studies III*, 1976

—, *Studies in the Topography of Chalcis*, Leiden, 1985

J.L.S. Bartholdy, *Bruchstücke zur nähern Kenntniss des heutigen Griechenlands ... im Jahre 1803–1804*, Berlin, 1805

J.A. Buchon, *La Grèce continentale et la Morée*, Paris, 1843

—, *Atlas des nouvelles recherches historiques*, Paris, 1843

—, *Voyage dans l'Eubée, les îles Ioniennes et les Cyclades en 1841*, Paris, 1911

John B. Bury, 'The Lombards and Venetians in Euboia', *Journal of Hellenic Studies*, vii–ix, 1886,7

John Campbell, *Honour, Family and Patronage*, Oxford, 1964

Jean D. Carpenter and Dan Boyd, 'The Dragon Houses of Southern Euboia', *Archaeology*, 29, 1976

Richard Chandler, *Travels in Greece*, Oxford, 1776

Lord Charlemont, *The Travels of Lord Charlemont in Greece and Turkey in 1749*, London, 1984

Angeliki Chatzimichali, *Sarakatsani*, Athens, 1957
Dio Chrysostom, 'The Evian Hunter' (The Seventh Discourse), Loeb edition, 1932
Diodorus Siculus (various editions)
Edward Dodwell, *A Classical and Topographical Tour through Greece during the Years 1801, 1805 and 1806*, London, 1819
Yeorgios Drosinis, '*Agrotikai Epistolai*', *Estia*, July–December 1882
Juliet du Boulay, *Portrait of a Greek Mountain Village*, Oxford, 1974
George Finlay, *A History of Greece*, Oxford, 1877
Fritz Geyer, *Topographie und Geschichte der Insel Euboia*, Berlin, 1903
Y. Gikas, *I Alosi tis Chalkidas apo tous Tourkous*, Athens, 1959
Jules Girard, *Mémoire sur l'île de l'Eubée*, Paris, 1852
K.A. Gounaropoulos, *Istoria tis Nisou Euboias*, Thessaloniki, 1930
Vronwy Hankey, 'A Marble Quarry at Karystos', *Bulletin du Musée de Beyrouth*, xviii, 1965
J. Hawkins, 'The Syrinx of Strabo and the Bridge over the Euripus', in *Memoirs Relating to European and Asiatic Turkey*, ed. Robert Walpole, London, 1817
—, 'Discovery of a Very Ancient Temple on Mount Ocha', in *Travels in Various Countries of the East*, ed. Robert Walpole, London, 1820
Herodotus, *The Histories* (various editions)
W. Heurtley, Travel Diary, unpublished papers, British School at Athens, 1924
John Hobhouse, *Travels in Albania and Other Provinces of Turkey in 1809 and 1810*, London, 1813
Christopher Isherwood, *Down There on a Visit*, London, 1962
Franklin P. Johnson, 'The Dragon Houses of Southern Euboea', *American Journal of Archaeology*, xxix, 1925
I. Kaditis, *O Angelis Govios kai i Epanastasi tou 21 stin Euboia*, Athens, 1979
Richard Knolles, *Generall Historie of the Turkes*, London, 1603

Osbert Lancaster, *Classical Landscape with Figures*, London, 1947
John Cuthbert Lawson, *Modern Greek Folklore and Ancient Greek Religion*, Cambridge, 1910
William Martin Leake, *Travels in Northern Greece*, London, 1835
I. Liapis, *Mesaionika Mnimia tis Euboias*, Athens, 1971
Livy, *History of Rome* (various editions)
Peter Lock, 'The Frankish Towers of Central Greece', *Annual of the British School at Athens*, 81, 1986
Paul Lucas, *Voyage du Sieur Paul Lucas dans la Grèce*, Paris, 1712
H.J. Mason and M.B. Wallace, 'Appius Claudius Pulcher and the Hollows of Euboia', *Hesperia*, 41, 1972
William Miller, *The Latins in the Levant*, London, 1908
Jan Morris, *The Venetian Empire*, London, 1980
Ramon Muntaner, *The Chronicle of Muntaner*, transl. Lady Goodenough, London, 1920.1
Murray's Handbook to Greece, London, 1884
John Julius Norwich, *A History of Venice*, London, first published in one volume, 1982
—, *Byzantium, The Early Centuries*, London, 1988
A. Orlandos, *Archeion ton Bizantinon Mnimion tis Ellados*, vol. 7, Athens, 1951
H.W. Parke, 'Athens and Euboea, 349–8 BC', *Journal of Hellenic Studies*, xlix, 1929
Pausanias, *Guide to Greece* (various editions)
M.R. Popham and L.H. Sackett, *Lefkandi I*, Athens and London, 1980
M.R. Popham, 'Why Euboea?', *Annuario della Scuola Archeologica di Atene e delle Missioni Italiane in Oriente*, 59, 1981
Barry P. Powell, *Homer and the Origin of the Greek Alphabet*, Cambridge, 1991
Benjamin Powell, Trips in Euboea, unpublished papers, American School of Classical Studies, Athens, 1899
Henry Raikes, 'Journal through Parts of Boetia and Phocis', in

Memoirs Relating to European and Asiatic Turkey, ed. Robert Walpole, London, 1817

Bernard Randolph, *The Present State of the Islands in the Archipelago*, Oxford, 1687

M. Rangabé, *Mémoire sur la partie meridionale de l'île d'Eubée*, Paris, 1852

L.H. Sackett and others, 'Prehistoric Euboea: Contributions towards a Survey', *Annual of the British School at Athens*, 61, 1966

A. Sampson, *I Neolithiki kai Protoelladiki I stin Euboia*, Athens, 1980

—, *Euboiki Kimi*, Chalkis, 1981

—, *Manika*, Chalkis, 1985

John Sibthorp, 'Extracts from the Papers of Dr Sibthorp', in *Travels in Various Countries of the East*, ed. Robert Walpole, London, 1820

Theodoros Skouras, *Ta Drakospita tis Euboias*, Chalkis, 1991

Fotini Spirou, *Economie et société de l'île d'Eubée à travers les récits des voyageurs (1630–1815)*, unpublished thesis, Pau, 1985

Strabo, *Geography* (various editions)

Chrisostomos Themelis, *Archai kai Diadosis tou Christianismou en Euboia*, Thessaloniki, 1954

— *Euboiki Monastirologia*, Athens, 1965

Thucydides, *History of the Peloponnesian War* (various editions)

various authors, *Anthropologika kai Archaiologika Chronika*, I, 1986

various authors, *Nouvelle contribution à l'étude de la société et de la colonisation eubéenes*, Naples, 1981

Richard Vedder, Ancient Euboea: Studies in the History of a Greek Island from Earliest Times to 404 BC, unpublished thesis, Arizona, 1978

Epam. Vranopoulos, *Ellinistiki Chalkida*, Athens, 1972

—, *I Istoria tis Archaias Euboias*, Athens, 1987

M.B. Wallace, The History of Karistos from the Sixth Century to the Fourth Century BC, unpublished dissertation, Toronto, 1972
W.P. Wallace, 'The Demes of Eretria', *Hesperia*, 16, 1947
—, *The Euboian League and its Coinage*, Numismatic Notes and Monographs 134, New York, 1956
—, 'A Tyrant of Karistos', in *Essays in Greek Coinage*, ed. Kraay and Jenkins, Oxford, 1968
George Wheler, *A Journey into Greece*, London, 1682
S.S. Wilson, *A Narrative of the Greek Mission*, London, 1839
Christopher Wordsworth, *Greece – Pictorial, Descriptive and Historical*, London, 1839
Thomas Wyse, *Impressions of Greece*, London, 1871
R.S. Young, A Short Description of South Euboea, unpublished papers, American School of Classical Studies, Athens, 1930

Index